FROM
Defender
TO Critic

Other Jewish Lights Books by Dr. David Hartman

The God Who Hates Lies:
Confronting and Rethinking Jewish Tradition

A Heart of Many Rooms:
Celebrating the Many Voices within Judaism

A Living Covenant:
The Innovative Spirit in Traditional Judaism

Love and Terror in the God Encounter:
The Theological Legacy of Rabbi Joseph B.
Soloveitchik

FROM
Defender
TO Critic

The Search for a New Jewish Self

Dr. David Hartman

For People of All Faiths, All Backgrounds
JEWISH LIGHTS Publishing
Woodstock, Vermont

From Defender to Critic:
The Search for a New Jewish Self

2012 Hardcover Edition, First Printing
© 2012 by David Hartman

Library of Congress Cataloging-in-Publication Data
Hartman, David, 1931–
From defender to critic : the search for a new Jewish self / David Hartman. — 2012 hardcover ed.
p. cm.
Includes bibliographical references.
ISBN 978-1-58023-515-0 (hardcover)
1. Jewish law. 2. Spiritual life—Judaism. 3. Joy—Religious aspects—Judaism. 4. Soloveitchik, Joseph Dov. I. Title.
BM520.3.H375 2012
296.3—dc23
2012004291

10 9 8 7 6 5 4 3 2 1

Manufactured in the United States of America

Jacket Design: Tim Holtz

Published by Jewish Lights Publishing
A Division of LongHill Partners, Inc.
Sunset Farm Offices, Route 4, P.O. Box 237
Woodstock, VT 05091
Tel: (802) 457-4000   Fax: (802) 457-4004
www.jewishlights.com

To all my children and grandchildren.

Contents

Part II: Abraham's Argument:
Reclaiming Judaism's Moral Tradition

Introduction

From Loving Defender to Loving Critic
An Intellectual Autobiography

In the early 1970s, not long after making *aliyah*, I had the wonder-ful opportunity to dialogue with many serious Christian theolo-gians from all over the world. At a certain point, a group of these colleagues asked that I write an article on the topic "The Joy of the Law," specifically using the lens of Buber's work on Hasidism, with which they were familiar. Buberian neo-Hasidism, they felt, could potentially be a productive lens for understanding how joy might be extracted from the tradition of mitzvah and halakha.

While I liked and admired these other theologians, there was something about their narrow emphasis on Buber that distressed and disturbed me. For them, the only mediator of opportunities for spiritual joy in the Jewish experience are those rooted in mystic traditions. It was clear to them—indeed, it was taken for granted—that the halakhic tradition per se is a burden, a source of guilt and spiritual deadness, empty of any claim to spiritual vitality. As a serious young rabbi and yeshiva student who spent most of his life studying Talmud, I held the perspective that halakha was *the* central value in Judaism: the ultimate source of joy, of vitality, of meaning itself. It disturbed me to realize that it was seen by so many as an obstacle to spirituality, a source of guilt and oppression.

Upon further conversation and reflection, I came to realize that Judaism was actually incomprehensible to many serious Christian thinkers. Hasidic storytelling as understood by Buber was not the major carrier of living Judaism. It had its place, but it was not the central organizing framework for understanding Jewish tradition.

If the only focus for any sense of spiritual joy would be Hasidism or some mystic escapism, the essence of the Judaism I knew and loved had been totally missed. After further consideration, I realized that fundamentally this perspective is rooted in the Pauline critique of Judaism. For Paul, the major obstacle for rapprochement between Christianity and Judaism was the halakha, which he characterized as antithetical and destructive to the true life of the spirit. This lack of understanding has been a major stumbling block for Christian thinking about Judaism ever since. Moreover—and perhaps even more troubling—the critique of "pharisaic legalism" deeply infiltrated the Western intellectual tradition, most prominently through Spinoza.

I viewed it as my sacred task, then, to correct what I saw as a distorted view of the Jewish tradition: to respond to the Pauline and Spinozan critiques of Judaism, which centered fundamentally around the meaning of halakha. In my earliest writing and thinking, I set before myself the task of developing a phenomenology of halakha that might silence the critiques of Paul, Spinoza, and their contemporary inheritors.

What resulted from this serious encounter with Christianity was my first book, *Joy and Responsibility*. The major essay that sparked much of my subsequent thinking that went into the book was "The Joy of Torah," which began my intellectual adventure of defending Talmudic tradition—for which halakha is the fundamental carrier of living Judaism—as filtered in modernity through the religious culture of my upbringing, the Orthodox yeshiva. I saw my work, in a sense, as translating the lived experience of a yeshiva student—whose spiritual and intellectual life centered around a total dynamic engagement with halakha—into terms that could be understood as reasoned and compelling within a Western philosophical frame of mind.

In "The Joy of Torah" I argued that there is a type of profound spiritual joy that emerges from feelings of adequacy, responsibility, and solidarity with community. The description of the community of Israel in the Bible is for some theologians a shocking account of rebellion and sin; for me, however, it is an inspiring testimony to the fact that God gave the Torah to human beings and not to angels. The continuous renewal of divine demands, despite repeated human failures, indicates that God did not operate with an idealized concept of covenantal humanity. The giving of the Torah to a people who are prepared to return to slavery in Egypt the first time they are thirsty—God's faith in human adequacy to fulfill the law—fills me with feelings of deep joy. God believed that fragile human beings were capable of becoming responsible and mature. Rabbinic Judaism's expansion and elaboration of halakha further illustrates the belief in the community's ability to realize the historic task of becoming a holy people. The joy of mitzvah stems from recognizing that God is prepared to give limited, imperfect human beings a great covenantal task. The continuous demand of Torah confirms God's love and faith in humanity.

"The Joy of Torah" and the essays that followed it were also profoundly informed by my years in the rabbinate, an experience that forced me to seek ways to talk about Judaism so as to enable Jews of various backgrounds to find meaning in what was being said. Although I was an Orthodox rabbi of Orthodox pulpits in the Bronx and in Montreal for seventeen years, my congregations comprised people of vastly different backgrounds, beliefs, and levels of observance.

Like many rabbis, I noted in most of my congregants—indeed, in most of the Jewish world at large—a deep estrangement from the religious framework of the Torah. Jewish tradition was not deemed worthy of serious attention; it was not, in William James's words, a live option. I realized then that my task was not to proselytize, but to counter indifference by cultivating an awareness of Jewish tradition as a theological and cultural option that commands attention, that cannot easily be dismissed.

My years in the rabbinate taught me pedagogical empathy: a teacher must begin at the place of the students, listen before speaking, hear and share in the deep estrangement of Jews from their tradition—to enter that estrangement and to try to understand the roots of modern Jewish alienation.

Maimonides's approach to Torah as expressed in *Guide of the Perplexed* was then, and has remained, a powerful source of inspiration and guidance for me. In Maimonides, I beheld a master halakhist whose authoritative halakhic works have guided Jews for generations. This singular pillar of Jewish tradition was prepared to understand many mitzvot of the Torah in the light of the particular human conditions of the community of slaves that left Egypt. God, says Maimonides, speaks in the language of human beings; God takes into account the lived reality of people when formulating norms and directives. God listens carefully and sympathetically before speaking.

In the essays of *Joy and Responsibility*, I strove to incorporate this model of teaching, emulating God through the prism of Maimonides. I realized that in addressing a people that has experienced the tragic consequences of God's silence in history, we must not begin by teaching dogmatic theology. To a generation that has lost an appreciation for the human significance of mitzvot, we should not emphasize a theocentric orientation to halakha. Rather than articulating a clear theology, my concern was with formulating aspects of a religious anthropology.

How do the practices and the conceptual framework of halakha affect a person's character and perspective on life? I was not concerned with proving that God created the universe in seven days, but, rather, with understanding the human implications of accepting the doctrine of a Creational universe. How does the notion of Creation affect the way a human being organizes his or her daily life?

In "Embracing Covenantal History: Compassion, Responsibility, and the Spirituality of the Everyday," I set out to show how belief in Creation leads us to reject human passivity (religion as the opiate of the masses) and adopt an active, self-reliant attitude toward history as well as the everyday life of the spirit. According to Joseph B. Soloveitchik in "The Lonely Man of Faith," the idea of God the Creator serves as a model for humanity to imitate. We must imitate God not only by internalizing God's moral attributes but also by becoming active and responsible agents seeking to perfect an imperfect reality.

In "Democratizing the Spiritual: The Risks, and Rewards, of Halakha," I tried to correct the mistaken notion that the "halakhic person" is naïve, arrogant, and spiritually complacent. Rabbinic Judaism was fully awake to the various risks that Jewish communal spirituality entails. When you strive to build your spiritual life within a living community, you must give up viewing religion in terms of salvation of the soul; you must be spiritually prepared to get your hands dirty and to take great risks. Unless you are prepared to take risks and to make compromises, you cannot build a relationship to God within the framework of community. In Judaism, love for God must lead to a love for real people. If you can only love an idealized community of the elect, you remain the victim of messianic abstractions, unable to embrace the community of real Jews in this imperfect world.

In "Learning to Hope: A Halakhic Model of History and Redemption," I sought to elucidate a critical aspect of the significance of Zionism for modern Jews: its unique potential to enable the Jewish people to rediscover the vitality of Torah as a way of life. The religious value of events in history is not measured solely by their relationship to a future messianic age, but by how they expand the area of responsibility for the implementation of halakha. All my tradition asks of Jews is that in each generation they renew the covenantal moment of Sinai. Though I am ignorant of how contemporary Israel is related to the end of history, I do know how Israel is related to the beginnings of covenantal history.

In "Creating a Shared Spiritual Language: The Urgency of Community and the Halakhic Roots of Pluralism," I examined the implications of the fact that the movement to Sinai is preceded, in the symbolic structure of the biblical narrative, by Egypt. A religious community deeply committed to and concerned about the fate of all Jews must not only participate in bearing burdens of survival and security but must also strive to build spiritual bridges among themselves. The sense of community that precedes the revealed word of God and the obligations of mitzvah must also influence our attitude and approach toward the observance of commandments. Halakha is addressed primarily not to the singular individual, but to the individual rooted in the historical destiny of a community.

The quest for unity and community, I suggest, ought not to be expressed solely in terms of survival. Religious leaders and teachers who stress the centrality of Jewish peoplehood for Jewish spirituality must strive to formulate an approach to mitzvot that would enable their students to share a common spiritual language with the rest of the Jewish people. The need to formulate a shared spiritual language is most evident in the State of Israel, where the common struggle for survival loses much of its meaning in the absence of shared beliefs about the significance of Jewish communal existence.

My hope in writing these essays was that the shift of emphasis from dogmatic theology, leaps of faith, eschatological pronouncements, and miraculous expectations, to an analysis of the human implications and significance of religious concepts, would provide the groundwork for discovering a shared spiritual language for a society seeking a way to return to Sinai.

As I look back over the decades since the publication of *Joy and Responsibility*, I realize how far I've come from being the defender of traditional halakha. In the interim, I have found many distortions and perversions in the perception of halakha as the dominant carrier of meaningful Judaism. In a sense, the second section of this book, drawn from my public lectures from the past fifteen to twenty years, is the story of how I came to question the authoritarian control of the halakhic system and develop a theology of halakhic critique: an experiential process of evaluating the system against its own teleology, the deep structure of values it advocates and to which it encourages its adherents to aspire.

One of the primary voices with which I have grappled in my shift in focus from defender to critic of halakha has been that of Rabbi Joseph B. Soloveitchik. He was, and to some extent will always remain, my master who taught me everything I know about Judaism. At the same time, as the years passed and my thinking evolved to flesh out, in increasing scope and detail, the implications of a covenantal theology—a theology of empowerment that encourages individuals and communities to take ever greater levels of responsibility for their religious lives—I became more critical of his emphasis on formalist abstraction, self-abnegation, and halakhic stasis. As discussed at length in my previous book, Soloveitchik insisted, as a faith article of Orthodoxy, upon assigning to every Talmudic statute a sacred ontological status so riveted in the patterns of tradition that it is "protected" from any currents of thought that might lead to meaningful substantial change.

Thus, one of the emphases in my own thinking has been to find alternative paths within the tradition, paths that seem to challenge and reframe the legacy of this master halakhist. A major focus has been to take halakha beyond formalism and authority, to greater emphasis on the individual and his or her subjective, experiential role in creating a meaningful Judaism. My concern has shifted from the centrality of mitzvah obligation to the spiritual character of the personality shaped by the encounter with halakha. What type of human being emerges from this rule-dominated system? Where does this person stand in relation to the values at the tradition's core?

My central critique of traditional halakha could be described as an attempt to free the individual to experience the system while at the same time taking personal responsibility for his or her religious life—allowing anyone to stand independently before the massive weight of halakhic tradition. There is a greater focus now on inwardness and covenantal responsibility, a perspective that empowers Jews at any stage of halakhic involvement to stand in opposition to various elements of inherited halakha as a legitimate expression of halakhic Judaism. This approach elicits much more concern with the depth of spiritual experience that an individual brings to the norms he or she has chosen to live by.

Ultimately, I have found Soloveitchik's halakhic "heroism"—the moment of *Akedah*-like self-sacrifice in which individual perspective is suspended and personal intuition is subjected to the objective divine will of halakhic tradition—to be masochistic and tragic. For the Rav, a signal moment of halakhic spirituality is the moment in which the bride and groom, on their wedding night, refrain from sexual intercourse upon finding any trace of female bleeding. As a rabbi, I have followed the young *chasan* and *kala* to the door of their wedding room, in which the passion of their love could find fulfillment, and have felt the tragic pain of the halakhic demand that they withdraw from consummating their love if she finds, in her underwear, a drop of blood. This is not heroism, but cruelty. It carries a great risk of trampling intimacy, distorting natural love and spontaneous relationship. Spiritual heroism must find an alternative orientation than halakhic repression. Interpretive room must be created for such alternatives; the world must be open to its multiple possibilities of meaning as I choose to live within the patterns of traditional halakha.

The essays gathered in this section will give the reader some inkling into my struggle and the halakhic spirituality I have come to embrace. In the process of teaching and discussing this evolution of my theology, I have heard several consistent critiques, which I would like to take a moment to outline and address in broad strokes.

Some have criticized my more recent approach to Judaism as having undermined the fundamental ground and structure of what, for most of our history, has been the major unifying force of the Jewish people: clear commitment to the authority of halakha. Subjectivity and autonomy have a place, but we must be careful that in emphasizing personal responsibility we don't lose the sense of collective obligation that binds us together. I have undermined the very concept of a minyan, the possibility of finding ten people who would join together in worship. Weakening halakha, they argue, is an anarchic gesture that weakens Jewish community. What can I claim as a unifying force for Jewish continuity and communal spirituality?

As these essays repeatedly suggest, my intent is not to strip halakha, or the past, of all authority, but rather to create a space for questioning and critique in the areas where it conflicts with an individual's ability to appropriate reality—for example, when it prohibits me from acting out a moral life in tune with modern experience. Of course, it is possible to appropriate voices of authority as well, and indeed I want to preserve a voice of authority—just not one with the unilateral prerogative to drown out voices of religious autonomy and subjectivity. Ultimately, I want to preserve the tension between an individual's inner voice and the voice of the past, for this is precisely what creates vitality in living Judaism.

There are others who claim I have lost something very deep as I moved away from the culture of the yeshiva. They say I am too responsive to modernity and less seriously committed to the past. In fact, the past continues to claim me deeply—but only if it illuminates the present, imbuing life as I see it and live it with vitality, resonance, and spiritual intimacy. A past that denies anything has changed, that claims exclusive authority over my individual point of view, is one I am content to leave behind.

Others, approaching this set of ideas from a different angle, have raised a different type of critique: that I offer nothing new. What am I doing, they ask, beyond recycling the founding principles of Conservative Judaism? My primary response to this suggestion is that I am happy to participate with Conservative Jews, and with all

Jews who find resonance in my religious perspective, in creating a Judaism that is anchored in reverence of the past and prepared to absorb the new currents of experience and value that have emerged in the contemporary world. I do not claim exclusive creativity.

For the sake of clarity, however, I would add that while various elements of my synthesis of tradition and modernity may share motifs with Conservative thought, my theology has not emerged from within the Conservative intellectual milieu. Rather, it reflects a deep grounding in the religious sensibilities and currents that have been present in Jewish history, primarily in the culture of the yeshiva. In this sense, it represents a different take on the core dialectic among memory, past, and present.

This is a dynamic that must be continuously reexamined and reconsidered; clearly, as a people, we have not exhausted the possibilities of how to integrate the traditions we inherit with our situated, lived experience. Conservative Judaism offered one version of this synthesis, and the question of why it has failed as a movement to capture the religious sensibilities of contemporary Jewry is an intriguing and significant one. Their hearts and minds had, it seemed to me, the right intention. What blocked them from bringing the Jewish people along and providing a framework for the rebirth of Judaism in the modern world?

One suggestion is that the movement was weighed down by always "having" to prove that it is halakhic. Jewish meaning gets reduced to one's ideological stances on a set of politically tinged religious issues—women rabbis, homosexuality—and as a result of this narrow focus on signal issues, the prosaic rhythms of daily life in the religious community suffer. In this way Conservative Judaism, and Conservative Jews, have left the daily routines of Judaism to wilt away.

My own variation on the synthesis of tradition and modernity is not a philosophy meant to serve as the platform for a new movement or institution, but a process of living experience among individuals and communities that choose to adopt its angle of vision.

It is a process that demands constant introspection and renewal and cannot be branded or co-opted by any formal or official frame of reference. It stands separate from all expressions of institutionalized Judaism, because it never knows what new forces it will absorb as it moves into the future.

In this sense, in my thinking I have tried to capture something of the open-endedness that is constitutive of halakhic Judaism at its very core. The last word on the Oral Torah has not been written, and never will be. Torah is meant to be a catalyst for new experiences and thinking that will nurture its vitality forever.

Part I

The Spirituality of Halakha

Early Essays

1

THE JOY OF TORAH

Halakha: The Antithesis of Joy?

The term "joy of Torah" might strike many as an oxymoron—especially if Torah is understood to encompass the binding legal system of halakha. The notion arouses a number of possible objections, from both within the tradition and without. Halakhic Judaism is often presented in this (as I hope to show, distorted) light; it is not uncommon to be questioned by serious Christian and Jewish people who are perplexed by the notion of the joy of halakha. While accepting the possibility of joy in a Buberian-Hasidic approach to Judaism, they cannot imagine any sense of joy in approaches to Judaism that emphasize the practice of halakha and an intellectual involvement with details of the halakhic system. They automatically identify this type of Judaism with "pharisaic legalism," that is, with submissive obedience to the merciless letter of the law.

It must be acknowledged that many features of halakha indeed appear to mitigate against the experience of joy.

For example, consider the halakhic principle "commandments were not given to provide enjoyment," about which Rashi comments that commandments were not given to Israel so that their performance would be a source of pleasure but rather so that they would be a yoke on their necks.[1] Similarly, *Tosafot*, regarding the statement "Greater is he who does an act that he is commanded to do than he who does an act that he is not commanded to do," suggests that a person who is commanded is greater because his life is of constant worry to fulfill the commandments of the Creator and to negate his inclinations to transgress.[2]

The picture of halakha reflected in these two statements seems totally at odds with the experience of joy. More generally, the expression "yoke of the commandments," frequently used in halakhic writings, conveys the idea that mitzvot (commandments) are a heavy weight pressing hard upon a person. This attitude of "pharisaic legalism" with its submissive obedience to the letter of the law hardly seems conducive to joy, an experience normally associated with feelings of ease and spontaneity.

In addition to the weight of command and authority, another feature of halakha that may be incompatible with the experience of joy is the emphasis on uniform practice. Individual uniqueness and spontaneity seem to be ignored by a spiritual life that elaborates detailed patterns of behavior for all to follow.[3]

In this chapter, we shall analyze some of the practical and conceptual features of halakha that provide conditions for the experience of joy.[4] We shall indicate the circumstances and the conditions characteristic of three widely recognizable types of joy, then show how these conditions are met in the practical and the conceptual areas of halakha.

Three Types of Joy

Our approach falls within a tradition of Jewish thinkers best exemplified by Maimonides and Soloveitchik. In contrast to a mystic theocentric orientation to halakha, this way of thinking focuses primarily on the anthropocentric significance of the law, or what it means for the people living it.[5]

The concept "joy," for example, is unquestionably an ordinary concept, that is, a concept used regularly by people lacking erudite analytical skills or precise, sophisticated definitions. Also, joy is not a single concept but constitutes what Austrian philosopher Ludwig Wittgenstein called a "family concept." To understand its meaning, we must be able to use it in a variety of contexts.

We will focus on the concept of joy as it appears in three contexts that are familiar and recognizable:

1. *Joy as the feeling of dignity and of adequacy.* Joy may be ascribed to you when you regard yourself with dignity and strength. In contrast to a person who feels powerless and insignificant, you feel joy in the belief that you have power to act and be creative, to direct life, and to assume responsibility for spiritual development. The feeling of adequacy associated with this sense of joy may reflect your attitude to yourself or may result from your feeling of full acceptance by another. You experience joy when another moves toward you in genuine acceptance. When you feel that someone responds to you and accepts you as the person and not as the embodiment of some idealized image, you gain a sense of dignity. You experience yourself as someone capable of assuming responsibility and of entering into human relationships. Thus, both from a personal and from an interpersonal perspective, the notion of joy is closely related to experiences of adequacy and acceptance.

2. *Joy as the product of complete actions.* There is joy in the completion and in the fullness of an action. Actions complete unto themselves do not have an extraneous purpose. Such actions, if placed within a means-ends nexus, are felt to be ends in themselves, not serving any other goal.

3. *Joy as the feeling of expansion.* This type of joy is associated with the feeling best described as going beyond yourself or of no longer feeling self-enclosed or trapped within yourself. It

is the joy of being loved and of feeling capable of love, that is, the feeling that another has become part of your consciousness. Joy in this sense involves a feeling of expansion, when community or another person becomes part of your "I."

Regarding the term "Torah," there are two senses that should be distinguished:

1. *Torah as a mitzvah (commandment)*. Given this sense, the joy of the Torah means the joy of mitzvah, the joy of a commandment.[6]

2. *Torah as a body of material we may study and analyze.* When we speak of joy of the Torah, therefore, we ought to distinguish between the joy of mitzvah (commandment) and the joy of Torah.

God as Artist and Teacher: The Divine Speech(es) of Creation and Sinai

From a theological perspective, the creation of the world and the revelation at Sinai are the two most significant moments described in the Torah. Both involve moments of divine speech: the Word that constitutes creation out of nothing, and the Word that constitutes the covenant of Sinai. To elucidate the spiritual significance of these theological moments, we shall distinguish between two models of speech: the artist model and the teacher model.

The artist expressing him- or herself in creative activity is not necessarily concerned that his or her words be easily understood or work of art be appreciated. These goals are not essential to the creative impetus. The artist may be said to create because of an overflow within the self. The resulting speech is primarily a monologue.

In contrast to artistic speech, the speech of the teacher is intended as communication. The essential element is not self-expression alone, but the desire to be understood. Such speech emerges only after listening, for unlike the solitary context of the artist, it is essentially a response to others. Concern with the listener's capacity to understand is integral to this form of speech, whose goal is to guide and persuade. Artistic speech is primarily self-expression; concern with how others will react often signals the end of the true artistic creativity.

Using these two models of speech, we can clarify the two central theological moments of the Torah: Creation and Sinai. Creation fits the model of the artist, that is, the speech of self-sufficiency. Sinai, on the other hand, reflects the speech that responds to an audience and aims at influencing and guiding. To Maimonides, Creation is a moment of divine self-expression. *Olam chesed yibaneh*—the world emerges out of an overflow of God's creative power.[7] Being and nature are the product of the divine overflow.

In Creation, that is, in the Word that established being, divine speech is divine self-expression—a monologue. For Maimonides, reflection on nature heals human grandiosity, because comprehension of God's revelation in nature leads to the awareness that we are not the center of Creation.[8] Humanity is not the central figure in the cosmic drama that expresses God's infinite power and wisdom.

In contrast, at Sinai humanity plays an indispensable role as listeners, the receivers of communication. Reflection on the revelation of the Torah leads to an anthropocentric worldview, for the covenantal speech of Sinai is addressed to an audience with the intention that they understand.

Critically, the divine speech to the people at Sinai followed the divine listening to the suffering and moral condition of the people in Egypt. In Maimonides's view, we cannot understand much of biblical legislation if we do not take into account the influence of Egyptian culture and slave life on the Hebrews. The particular social and historical conditions of the Jewish people (the "students") determine the approach of the divine educator at Sinai.[9]

It is not surprising, then, that one of the ways divine speech at Sinai is understood by the Rabbinic tradition is through the model of a teacher:

Because the Holy One appeared to Israel at the Red Seas as a warrior, *and appeared to them at Sinai as a pedagogue who teaches the day's lesson and then again and again goes over with his pupils what they have been taught, and appeared to them in the days of Daniel as an elder teaching Torah* ... Rabbi Hiyya bar Abba said that He appeared to them in a guise appropriate to each and every place and time. At the Red Sea He appeared to them as a mighty man waging their wars; at Sinai He appeared to them as a pedagogue, as one who stands upright in awe when teaching Torah; in the days of Daniel, He appeared to them as an elder teaching Torah, for the Torah is at its best when it comes from the mouths of old men.... At Sinai, when He said, *"I am the Lord thy God,"* appropriately He appeared to them as a pedagogue teaching Torah.[10] [emphasis added]

Jews who recite the *Birkat ha-Torah* (the Blessing on the Torah) in the daily prayer service identify God as the one "who teaches Torah to His people Israel." The teaching of Torah was viewed by halakhic authorities as *imitatio dei*, an imitation of God who is the teacher par excellence.[11]

The Rabbinic perception of the revelation at Sinai from the viewpoint of God as teacher is not alien to the biblical portrayal of God's relationship to humanity. The unfolding of the biblical narrative connecting Creation with the covenant at Sinai is supportive of the Rabbinic image of God as teacher.

Covenant as Dialogue:
Divine Aspiration and Human Reality

In the beginning, amidst the exhibition and the excitement of the creation and the ordering of the universe, the Creator God proclaims majestically, "Let us make a human being!" (Genesis 1:26). The God who is limited by nothing, who need but say, "Let there be ..." for anything to come to be, creates a being in the image of God. It is not long before the Torah describes God's punishing response as humanity fails to realize divine expectations. The corruption of the generation of the flood results in God's nearly destroying all of creation. In the early chapters of Genesis, God is portrayed as reacting violently to humanity's moral failures.[12]

The covenant and halakha emerge when God's aspirations for humanity come to terms with human reality. God's saying, "Never again will I doom the earth because of man, since the devisings of man's mind are evil from his youth ..." (Genesis 8:21), is the beginning of a process culminating in the revelation at Sinai. In contrast to the rage of the flood, the giving of the law reflects the acceptance by God of humanity with its imperfections and weaknesses. God no longer looks at us simply as the (often failed) expression of God's image, but as complex creatures for whom true self-realization is the rare and often momentary result of much effort and concentration. The Torah does not prescribe the living out of platonic perfect forms. It assumes and embodies, rather, a dialectical tension between divine aspiration and human imperfection.[13]

Perhaps the Torah was given in the desert because the desert experience exposes our fragility and limitations.[14] God proclaims, "You shall be to Me a kingdom of priests and a holy nation" (Exodus 19:6). In the desert, however, with neither food nor water, the people cry out, "Why do we need to put up with the insecurity of freedom? We may as well go back to Egypt!" The desert reveals our animal dependencies, our weakness in the face of biological need and psychological fear.

For Buber, the lofty "Eagle Speech" of Exodus expresses the essence of the covenant between God and Israel:[15]

> You have seen what I did to the Egyptians, how I bore you on eagles' wings and brought you to Me. Now then, if you will obey Me faithfully and keep My covenant, you shall be My treasured possession among all the peoples. Indeed, all the earth is Mine, but you shall be to Me a kingdom of priests and a holy nation.
>
> (EXODUS 19:4–6)

We suggest that a more poignant prelude to the establishment of the covenant is the biblical account of God's giving manna to the people in the desert. God tells the people, "I will give you enough food each day, but please do not hoard it. Trust Me each day." How do the people respond? They go out to gather manna and take extra, at least enough for the next day. On Friday, God allows them to take a double portion of manna so that on the Sabbath they will not have to work. Despite God's causing a double portion of manna to fall on Friday, the people go out on the Sabbath to gather more.

This incident reveals the problematics involved in the relationship between God and Israel. "You shall be to Me a kingdom of priests and a holy nation" (Exodus 19:6) reveals God's dream for humanity. The manna incident reveals the reality with which God must come to terms. The desert repudiates the romanticization of humans—and the Torah is given in the desert. The law is the expression of God's realistic acceptance of human beings with their limitations.

The spirit of what we are suggesting is beautifully described in the following midrash:

> When Moses ascended on high, the ministering angels spoke before the Holy One, blessed be He: "Sovereign of the universe! What business has one born of woman among us?" "He has come to receive the Torah," answered He to them. Said they to Him, "That secret treasure, which has been hidden by Thee for nine hundred and seventy-four generations before the world was created, Thou desirest to give to flesh and blood! 'What is man, that Thou art mindful of him? And the son of man, that Thou visitest him? O Lord our God, how excellent is Thy name in all the earth! Who has set Thy glory [the Torah] upon the heavens!' (Psalm 8:5, 8:2)." "Return them an answer," bade the Holy One blessed be He, to Moses.... He [then] spoke before Him: "Sovereign of the universe! The Torah which Thou givest

me, what is written therein? 'I am the Lord thy God, who brought thee out of the Land of Egypt' (Exodus 20:2)." Said He to them (the angels): "Did ye go down to Egypt; were ye enslaved to Pharaoh? Why then should the Torah be yours? Again, what is written therein? 'Thou shalt have no other gods' (Exodus 20:3). Do ye dwell among peoples that engage in idol worship? Again what is written therein? 'Remember the Sabbath day, to keep it holy' (Exodus 20:8). Do ye then perform work that ye need to rest? Again what is written therein? 'Thou shalt not take [tissa] (the name ... in vain)' (Exodus 20:7). Is there any business [massa] dealing among you? Again what is written therein? 'Honor thy father and thy mother' (Exodus 20:12). Have ye fathers and mothers? Again, what is written therein? 'Thou shalt not murder. Thou shalt not commit adultery. Thou shalt not steal' (Exodus 20:13). Is there jealousy among you; is the Evil Tempter among you?" Straightway they conceded to the Holy One, blessed be He.[16]

The essential point of this midrash is expressed by numerous concepts frequently used in halakhic discourse, for example, "the Torah speaks in human language"[17] and "the Torah pitches its speech to the evil instinct."[18] In other words, Torah is not a heavenly law addressed to perfect beings; Torah is a response to what people are. Halakha is an attempt to educate and to guide people who have passions and jealousies, who may steal from one another or feel desire for another's spouse.

Whereas nature reflects divine self-sufficiency, the Torah reveals God addressing people in terms of their imperfect reality.

Halakha and the Spirituality of Partial Meaning in an Unredeemed World

Halakhic themes are not always spiritually uplifting and beautiful; they often presuppose harsh and brutal realities. People are often puzzled and embarrassed by the section in Deuteronomy 21:10–14, dealing with a soldier who takes a woman captive. The situation is that of a man who is away from his home, his family, his friends, and his familiar social context, who is engaged in the violence and brutality of war. Addressing this context, the Torah says: If you desire her, you may have her, but you must wait until you take her home.

The significance of this biblical legislation lies in the fact that God does not abandon humanity in the jungle, but goes into the jungle to help us try and salvage whatever is possible. Rather than naively pretend that we will transcend our desires and hungers no matter what the circumstances, the Torah aims at retaining some degree of dignified conduct within an otherwise brutal and anarchic situation. Halakha does not presuppose a perfect society composed of perfect people; its norms and practices are often directly aimed at the concrete problems and acute moral conflicts that we face.

Similarly, much halakhic discussion deals with the minute details of everyday life. In their attempt to encompass almost every aspect of human existence, the writers of the Talmud and those who follow in their tradition refuse to regard any aspect of the human condition as unworthy of divine concern. Halakhic discussions anchor the dialogue with God within the multiple possibilities of the concrete.

The first mishnah most people are taught when they begin the study of the Talmud often arouses disappointment. This mishnah deals with the problem of two people holding a garment and each one saying, "It's mine!" Perhaps, for the sake of spiritual edification, we ought to rewrite the mishnah: two people find one garment and each says to the other, "You may have it!" The mishnah, however, speaks to the reality of scarcity and conflict: we do not live in an ideal world. Much of halakha is a detailed involvement with the mundane realities of life; it reflects a sustained struggle to achieve *kedushah* (sanctity) in an imperfect reality.[19] *The courage to establish partial meaning in an unredeemed world is one of the most profound dimensions of halakhic spirituality.*

If we are prepared to seek within halakha the basic philosophical orientations of Judaism, we will recognize the centrality of the notion of *the divine acceptance of human limitation*.[20] (This acceptance is the ground for the belief in the permanent possibility of *teshuvah*, the repentance and renewal of people.) The fantastic involvement of halakha with details, the legal minutiae in the case of someone's ox goring someone else's ox or of someone lighting a fire that destroys another person's property—in halakha we encounter, again and again, a God who accepts and is involved with the world of ordinary people.

From Fear to Love: The Joy of Acceptance

People experience God's love and full acceptance in the knowledge that God gave human beings halakha:

> Thou hast loved the house of Israel Thy people with everlasting love; Thou hast taught us Torah and precepts, laws and judgments. Therefore, Lord our God, when we lie down and when we rise up we will speak of Thy laws, and rejoice in the words of Thy Torah and in Thy precepts for evermore. Indeed, they are our life and the length of our days; we will meditate on them day and night. Mayest Thou never take away Thy love from us. Blessed art Thou, O Lord, who lovest Thy people Israel.[21]

For the covenantal Jew, the giving of the Torah in the desert confirms that God's love is a response to our humanity, and not exclusively an expression of divine aspiration. Biblical descriptions of Israel in the desert allow for no illusions about the unique "spiritual genius" of Israel. Even Moses, in his final speech to the people, recognized how far they were from embodying their covenantal mission. The Bible does not allow even an old dying leader to have illusions about the spiritual grandeur of Israel! Still, God has loved the house of Israel by giving them Torah. And the people rejoice in it.

Halakha, therefore, is inherently related to the joy of feeling accepted and confirmed by another. Realism and responsibility are not only not antithetical to love and joy but are also their very grounds.

Thus, the dynamic the covenant seeks to initiate between God and humanity can be summarized as follows: when the Jew deeply feels and understand how halakha mirrors divine acceptance of human reality, he or she is encouraged to move toward a full acceptance of God and of the revealed mitzvot. We manifest our love for God by performing the commandments with joy, that is, for their own sake, and not as a means to receive reward or gratify our needs.[22]

God, however, is such an accepting teacher that God is prepared to say, "You need not accept Me for My own sake as long as you perform the mitzvah." It is as if God were saying, "I am secure because I, the Creator of the universe, am self-sufficient. I welcome and encourage anthropomorphic descriptions if they are helpful for people, because the full expression of My wisdom and power is not dependent exclusively on My role as teacher.[23] I accept your worship of Me because of My promising you rain, children, wealth, and security. I do not mind if you fulfill My commandments in order to receive these material goods: this is but the starting point of your development and growth."

Israel may start to worship God in *yir'ah*, that is, action motivated by the expectation of rewards. Ideally, we should aspire to move from *yir'ah* to the *ahavah* (love) that is bound up with *simchah shel mitzvah* (the joy of a commandment).[24] Love and joy become identical experiences when a person reaches the point where she or he can say, "I do the mitzvah because it is a mitzvah. I serve God because God is God and not because of any rewards."

To love God to this extent and to perform acts for their own sake is to experience the joy of being engaged in actions sufficient unto themselves. This notion of *simchah shel mitzvah*, which is equivalent to the second notion of joy defined above, is psychologically tied to the joy of experiencing God's acceptance.

The joy of personal adequacy and dignity may liberate us from the need to manipulate relationships for the sake of gratifying personal hungers.[25] Human fears and deprivations act as a prison, preventing us from recognizing and appreciating that which is independent of our needs.[26]

To Maimonides, the study of philosophy, that is, physics and metaphysics, liberates people to appreciate objective reality. Philosophy, by clarifying the structure of reality and the ultimate significance of knowledge, provides the liberating power enabling people to move from a relationship grounded in *yir'ah* to one based upon *ahavah*.[27]

Our position is that an understanding of the halakhic process in itself provides the conditions for moving from *yir'ah* to *ahavah*. When we internalize the affirmation of worth and dignity implicit in a relationship to God built upon halakha, we may discover psychological resources enabling us to respond to mitzvot with love. Knowledge of God as God is revealed in nature may be the way for modern people to learn to worship God out of love.[28]

Partners in Creation:
Adequacy, Dignity, and the Joy of Learning

Our analysis of the joy of the Torah has so far dealt with the Torah as mitzvah, the joy of the commandments. As mentioned earlier, Torah also denotes a specific body of material that is the object of study and analysis. In the *beit ha-midrash* (hall of study) of a yeshiva, people often sing while learning. On seeing such people swaying and singing, an observer might mistakenly believe them to be praying, when in fact they are engaged in a profound intellectual activity.

I have had the rare privilege of studying with a Talmudic master who experienced total joy while intellectually grappling with Talmud and with the vast corpus of legal and aggadic material. Within the world of learning, often referred to as "the world of Torah," one discovers notions of joy similar to those discussed above.

The Jewish tradition of study began with Talmudic Judaism, that is, with the development of the oral tradition. The centrality of learning in Rabbinic Judaism, as expressed in the saying *Talmud torah keneged kulam* (the study of Torah over and above all else), characterized Jewish values and practice throughout history.

The tradition of Torah learning reflects a deep sense of human adequacy and an acknowledgment of human dignity.[29] Within the Jewish tradition, the importance of learning is closely related to the model of God as the accepting, loving teacher. Students who feel the warmth and the love of their teacher are often encouraged to work out the implications of what their teacher has given them. The teacher's love liberates students to create, yet to regard their creation as an expansion of what they have received. This experience underlies such Talmudic statements as "Everything that an accomplished student shall say before his teacher was given by Moses at Sinai," as well as the following beautiful story:

> When Moses ascended on high, he found the Holy One, blessed be He, engaged in affixing coronets to the letters. Said Moses, "Lord of the universe, who stays Thy hand?" He answered, "There will arise a man, at the end of many generations, Akiba ben Joseph by name, who will expound upon each title heaps and heaps of laws." "Lord of the universe," said Moses, "permit me to see him." He replied, "Turn thee round." Moses went and sat down behind eight rows [and listened to the discourses upon the law]. Not being able to follow their arguments he was ill at ease, but when they came to a certain subject and the disciples said to the master, "Whence do you know it?" and the latter replied, "It is a law given unto Moses at Sinai," he was comforted. Thereupon he returned to the Holy One, blessed be He, and said, "Lord of the universe, Thou has such a man and Thou givest the Torah by me!" He replied, "Be silent, for such is My decree."[30]

Although it is correct to say that the halakha derives from Moses, it is Akiba, the student of Moses, who continues the tradition and creates within the framework of the teachings received from Moses.[31] The secure student is not paralyzed by the authoritative words of the teacher, but recognizes in them multiple possibilities and is prepared to expand on them.

Moreover, just as intense love relationships often provoke the feeling that all one is or has is due to the other, so too the student intensely committed to the words of his or her teacher will not necessarily distinguish between what he or she has created and what he or she has received. It is important to differentiate between creativity grounded in love and relationship, and the creativity that emerges from a sense of separation and individuality. Midrashic writers reflect the relationship of a lover to a beloved; the feeling that the Torah is a gift of love from God permeates all their writings. Because the Torah was given in love and studied with love, it contains all that future generations will "discover" to be "included" in God's message.[32]

With the development of the oral tradition, Israel becomes a co-partner in the creative process of the Word; revelation ceases to be a Word given once and for all at Sinai, but becomes a Word that is continuously discussed and developed by students. The Word that mediates divine love becomes integrated with human response; the creative development of the Torah by the student and the teacher's guidance become part of one Torah. The Oral Torah and the Written Torah become one. In fact, some go so far as to say that the covenant is not based on the written Word but on the oral Word.[33] *The covenant experience truly emerges when Israel, the listener, turns the received Word into a creative Word that is, so to speak, open-ended.*

Learned in love, the content of Torah can never be exhausted; it is received and expanded in each generation. The student experiences God as the Giver of the Torah through intellectual engagement, even in those aspects of Torah created by people. Prophecy is no longer the sole mediator of the word of God; a student of Torah, with no credentials other than his/her intellect, may mediate God's word.[34] That is why a student recites *Birkat ha-Torah*, the Blessing over Torah, even when studying the writings of contemporary teachers.

The covenant, which calls upon humanity to be responsible, is strengthened when Israel feels adequate to expand the implications of the spiritual guidance that began at Sinai. Revelation then becomes a *derekh*, a pointing, a way, a direction. Intense intellectual engagement with Torah transforms the individual from a passive recipient of the tradition to an active shaper of the future direction of Torah; the student of Torah trusts his or her mind.[35] The experience of learning reflects and develops a sense of adequacy that finds expression in the intense joy of *limud Torah*.

The Joy of Community: Expanding the "I," Personalizing the "We"

According to Maimonides, the concept "mitzvah" and the normative system of halakha are fundamentally grounded in the inception of a people.[36] Mitzvah is not rooted in the "leap of the alone to the Alone"; it is the spiritual road of an individual who serves God within the context of community.

It is not primarily a private experience, but a collective language giving expression to a shared spirituality. Individuals meet through the medium of the shared form to build a joint spiritual life. In the traditional prayer book, the prayers are formulated in the first person plural, because it is not "I" as a single individual but "we" as a collective community that is praying. The liturgy symbolizes its connection to the collective in the requirement of the minyan, for it is only in the midst of ten people or more, the symbol of community, that the individual fully gives expression to the collective dimensions of prayer.[37] Mitzvah and halakha give expression to the spiritual concerns of the person who wants "we" to be part of his or her "I," mediating a collective spirituality that inculcates the joy of self-expansion.[38]

While creating a framework of collective spirituality, halakha also embraces the individual who stands before God. Torah study—in addition to the theological significance discussed above—enables individuals to grow and enrich themselves within the context of community, interpreting and internalizing the meanings of their lived practice in their personal language. On one level, the total community stands as one before the mitzvah; on another level, individuals develop according to their particular sensibilities and capacities.

The emphasis on learning loosens the rigid uniformity of community and makes room for individual spirituality. You participate in community and in its shared forms of behavior. As you learn and understand more, however, you discover new meanings for the concepts and the practices shared with others. You act, to begin with, as a collective person; you understand, however, as a single person. The individual appropriates a collective language, but through learning transforms it into a personal language. Learning, then, is one way a collective, covenant people allows for the possibility of individual spirituality.[39]

Although, to the traditional halakhic person, the forms used to express his or her relationship to God are collective, the significance the individual attributes to a mitzvah may be personal. In traditional Judaism, individuality finds expression in the way we internalize the collective language of halakha:

> The Divine Word spoke to each and every person according to his particular capacity. And do not wonder at this. For when manna came down for Israel, each and every person tasted it in keeping with his own capacity—infants in keeping with their capacity, young men in keeping with their capacity, and old men in keeping with their capacity.... Now if each and every person was enabled to taste the manna according to his particular capacity, how much

more and more was each and every person enabled according to his particular capacity to hear the Divine Word.[40]

The emphasis in Jewish tradition upon learning may be one of the
reasons why the Torah, throughout history, has been able to address
so many types of individuals despite vast differences of background
and mentality. Commitment to the collective past need not negate
a person's conception of who he or she is in the present. Through
learning, we gain an understanding of the directives of the past, as
well as an understanding of how to respond to and build upon the
past. Learning moves the individual from the joyous sense of the
collective to the joy of personal spirituality.

Similarly, the scope of halakhic obligation has both collective
and individualistic expressions. Halakha is a system of laws
prescribing actions that every member of the community must
follow. But obligations based on the legal authority of God do not
exhaust its scope. Besides the precise detailed system of standards
that obligates every individual in the community to specific actions,
Maimonides's *Mishneh Torah* includes another description of the
essence of halakhic life:

> A man should aim to maintain physical health and vigor, in
> order that his soul may be upright, in a condition to know
> God.... Whoever throughout his life follows this course will
> be continually serving God, even while engaged in business
> and even during cohabitation, because his purpose in all that
> he does will be to satisfy his needs, so as to have a sound
> body with which to serve God. Even when he sleeps and seeks
> repose, to calm his mind and rest his body, so as not to fall
> sick and be incapacitated from serving God, his sleep is service
> of the Almighty. In this sense, our wise men charge us: "Let
> all thy deeds be for the sake of God" (*Mishnah Avot* 2:17). And
> Solomon, in his wisdom, said: "In all your ways acknowledge
> Him, and He will direct your paths" (Proverbs 3:6).[41]

This description of how halakhic Jews relate all of their activities to God is not a description of action grounded in legislative authority. The statement "Let all thy deeds be for the sake of God" is not a formula yielding precise legal norms of behavior. Its comprehensiveness reflects the aspiration of the individual who desires to sanctify every aspect of human conduct. Halakhic norms stemming from legislation are related to specific actions and specific times. "In all your ways acknowledge Him" embodies the aspiration to approach God in every aspect of our behavior. The statement "In all your ways acknowledge Him" reflects the aspiring movement from people to God, as opposed to the legislative moment from God to people. The attempt to endow all of human action with religious significance leads the individual to seek a perspective that would enable him or her to say, "I have set the Lord before me continuously" (Psalm 16:8).

This single-minded pursuit of God indicates that halakha is more encompassing than a collection of specific legal commandments addressed to community. In endowing sleep and physical exercise with religious significance, we are not merely following a stated commandment. The all-pervasive longing for God—not simply obeying specified norms embodying God's will—is the source of this comprehensive understanding of halakha. Singular individuals understand that what God requires of us cannot be confined and exhausted within a precise, delimited structure of norms. They are drawn to a God who inspires action not only on the basis of God's legislative will, but also by God's infinite perfection. They do not look solely to the practice of the community to determine what is expected from them.

The difference between the unique individual and the community goes beyond a person's ability to develop a comprehensive understanding of halakha. Even within the circumscribed world of halakhic norms, we can discern both communal and individual orientation. The two halakhic categories reflecting this are (1) *din*, law that defines the line of legal requirement, and (2) *lifnim mi-shurat ha-din*, law that is beyond the line of legal requirement.

When a man, great in the knowledge of the Torah and reputed for his piety, does things that cause people to talk about him, even if the acts are not express violations, he profanes the Name of God. As, for example, if such a person makes a purchase and does not pay promptly, provided that he has means and creditors ask for payment and he puts them off ... or if his mode of addressing people is not gentle, or if he does not receive people affably, but is quarrelsome and irascible. The greater a man is the more scrupulous should he be in all such things, and do more than the strict letter of the law requires. And if a man has been scrupulous in his conduct, gentle in his conversation, pleasant toward his fellow creatures, affable in manner when receiving them, not retorting, even when affronted, but showing courtesy to all, even to those who treat him with disdain, conducting his commercial affairs with integrity... and doing more than his duty in all things... such a man has sanctified God, and concerning him, Scriptures saith: "And He said unto me, 'Thou art My servant, O Israel, in whom I will be glorified'" (Isaiah 49:3).[42]

Thus we see how the tradition distinguished between practice stemming from a uniform law obligatory for each member of the community and practice expressing the spiritual capacities of certain individuals within the community and, in essence, allowed for the spontaneity of individual spiritual creativity.[43]

Whether the scope of such spontaneous spirituality is sufficiently broad to satisfy the great variety of spiritual sensibilities present in a pluralistic and an individualistic society is a serious question. While not attempting to resolve this problem, we propose that despite the concept of "the yoke of the commandments" mentioned at the beginning of this essay, the notion of joy is an integral part of the religious experience of the halakha.

While not denying that submission to authority is a central experience of the halakha, we maintain that our understanding of Judaism is incomplete if it fails to appreciate the various opportunities for joy embedded in the experience of being a halakhic Jew. The joy of being intellectually engaged in the study of Talmud, the profound intellectual autonomy found in halakhic writings, and the feeling of self-respect and dignity that emerges from being commanded and charged with the responsibility of implementing Torah in the daily life of the community are also features that characterize halakhic Judaism. In the conceptions of God that penetrate and underlie the halakha, as well as in its characteristic methods, practices, and concepts, one encounters the elements out of which emerges the joy of Torah.

2

THE BODY AS A
SPIRITUAL TEACHER
LEARNING TO ACCEPT INTERDEPENDENCY

The bearing of a religious tradition on contemporary moral issues is sometimes understood as the relationship of a set of statutes and decisions to a particular practical problem. This orientation seeks to formulate traditional legal or theological categories that, if accepted, can "resolve" the dilemmas of our time. The project of offering Jewish "solutions" to moral problematics holds little interest to me. More useful, in my opinion, is the cultivation of a way of thinking, developing a process through which a person living within a particular tradition (in this case, halakhic Judaism) might begin to use it as a lens though which to contemplate the moral and spiritual challenges life presents.

The moral dilemmas of the physician confronted with decisions involving life and death capture public attention because of their dramatic nature. However, the physician daily faces profound moral ambiguities that are rooted in the very relationship of the doctor and the patient. What happens to the doctor and to the patient in a situation where the basis of the encounter is need and helplessness? An appreciation of the dynamics of dependency relationships and the different human responses to such relationships brings us to the very heart of traditional Jewish spirituality.

Traditions of Autonomy and Dependency

For the sake of analysis and at the risk of oversimplification, we can divide what is generally referred to as Western thought into two distinct traditions. One tradition is characterized by the desire for *autonomy* and *self-sufficiency*. The highest human perfection is intellectual excellence, which, ultimately, is an individual achievement. Though a person may be seriously concerned with justice and with the needs of others, the individual aspires to overcome this need for others and to reach perfection where he or she no longer feels dependent on anyone or anything. Perhaps it is more correct to describe this approach as choosing certain needs above other types of needs, that is, intellectual above physical or social needs.

In Plato's *Phaedo*, for example, the metaphor used to describe the relationship of the body and the soul is that of a person locked in a prison. Platonic philosophy aims at liberating humanity from the prison of the body. To anyone schooled in Western thought, the prisoner metaphor is most appropriate to the description of the relationship of the soul or mind and the body to the process of self-perfection. For Aristotle, although ethics and politics are the objects of serious attention and analysis, the essence of humanity, that activity which is distinctly human, is intellectual contemplation of eternal truths. Unlike practical deliberation, contemplation need have no practical value. The highest human achievement lies in the privacy of one's thoughts; its content has no human utility; its subject, the philosopher, must be free of the claims of the body that interfere with this activity.

In contradistinction to this tradition is one in which *relationship* is an integral part of human perfection. The perfection aspired to is realized in relationship with others and is associated with a pattern of life where the main focus is upon fulfilling normative demands within community and history.

"Not Good" to Be Alone:
Existential Incompleteness and the God of Relationship

The biblical tradition that expresses the relationship of God and the people of Israel is a paradigm case of this relational ontological outlook. The God of the Bible, unlike the God of Aristotle, is described almost exclusively in terms of God's relationship with human beings. Indeed, many religious Jews consider that negating God's providential relationship to history and to humankind—the relationship—is tantamount to espousing atheism.

People are drawn to the Aristotelian God by virtue of the perfection they wish to realize. In this tradition, the "relationship" to God is like the "relationship" between a person and an object of his or her curiosity or aesthetic appreciation, perhaps ultimately of some form of emulation. It is no wonder that in the Middle Ages, a very serious distinction was drawn between belief in the eternity of the universe and belief in creation. The God of Aristotle was an object of intellectual contemplation. Only a God who could be conceived as the Creator, as acting at a particular time, could give law to humanity and could be conceived of in terms of a relationship.

On the inter-human level, the verse epitomizing the biblical outlook is "It is not good for a person to be alone" (Genesis 2:18). As Soloveitchik explains in "The Lonely Man of Faith," the phrase *lo tov*, "[it is] not good," is not to be understood in the light of utilitarian or pragmatic considerations. The unqualified judgment that it is not good for a person to be alone has an existential basis. The biblical statement declares that a human being is incomplete by him- or herself; biological, social, economic, etc., interests aside, it is simply not good that a person be alone.

In the Greek tradition, with its ideal of intellectual perfection, it makes sense for us to seek to be liberated from human relationships that demand intense emotional involvement. The contemplative love of the philosopher places the lover in a situation of control. Interpersonal love, however, places the lover in a context where he or she is vulnerable and dependent. The freedom of the beloved (an essential condition of mature love) precludes the possibility of absolute control and self-sufficiency. In contrast, the relational perfection sought in the biblical tradition leads humanity to accept dependency as a permanent, positive feature of the human condition.

The distinctive approaches of these two traditions—autonomy and relationality/interdependency—extend to many more specific issues. Let us consider their differing implications for attitudes to the body—and then extend these to some practical considerations with respect to our approach to medical care.

Common to the various expressions of the Greek tradition is the metaphor of "the prison of the body." The desire to escape the body and the glorification of the life of the "disembodied intellect" are psychologically tied to feelings of embarrassment at having a body with weaknesses and needs. In biblical thought, however, the body is not perceived as being in conflict with the soul. *The distinction between body and soul is similar to a difference in organic functions; it does not reflect that radical dualism that is implicit in Plato's prison metaphor.*

The difference may not be accidental. As suggested above, the God of the Torah covenant differs from the God of Greek metaphysics in that the covenantal God has a personal relationship with people. However scandalous it may sound to the ears of the metaphysical theologian, God in the Bible chooses interdependency with humankind. The God of History, who sends prophets, gives law, acts and reacts to what people do, is a God who, in some sense, "needs" humanity. Heschel's striking title *God in Search of Man* and his use of such notions as "divine pathos" penetrate to the heart of the biblical outlook. In choosing a covenantal relationship, God, in effect, chose interdependency.

In this framework, interdependency is an ultimate datum of reality. If to be fully human is to give up the quest for total self-sufficiency, and if to be whole a person must learn to love, to accept dependency, and to be able to say, honestly, "I need you," then spiritual liberation must consider the significance of the human body. The Greek tradition must be turned on its head. Our bodies can humanize us and dispel delusions of self-sufficiency.

Dependency and Humility:
The Body as a Spiritual Teacher

The source of human hubris can often be traced to the exaggerated emphasis on the intellect at the expense of recognizing the limitations of the body. The body gives us a sense of our humanity and dependency and, hence, teaches humility. And, in the Bible, humility is perhaps the most notable characteristic one can attribute to people of distinction: "Moses was a very humble man, more so than any other man on earth" (Numbers 12:3). To the degree that we are alienated from the rhythms of the body, to that degree are we out of touch with the spiritual outlook of the biblical tradition.

The body and its functions are dealt with extensively in halakha, which prescribes a blessing even after excretion:

> Blessed art Thou, Lord our God, King of the universe, who hast formed man in wisdom, and created in him a system of veins and arteries. It is well known before Thy glorious throne that if but one of these be opened, or if one of those be closed, it would be impossible to exist in Thy presence. Blessed art Thou, O Lord, who healest all creatures and doest wonders.

It is significant that, in the normative sequence of prayers, this blessing is considered the antecedent of the following:

> My God, the soul which Thou placed within me is pure. Thou hast created it; Thou hast formed it; Thou hast breathed it into me. Thou preservest it within me, and restorest it to me in the hereafter. So long as the soul is within me, I offer thanks before Thee, Lord my God and God of my fathers,

Master of all creatures, Lord of all souls. Blessed art Thou,
O Lord, who restorest the souls to the dead.[1]

Rather than ignore the body, halakha draws a person's attention
to its complex functioning. The "body" heals human delusions of
grandiosity. The body places us firmly in a world in which humanity
cannot survive alone. In hunger and in need, in the interlinking
of sexual desire and love and self-transcendence, in disease and in
decay, the body is an important spiritual teacher. To gain spiritual
wholeness, our soul must make contact with our body.

Humiliation and Hubris in the Doctor-Patient Relationship

The link between body and soul has important implications for
medical practice in general and for the doctor-patient relationship
in particular.

The relationship of the physician to the patient involves more
than curing a disease. The medical question is but one aspect of a
complex human problem. The relationship is a test of whether a person
finds dependency an embarrassing or a valuable human experience.

The problematics of the relationship between the doctor
and the patient can be understood, in many instances, in terms
of dependency exploitation. The patient approaches the doctor in
humility. The limitations of the body expose the delusion of our
self-sufficiency and place us in a position of dependency. Yet the
very dependency that creates humility in one party allows for the
possibility of hubris and manipulation in the other.

The dependency situation can set into motion either love—
human interactions where people are not embarrassed to need
one another—or manipulation—human interactions where one
person's vulnerability is the occasion for another's mastery and
dominance. The latter situation links feelings of helplessness
with expectations of humiliation and, thereby, promotes passivity
and withdrawal. At one pole of the dependency experience is the

frightened, guarded patient standing naked before the awesome knowledge and power of the physician, whom he or she needs. At the other pole, embarrassment and fear of manipulation are absent, and the doctor-patient encounter is marked by warmth, spontaneity, and constructive openness.

At this point, it is imperative that we place our remarks on the doctor-patient relationship in their proper perspective. Unquestionably, the crucial condition for being a good doctor is medical competence—the ability to contribute to a person's health. We are justifiably more fearful of medical incompetence than of callousness or indifference. Nevertheless, a case can be made for the *medical* importance of trust between patient and doctor.

Lacking the divine power of knowing what is in another's mind, the doctor must gain crucial information from the patient. An essential feature, then, of a patient-doctor relationship is that the patient is not afraid to tell the doctor what is wrong. But to reveal what is wrong may be a very painful experience; it is an exposure of our weakness and vulnerability.

It is not unusual for a person to postpone going to a doctor; sometimes the delay can be fatal. This often stems from a person's fear of admitting, "I am helpless." If the body is "the prison of the soul," and if we seek to see ourselves as fundamentally self-sufficient, how dare we succumb to the limitations of the body and expose ourselves to humiliation?

The reluctant patient is just one example of a general orientation to human dependency. To feel free to expose our dependence on another, to move from feeling sick to being cared for, involves such considerations as: "How vulnerable will I be? Can I afford giving a stranger so much power? Can I afford, in the psychological-existential sense, to expose my nakedness to another human being? Can I say to another: I need you?"

Good medical practice requires knowledge that depends, in part, on cultivating relationships based on trust and the absence of the embarrassment of dependency.

Preemptive Dignity:
Avoiding Crisis Dependency
through Preventive Care

There is an interesting midrashic comment on one of the biblical verses dealing with assisting those in need. The text reads:

> And if your brother becomes poor and his means fail him with you, then you shall strengthen him, be he a stranger or a settler, he shall live with you.
>
> (Leviticus 25:35)

Rashi's commentary on this verse (paraphrasing the midrash in *Torat Kohanim, Behar,* 5:1) focuses on the clause "you shall strengthen him":

> Do not let him slip down until he falls completely, for then it will be difficult to raise him; rather strengthen him as he begins to fall. To what is this comparable? To a burden upon an ass: while it is still on the ass, one person can hold it and set it in place; if it falls to the earth, even five people cannot set it back.

One can understand this midrash as making a commonplace point about the difficulty of assisting a person who has fallen into total poverty. The midrash tells the reader, don't wait for him to fall completely. Who, we may wonder, would wait for him to fall? Given our willingness to help, would one not heed common sense and assist a person when it is easiest—when one person can easily do what, later, five people will have difficulty accomplishing?

Perhaps the psychological insight underlying this midrash is that people often prefer responding to the needs of others where there is total helplessness rather than where the dependency is not so obvious. A person may watch the burden slipping off someone's ass and refuse to offer the small effort required for straightening the load, yet this same person may gladly exert much effort to help once the burden has fallen to the ground. There is a particular difficulty in responding to a dependency situation when we are not certain that the recipient will be fully aware and appreciative of our help and concern.

In a discussion of the norms involving human dependency, Maimonides writes:

> There are eight degrees of charity, one higher than the other. The highest degree, exceeded by none, is that of the person who assists a poor Jew by providing him with a gift or a loan, by accepting him into a business partnership, or by helping him find employment—in a word, by putting him where he can dispense with other people's aid. With reference to such aid, it is said, "You shall strengthen him, be he a stranger or a settler, he shall live with you" (Leviticus 25:35), which means strengthen him in such manner that his falling into want is prevented.[2]

The feature common to the acts of the highest degree of charity is that they put the recipient "where he can dispense with other people's aid." The highest form of responding to dependency is to eliminate the need for the crisis-dependency relationship.

The second highest stage of charity, says Maimonides, is to give to the needy "in such a manner that the giver knows not to whom he gives and the recipient knows not from whom it is that he takes."[3]

While not negating the value of responding to a person's need, whatever the motivation (the two stages are but the highest in a series of eight), Maimonides, like the midrash referred to above, draws attention to a form of response to dependency where the answer is directed not only to a particular lack but also to the human predicament of the person in need. The ability to respond to the *person* in the condition of need is the sign of exceptional human sensitivity and refinement.

Within the particular context of the practice of medicine, this type of dependency response is referred to as "preventive assistance." The doctor strives to bring the patient to a situation where she or he does not require the physician. Preventive medicine is an expression of a dependency relationship in which human integrity is respected.

The model for this relationship is that of the teacher-student. The asymmetry of the relationship is not a result of an essential difference between the two parties, nor is it a permanent condition. The ability to see beyond the given dependency relationship to the human beings in question and the attempt to enhance feelings of worth and dignity underlie this ideal response. The midrash and Maimonides stressed the clause "You shall strengthen him" to place the emphasis on the *person* in need, and not on what he or she needs. The human being must be seen in his or her entirety.

Preventive medicine instills a sense of worth and self-sufficiency in patients, who come to feel that they are able, by their own efforts, to ameliorate their problems. Can we create a situation of doctor-patient relationships and medical care where the preventive role predominates? Must we always wait until the person falls in order to respond?

The Challenge of Empathy

In the same chapter of *Mishneh Torah* where Maimonides discusses the eight degrees of charity, he writes:

> Whosoever gives charity to a poor man ill-manneredly and with downcast looks has lost all the merit of his action even though he should give him a thousand gold pieces. He should give with good grace and with joy and should sympathize with him in his plight.... He should speak to him words of consolation and sympathy.[4]

This paragraph indicates clearly that the normative practice of giving charity—"the sign of the righteous man, the seed of Abraham our

Father"—involves more than what we today call "giving charity." A necessary condition for fulfilling the normative halakhic requirement of *tzedakah* (charity) involves the *manner* in which we respond to the person in need. Not only *what* I do but *how* I do it enters into the necessary conditions of this norm. Maimonides stresses that we must see the whole person when we respond to need. Empathy is an element in the proper response to a dependent person.

The implication for medicine is that the patient is not simply the bearer of a disease. A patient presents the physician with more than a functional problem; the particular symptom is but one aspect of a complex, sensitive person. A doctor must recognize the whole person beyond the immediate illness, just as one who gives charity cannot fulfill the norm merely by giving money and ignoring the person.

Few would disagree with this guideline, and its inclusion in Maimonides's laws regarding charity is reasonable and clear. Not so clear is the paragraph immediately following the one quoted above:

> If a poor man requests money from you and you have nothing to give him, *speak to him consolingly*. It is forbidden to upbraid a poor person or to shout at him, because his heart is broken and contrite.... Woe to him who shames a poor man.[5] [emphasis added]

Why, we may ask, must Maimonides enjoin us not to shout at a poor person when we have no money to give? Who would dream of attacking a person in need simply because one was unable to respond to the request?

But Maimonides is sensitive to a problem that people, in general, and doctors, in particular, must face. How do we respond to people we *cannot* help? How do we react to the needy when our inability to satisfy their needs exposes *our* inadequacies?

In the preceding paragraph Maimonides addressed the problem of accepting the person in need as a total human being. In the present paragraph, Maimonides deals with the problem of learning to accept our limited capacities to help someone in need. The ability to respond to another, even though this response will not solve the other's problems completely, is an important feature of mature interdependency.

Maimonides was aware of the fact that we feel threatened when we cannot meet people's needs. We are angry at those who, even unwittingly, expose our limitations and remind us of our circumscribed capacities.

Dependency relationships based on the delusion of omniscience and omnicompetence eventually lead to frustration and anger. Both the person cast in the role of omnicompetent benefactor and the expectant recipient eventually face the frustration of an imperfect reality.

As suggested, one of the major pitfalls in the practice of medicine is the doctor's being cast in the role of the parent in a crisis-dependency relationship. It is not surprising, then, to find considerable anger expressed against doctors in the common "doctor jokes." This anger reveals the frustration of the child who comes to recognize the parent's limitations and is compelled to live in an imperfect world. It masks the unarticulated anger of those impatient for the Messiah to arrive.

Dependency relationships can give rise to warm and open human encounters only if the humanity of the participants is fully recognized by both parties to the relationship. If both the patient and the doctor can accept the fact that the other is a human being—no more and no less—then dependency need not necessarily carry a pejorative connotation. As Maimonides ranked responses to the poor, and hence argued for recognizing the significant differences between the types of responses to those in need, this chapter has indicated the subtlety and complexity of the dependency relationship between doctor and patient.

A sensitive understanding of what is involved in various aspects of the practice of medicine leads to the notion of accepting the "body" as an integral part of being human. The covenant gave a law and acknowledged the inescapable humanity of people. Accepting the fact of our being dependent is a precondition of entering into a relationship with a God who seeks a covenant with people. In the deepest sense, then, the practice of medicine helps create a human world that enables human beings to live with interdependency and the covenantal experience.

Doctors, Patients, and the Wholeness of the "I-It" Encounter

One of the weaknesses of Martin Buber's writings is that the complexity of the "I-It" relationship is not adequately explicated. The "Buberian" is preoccupied with the dynamics of the "I-Thou." Buber writes, "But this is the exalted melancholy of our fate that every 'Thou' in our world must become an 'It.'"[6] Buber holds that authentic relationships can only be of the "I-Thou" type; "I-It" relationships are functional and somehow ultimately manipulative.

Is the doctor-patient relationship the occasion for an "I-Thou" encounter? Absolutely not. One doesn't go to a doctor for a love encounter. It would be absurd to expect to find in a routine medical checkup the qualities of spontaneity and "radical surprise." The doctor-patient relationship is a paradigm case of a functional relationship and, hence, in Buberian terms, clearly within the "I-It" class. Yet, it is certainly wrong to characterize the doctor-patient relationship as necessarily manipulative. The doctor does not have to "encounter lovingly" the whole person in order to prevent her or his relationship with the patient from degenerating into manipulation. "I-Thou" and "I-It" clearly do not exhaust all possible characterizations of human encounters. Relationships revolving around definite needs and interests may nonetheless be genuine human encounters.

We may not fault the doctor for focusing on a functional problem and not on the "whole" person. Nevertheless, there is an important place for the notion of the "whole" person in the doctor-patient relationship. Borrowing Buber's language, we can aspire to a situation where the relationship, though thoroughly functional, takes place within an "I-Thou" perspective. This means that when the physician is dealing with a particular problem—a diseased liver, a heart disorder, or a common cold—she or he ought to remember that a whole person has this problem.

Although a physician is engaged in a functional problem, she or he must consider the physical and psychological consequences of the treatment. Whether a patient will perceive him- or herself as ugly and unattractive as a result of a particular treatment is a relevant fact to be considered in prescribing treatment. "Wholeness," then, is not only relevant to encounters of friendship and love; it is also relevant to medical practice where considerations involving the total person affect specific functional decisions.

I am not claiming that the body defines the whole human being; we're more than our bodily needs. But it is universal experience that the body sometimes takes over; pain can lock a person into him- or herself. I'm claiming that we must be aware of the whole human being, including the body—dignity and self-respect in the bodily sense are no less important to the spiritual-existential condition. The doctor-patient example reflects the opportunity for a person to be sensitive to another's fears; it also gives us the opportunity for a person not to allow the body to define the whole human being, but to try to find channels of self-transcendence: the ability to appreciate the kindness of another human being toward us. This is not sentimental, but essential to the spiritual and indeed the medical health of human beings created in the image of God.

3

Democratizing the Spiritual

The Risks and Rewards of Halakha

Pious Certainty, Submissive Obedience, and Social Conformism: Spinoza's Critique of Judaism

Halakhic Judaism is often characterized as an extensive and detailed code of norms. The name of the celebrated codification of Jewish law the *Shulchan Arukh* (the Set Table) suggests Judaism is a way of life that is completely worked out and prepared. All that is required of a person is the willingness to sit at the table and partake of the meal, that is, follow the prescribed rules and regulations.

Similarly, halakha is often perceived as a finished, self-sufficient guide to human conduct. The only difficulty we may encounter is in the quantity of norms or the sacrifices demanded by certain practices. Aside from this, the *Shulchan Arukh* simplifies human life by reducing the complexity of alternatives to one straightforward choice: to obey or not to obey. Doubt, confusion, uncertainty, agonizing deliberation, and frustration in the face of complexity seem alien to the experience of a person committed to this way of life. Within the comprehensive framework of halakha we know exactly what to do "from the cradle to the grave," from the moment we wake up to the moment we go to sleep. Nothing in human existence is unregulated; there is a correct way of responding to each and every event of our life.

> Surely, this Instruction which I enjoin upon you this day is not too baffling for you, nor is it beyond reach. It is not in the heavens.... Neither is it beyond the sea.... No, the thing is very close to you, in your mouth and in your heart, to observe it.... I have put before you life and death, blessing and curse. Choose life....
>
> (DEUTERONOMY 30:11–14, 30:19)

Spinoza defined Judaism in light of the primacy of obedience. Using Judaism as a paradigm case of faith and theology, Spinoza, in *A Theologico-Political Treatise*, claims: "The sphere of reason is ... truth and wisdom; the sphere of theology is piety and obedience" (chap. 15); "Philosophy has no end in view save truth: faith ... looks for nothing but obedience and piety" (chap. 14); and with reference to Rabbinic Judaism (in contrast to Jesus, who sought "solely to teach the universal moral law"), "the Pharisees, in their ignorance, thought that the observance of the state law and the Mosaic law was the sum total of morality; whereas such laws merely had reference to the public welfare and aimed not so much at instructing the Jews as at keeping them under constraint" (chap. 5).

The type of personality most compatible with the essence of Jewish spirituality, as understood by Spinoza, is the obedient, submissive person. While philosophy and universal morality demand that one be intellectually open, inquisitive, and reflective, Judaism focuses entirely on subservience to laws ("Scripture ... does not condemn ignorance, but obstinacy" [chap. 14]).[1]

Although to Spinoza and to others this characterization is negative and discrediting, there are those who revel in the confidence, serenity, and certainty that such an orientation to life affords. The following analysis takes issue with this picture of Judaism, seeks to correct this misleading caricature, and will try to offer an alternate representation of halakhic spirituality—one that accepts the risk of uncertainty and is prepared to live within the challenging environment of the modern world. This is a picture of a halakhic system driven not merely by legalistic or "pharisaic" formalism but by an attempt to cultivate a certain set of human spiritual values. It is a halakha that understands itself as staking out a position of calculated risks and rewards in order to cultivate these values in the face of various mitigating human tendencies; that sees our personal relationship with God, individually and collectively, as preceding and transcending the disciplined life of halakhic judgment; that views the observance of sacred time as evoking and nurturing shared memories of that living relationship; that sees the legalistic dimension of halakha as an expression of "relational morality," outlining the types of normative expectations inherent in any relationship; that relates to the mitzvot as expressions of divine love, against a backdrop of unconditional divine love; and that takes certain normative risks for the sake of democratizing the spiritual and creating communities of action.

Beyond Formalism:
Halakha as a Values-Driven System

The picture of Judaism as a comfortable, rule-dominated spiritual way of life fails to do justice to Jewish thought and practice for a number of reasons. The identification of Judaism with behavioral conformity to the detailed norms of the halakha reveals a limited vision of the tradition—one controverted throughout its own Scripture and liturgy. On Yom Kippur, when worshipers atone for their sins, the following text from Isaiah is read:

> *Because you fast in strife and contention,*
> *And to strike with a wicked fist!*
> *Your fasting today is not such*
> *As to make your voice heard on high.*
> *Is such the fast I have desire,*

A day for men to starve their bodies?
Is it bowing the head like a bulrush,
And lying in sackcloth and ashes?
Do you call that a fast,
A day when the Lord is favorable?
No, this is the fast I desire:
To unlock fetters of wickedness,
To untie the cords of the yoke,
To let the oppressed go free.
        (ISAIAH 58:4–6)

The prophet's ringing repudiation of formalism bears witness to Judaism's acknowledgment that external compliance with norms may not only be inadequate, but may also lead to hateful and perverse religiosity. In the face of ethical indifference, ritual observance becomes pointless and decadent.[2]

The mistake of confining halakhic demands to the observance of positive norms and avoidance of negative ones is discussed by Nachmanides in his commentary on the Torah. With regard to the verse "You shall be holy, for I, the Lord your God, am holy" (Leviticus 19:2), Nachmanides develops the notion of a person becoming a "degenerate within the framework of the Torah":

> And such is the way of the Torah, that after it lists certain specific prohibitions, it includes them all in a general precept. Thus after warning with detailed laws regarding all business dealings between people, such as not to steal or rob or to wrong one another, and similar prohibitions, he said in general, "And thou shalt do that which is right and good" (Deuteronomy 6:18), thus including under a positive commandment the duty of doing that which is right and of agreeing to a compromise (when not to do so would be inequitable); as well as all requirements to act "beyond" the line of justice for the sake of pleasing one's fellowman.[3]

Nachmanides expands elsewhere with regard to the verse "What is right and good in the sight of the Lord" (Deuteronomy 6:18):

> Our Rabbis have a beautiful Midrash on this verse. They have said: "['That which is right and good'] refers to a compromise and going beyond the requirement of the letter of the law." The intent of this is as follows: At first he [Moses] stated that you are to keep His statutes and His testimonies which He commanded you and now he is stating that even where He has not commanded you, give thought, as well, to do what is good and right in His eyes, for He loves the good and the right. Now this is a great principle, for it is impossible to mention in the Torah all aspects of man's conduct with his neighbors and friends, and all his various transactions, and the ordinances of all societies and countries. But since He mentioned many of them—such as, "Thou shalt not go up and down as a talebearer" (Leviticus 19:16); "thou shalt not take vengeance, nor bear any grudge" (Leviticus 19:18); "neither shalt thou stand idly by the blood of thy neighbor" (Leviticus 19:16); "thou shalt not curse the deaf" (Leviticus 19:14); "thou shalt rise up before the hoary head" (Leviticus 19:32) and the like—He reverted to state in a general way that, in all matters, one should do what is good and right, including even compromise and going beyond the requirements of the law.[4]

According to Nachmanides, compliance with the explicit norms of Judaism is no guarantee of fulfilling the requirements of halakha. In fact, a person's conduct may be judged sinful and reprehensible even if he or she has not violated any explicit rule. Halakha is a normative system that is not restricted to conduct regulated by specified clear-cut rules but includes ethical and spiritual meta-standards such as "You shall be holy" and "You shall do that which is right and good." Such embracing norms, though vague and lacking the precision expected of typical legal systems, and the standards of conduct implicit in "going beyond the requirements of the law" are two operative elements that regulate halakhic conduct and justify critical assessment of what otherwise might be seen as blameless behavior.[5]

The important point is that these standards are operative within the legal system and are not simply moral evaluations of legally permissible behavior. As a religious system embracing all aspects of human conduct, halakha includes what in most secular legal systems would be considered extralegal morality. Hence, any description of halakhic Judaism that confines it to an enumeration of precise rules and regulations is incomplete and inadequate.

Nachmanides explains the need for general standards in the Torah by arguing that "it is impossible to mention in the Torah all aspects of man's conduct." The impossibility of stating precise rules to cover all conceivable situations explains and justifies vagueness and incompleteness in a legal system. This explains a judge's creative role in deciding the applicability of legal norms in unforeseen situations.[6]

A legal system committed to human values cannot offer people an absolute and final set of formal rules. No norm that regulates conduct can claim to be absolute to the degree that there are no imaginable situations where following this norm would be self-defeating, pointless, or damaging to other important values.

Nachmanides's reference to compromise, *peshura*, alludes to the Talmudic discussion of compromise in the form of arbitration where the following generalization is made: "Where there is justice, there is no peace; and where there is peace, there is no justice."[7] Arbitration aims at reaching a solution agreeable to all parties in a dispute, rather than a solution based on strict justice where one party may be found at fault. The interest in justice may conflict with another value, namely, the peaceful interaction of the parties in question. The crucial point is that both values cannot be strictly adhered to simultaneously.

"They Do Not Grant 'Halves' in Heaven": Necessary Evils and the Calculated Moral Risk of Halakha

The insoluble nature of some situations involving a conflict of values is vividly illustrated by a Talmudic debate. Rabbi Eliezer stated, "It is forbidden to arbitrate in a settlement, and he who arbitrates thus offends ... but let the law cut through the mountain." To which Rabbi Joshua ben Kovhah replied, "Settlement is a mitzvah [commandment, meritorious act]."[8]

The potential conflict of "goods" and the impossibility of formulating norms to cover all situations according to their intended purposes suggest that normative systems ought to be evaluated in light of the moral risks involved in the system. To speak of a perfect normative system is naïve if one believes that a set of rules per se can guarantee the implementation of the values and the type of society the system aims at realizing. Normative and legislative directives do not necessarily lead us to "turn away from evil and do good"; the wisdom of such practiced choices must be evaluated in light of a calculation of the moral risks the system is willing to take and, conversely, is conscientious about avoiding. Hence the importance of checks and correctives, lest a system become ossified and self-defeating.

The following story captures the crux of the inescapability of risks:

> "And they cried with a great [loud] voice unto the Lord, their God" (Nehemiah 9:4). What did they cry? Woe, woe, it is he [the evil inclination] who has destroyed the Sanctuary, burnt the Temple, killed all the righteous, driven all Israel into exile, and is still dancing around among us! Thou hast surely given him to us so that we may receive reward through him. We want neither him, nor reward through him! Thereupon a tablet fell down from heaven for them, whereupon the word "truth" was inscribed.... They ordered

a fast of three days and three nights, whereupon he surren-
dered to them. He came forth from the Holy of Holies like
a young fiery lion. Thereupon the Prophet said to Israel:
This is the evil desire of idolatry.... They said: Since this is a
time of Grace, let us pray for mercy for the Tempter to evil.
They prayed for mercy, and he was handed over to them.
He said to them: Realize that if you kill him, the world goes
down. They imprisoned him for three days, then looked in
the whole land of Israel for a fresh egg and could not find it.
Thereupon they said: What shall we do now? Shall we kill
him? The world would then go down. Shall we beg for half
mercy? They do not grant "halves" in heaven. [Then] they
put out his eyes and let him go. It helped inasmuch as he no
more entices men to commit incest.[9]

The statement "They do not grant halves in heaven" expresses the
insight that evil cannot be isolated and eliminated by miracle (let
alone by legislative fiat) as long as human society persists. Rabbi
Nachman explains that the phrase *tov me'od* (very good) in the
Creation story in Genesis includes the evil inclination, for without
it people would not build houses, marry, or have children.[10] Evil is
inextricably bound up with the human drive for power, assertion,
and creativity. Evil in general originates in the most basic impulses
of the human condition, which also supplies the motivation for eggs
being laid. Although one may know what is evil and may dream of
excising its sources and leaving only the good, reality refuses such
neat dissections.

The response to the request for half mercies—"They do not
grant 'halves' in heaven"—affirms the inescapability of risks. The
complexity of the human situation means that activities and projects
that are aimed at certain goals may unwittingly create the conditions
for undesired and counterproductive consequences. Complacent
trust in half mercies is the stuff of unanswered prayers; human
actions and institutions warrant constant scrutiny. To wish to create

a world without risks is to wish for a kind of existence that heaven cannot grant. Struggle is inherent in our world; that which brings forth good also spawns evil.

The arguments against describing halakha as a straightforward, uncomplicated system of rules require the presentation of an alternative description that can do justice to that system of norms. Rather than attempt to formulate definitions, we shall adopt an angle of vision in accordance with the insight that "they do not grant halves in heaven." The halakhic system, like any normative system, can be analyzed in terms of the risks involved. Any distinctive characteristic of halakha, such as the legalistic nature of Jewish spirituality, may be misunderstood unless it is perceived as a risk-laden alternative within a difficult dilemma. The decision to pursue a particular course of action does not preclude acknowledging the dangers implicit in one's choice. After weighing the risks of the alternatives, one may adopt a way of life in full awareness of its dangers. Unless this way of life is scrutinized and checked, it may become a distortion of its intended purpose.

Though normative systems are rarely, if ever, the products of a conscious thought-out act, there is value in analyzing a system in light of the risks it avoids and the risks it takes. To subject the halakhic system to such an analysis, we must indicate the problematic situations faced by halakha and thus elucidate the dangers associated with halakhic Judaism.

Jewish spirituality derives its meaning from two poles: *legal*, the divinely revealed norms humanity is expected to follow (halakha), and *relational*, the relationship between humanity and God. The struggle of halakhic spirituality is how to retain the relational ground that is the source, purpose, and animating principle of traditional norms in the face of a massive and seemingly self-sufficient legal framework. The development of Judaism into a comprehensive, all-encompassing legal structure often tends to overshadow its relational aspects and has led some to consciously identify worship of God with compliance with rules and statutes.[11]

The two poles, relational and legal, exist in a constant tension. On the one hand, legality can be interpreted as a response to the risks inherent in the unstructured passion of a spiritual relationship; on the other hand, the relational orientation counteracts the risks of a self-contained religious formalism. It is these risks that halakha attempts to balance with a series of checks and correctives.

Before the Law:
The Covenant as a Personal Relationship with God

The revelation of law at Sinai is an integral part of the establishment of a relationship between God and Israel. The striking parallels between the biblical covenant and the suzerainty treaties of the ancient Near East indicate, *inter alia*, the relational context of halakha. The biblical scholar Mendenhall argues that the first-person form of address ("I am the Lord ...") is related to the fact that (for the Hittites) "the covenant form is still thought of as a personal relationship, rather than as an objective, impersonal statement of law."[12]

In light of the analogy between the Sinaitic revelation and extra-biblical covenantal documents, one may ascribe to "I am the Lord your God who brought you out of the land of Egypt, the house of bondage" (Exodus 20:2) the function of a preamble, where a main party to the agreement is identified and the relational ground of the covenant is established. The stipulation of norms is part of the covenantal context and is not independent and autonomous. The repeated biblical references to God as Israel's God, and to Israel as God's people, indicate the soil in which biblical law and spirituality are rooted and nurtured.[13]

Rabbinic Judaism developed in a context that was in many important ways dramatically different from the biblical framework. Most important was the acknowledgment that prophetic revelation had ceased.[14] Unlike biblical accounts of direct unmistakable manifestations of divine will, Rabbinic Judaism encountered the "hiding of God's face," that is, powerlessness and national exile.[15]

The development by Rabbinic Judaism of the Torah that was "not in heaven" enabled the authority of legal reasoning to reach unprecedented heights. It is thus perhaps striking the extent to which Rabbinic thought continued to emphasize the centrality of the relational basis of Jewish law.

> "I am the Lord your God" (Exodus 20:2). Why were the Ten Commandments not said at the beginning of the Torah? They give a parable. To what may this be compared? To the following: A king who entered a province said to the people: "May I be your king?" But the people said to him: "Have you done anything good for us that you should rule over us?" What did he do then? He built the city wall for them, he brought in the water supply for them, and he fought their battles. Then when he said to them: "May I be your king?" they said to him: "Yes, yes." Likewise God. He brought the Israelites out of Egypt, divided the sea for them, sent down the manna for them, brought up the well for them, brought the quail for them. He fought for them the battles with Amalek. Then He said to them: "I am to be your king." And they said to Him: "Yes, yes."[16]

The authority of God to legislate is bound up with God's involvement in the historical drama of redemption. Events create a bond between Israel and God that in turn forms the basis of the covenant of God and Israel. The liberation from Egypt precedes the giving of the Torah at Sinai or, to use Soloveitchik's terminology, *berit goral* (the covenant of destiny) precedes *berit ye'ud* (the covenant of task). Halakhic norms are ultimately grounded in shared historical memories of significant moments in our people's relationship with God.

> When, in time to come, your children ask you, "What mean the decrees, laws, and rules that the Lord our God has enjoined upon you?" you shall say to your children, "We

were slaves to Pharaoh in Egypt and the Lord freed us from Egypt with a mighty hand. The Lord wrought before our eyes marvelous and destructive signs and portents in Egypt, against Pharaoh and all his household; and us He freed from there, that He might take us and give us the land that He had promised on oath to our fathers. Then the Lord commanded us to observe all these laws, to revere for our lasting good and for our survival, as is now the case. It will be therefore to our merit before the Lord our God to observe faithfully this whole Instruction, as He has commanded us."

(Deuteronomy 6:20–25)

Sacred Time:
Shared Memories of a Living Relationship

Even though postbiblical Judaism could not point to dramatic historical events like those described in the Bible and was compelled to explain God's silence rather than exalt in God's saving presence, halakhic Judaism nonetheless instituted structures to preserve the interrelationship of providential historical events and the normative system. Of inestimable importance in this regard was the structuring of experiences that vividly recreated events of the sacred past by dramatic rituals, public readings, and prayer. Through such frameworks, halakhic Judaism incorporated memory and history and a relationship with the Divine into the normative experience of the Jew.[17]

The notion of *sacred time*—rituals through which we evoke historical moments suffused with a manifest awareness of divine providential will—pervades the halakhic Jew's experience of the Sabbath and the historical festivals. The Exodus from Egypt, for example, became part of Jewish memory no matter where and when Jews lived.[18] Notwithstanding the silence of God in their everyday experience, Jews experienced God's redemptive, relational presence in halakhically structured sacred time. What was absent in daily reality was discovered through reenactment and remembering.[19]

Thus, historical memory became a fundamental feature of Jewish religious experience—a continual reminder of the relational basis of the normative system. The connection between halakha and the relationship between God and Israel was never severed. An accurate account of halakha, therefore, must describe the distinct nature of relational as well as legal morality.

Relational Morality:
The Normative Expectations of Social Roles

The notion of relational morality is not an unfamiliar one. Most people know of norms that are bound up with particular social relationships. Descriptions of socially defined roles or relationships, such as police officer, judge, or parent, are incomplete if they fail to mention the norms entailed by the roles in question. It makes no sense to want to be a police officer, for example, and at the same time refuse to be bound by the normative expectations entailed by this role.

The ethical autonomist who insists that personal decision separates what is factually and what is normatively applicable to an individual negates the normative component of many social realities. Rights and obligations enter into the very description of roles and socially defined relationships; a person who adopts or acknowledges certain roles cannot consistently negate the applicability of the relevant norms. The fact that the norms attached to certain relations, such as parenthood, may differ in various societies or that some relations may entail different expectations within the same society does not weaken this argument. The claim being made is that roles and relations generally entail normative expectations. This is what is meant by "relational morality."

Kant believed that an analysis of moral norms would reveal certain formal conditions by virtue of which rules become normative for human beings. The burden of this essay is not to uncover the ground of obligation of any particular norm. Rather, we claim that the relationship between God and a particular people constitutes the basis of a particular attitude to a certain set of norms. Saying that your identity, which is defined by your relationship to God, entails a commitment to a particular normative system does not commit you to negating the force of many of these selfsame norms outside of that relational context. Your relationship to God may be a *sufficient* condition for your commitment to certain norms and not necessarily a *necessary and sufficient* condition (e.g., it does not involve claiming that ethical norms lack normative force unless grounded in divine will). Characterizing halakha as a relationship-grounded normative system is compatible with the argument that moral concepts are logically prior to the theological concepts of the major Western religions, insofar as minimally acceptable definitions of God include moral concepts. Even if it is correct that the concept "God" is unintelligible unless moral concepts are assumed, this would in no way challenge the claim that entering into a relationship within the context of a covenantal relationship leads to the understanding that, for halakha, the relational condition is the dominant reason for complying with the norms of this system.

"Beyond the Requirements of the Law": A Case Study in Relational Morality

The relational feature of halakhic norms explains regulative features of halakha beyond explicit legal rules. The comments of Nachmanides on "You shall be holy" and "You shall do that which is right and good in the sight of God," quoted above, attest to the influence of standards within halakha that guide behavior "in the gaps" not covered by explicit rules and may even justify criticism of conduct ostensibly in conformity with halakhic rules. These nonformalistic standards are grounded in the relationship that underlies the legal system.

The order of the *Shema* portion of daily Jewish prayer, which is composed of two passages, one from Deuteronomy and one from Numbers, is explained by Rabbi Joshua ben Korhah as follows:

> Why do we read *shema* (Hear, O Israel! The Lord is our God, the Lord is One …) before *ve-haya im shamoa* (If ye shall

hearken diligently to My commandments ...)? Because one must first accept the yoke of the Kingship of God and then accept the yoke of the commandments.[20]

Rabbi Joshua ben Korhah acknowledges that allegiance to God and acceptance of the framework of commandments are two independent concepts. But even while identifying our relationship to God with the commandments, he insists that the acceptance of the yoke of the Kingship of God *precede* acceptance of the yoke of commandments. It is not one or the other, but the joining of the two, that shapes the character of the legal system.[21]

"More Delightful Than Wine": The Mitzvot as Expressions of Divine Love

Rabbinic Judaism perceived the mitzvot as expressions of divine love:

> Thou hast loved the house of Israel, Thy people, with ever-lasting love; Thou hast taught us Torah and precepts, laws and judgments. Therefore, Lord our God, when we lie down and when we rise up we will speak of Thy laws, and rejoice in the words of Thy Torah and in Thy precepts evermore. Indeed, they are our life and the length of our days; we will meditate on them day and night. Mayest Thou never take away Thy love from us. Blessed art Thou, O Lord, Who lovest Thy people Israel.[22]

The understanding of the mitzvah as a vehicle for experiencing and expressing the love relationship between God and Israel may explain the Rabbinic statement "Greater is he who does an act which he is commanded to do than he who does an act which he is not commanded to do."[23] The mitzvah as a relational norm loses its point if isolated from its context. While not ignoring the value of the rule as such, the Rabbis fought against severing the link between the norm and the religious passion for close connection with God.

Although the revelation at Sinai was understood as the ground of Rabbinic halakhic authority (i.e., as a formal legal category), this did not preclude the Rabbis from perceiving Sinai as the expression of an intimate love encounter between God and Israel.[24]

"Oh, give me the kisses of your mouth, for your love is more delightful than wine" (Song of Songs 1:2) refers, according to Rabbi Johanan, to the commandments given at Sinai. Rabbi Akiba, one of the great masters of the Talmudic method of legal inference and exposition, who was instrumental in establishing the authoritative foundation of the Talmudic legal tradition, understood the relationship between God and Israel in terms of the passionate poetry of the Song of Songs[25]: "All the ages are not worth the day on which the Song of Songs was given to Israel; for all the writings are holy, but the Song of Songs is the Holy of Holies."[26]

"Man does not sit, move, and occupy himself when he is alone in his house, as he sits, moves and occupies himself when he is in the presence of a great king," wrote Maimonides. Accordingly, those who achieve the perfection of *yir'ah* (awe before God) "know who it is that is with them and as a result act subsequently as they ought to."[27]

This is the aim of the law and, interestingly, is acquired after or by performing the actions prescribed by the law. The relational consciousness that is produced by the law impacts practice by adding to a person's normative practice the influence of his or her relationship with God. A person may be judged a "degenerate within the domain of Torah" or another person may act "beyond the strict requirements of the law" because the normative text of Jewish law contains not only "You shall ..." and "You shall not ..." but also "I am the Lord" (Exodus 20:2), "you shall be holy, for I, the Lord your God, am holy" (Leviticus 19:2), "Let all your deeds be for the sake of heaven" (*Mishnah Avot* 2:17), "In all your ways acknowledge Him, and He will direct your paths" (Proverbs 3:6), "I have set the Lord before me continuously" (Psalm 16:8), and "You shall love the Lord your God with all your heart and with all your soul and with all your might" (Deuteronomy 6:5).

Halakha is neither a self-contained, formalistic legal system nor a humanistic social contract. *Halakha is a relational ethic.* It is a covenant between a people and its God.

"Children of God": Halakha and Unconditional Divine Love

Although the importance of the relational feature of Jewish spirituality supports Buber's emphasis on the "I-Thou," halakhic Judaism merged the relational feature with the exacting rigor of legality. No account of traditional Judaism can be considered honest and complete unless it indicates how these two elements interact, each correcting the distortions that may result from an exclusive emphasis on one or the other.

Jewish spirituality is not characterized by conditional divine acceptance alone, but by the dialectical tension between *din* (justice, i.e., conditional acceptance) and *rachamim* (loving-kindness, unconditional love). According to the midrash,[28] God at first thought of creating the world with the quality of *din*. When God realized, however, that the world could not endure according to *din* alone, God introduced the quality of *rachamim*. This duality is not restricted to the characterization of ontological principles; it also applies to descriptions of God's relationship to God's people. Unlike the covenant at Sinai, the covenant with Abraham and his descendents does not stipulate conditions.

To what extent does the type of covenant with Abraham and the related notion of *berit avot* (the covenant of the fathers) shape the Jews' perception of their relationship with God? How is the legal-conditional understanding of the covenant counterbalanced by the idea of a permanent unconditional relationship?[29]

As discussed above, Jewish law is fundamentally a relational ethic. Thus, the relationship with God not only constitutes the ground of authority of Torah but also may influence the content of the law and the nature of our conduct. Relational morality may be called identity-based morality in the sense that the relationship not only influences our behavior but also constitutes the central category through which we define ourselves. Loss of identity signals loss of a source of normative conduct; choice of an identity provides a basis for action and evaluation.

The Mishnah attributes the following statement to Rabbi Akiba:

> Beloved is man in that he was created in the image [of God]. Greater love was proved to him in that he was created in the image of God, as it is said: "In His image did God make man" (Genesis 9:6). Beloved are Israel in that they are called children of God. Greater love was proved to them in that they were called children of God, as it is said: "You are children of the Lord your God" (Deuteronomy 14:1).[30]

While affirming the irreducible worth and dignity of all humanity, Rabbi Akiba underscores the applicability of the relational category "children" to Israel. The relational dimension involves a particular identity that, as explained above, brings with it particular normative conditions.

Whereas human dignity is based on a fixed unalterable condition, namely, the ontological status of having been created in the image of God, the permanence of the relational condition "children of the Lord" is the subject of a Rabbinic debate:

> "You are sons of the Lord your God" (Deuteronomy 14:1): when you behave as sons you are designated sons; if you do not behave as sons, you are not designated sons: this is Rabbi Judah's view. Rabbi Meir said: "In both cases you are called sons, for it is said, 'They are foolish children' (Jeremiah 4:22); and it is also said, 'They are sons in whom there is no faith' (Deuteronomy 32:20); and it is also said, 'A seed of evil-doers, sons that deal corruptly' (Isaiah 1:4); and it is said, 'and it shall come to pass that, in the place where it was said unto them, You are not My people, it shall be said unto them, You are sons of the living God' (Hosea 2:1)."

Why give these additional quotations? For should you reply, "Only when foolish are they designated sons, but not when they lack faith"—then come and hear: And it is said, "They are sons in whom is no faith." And should you say, "When they have no faith they are called sons, but when they serve idols they are not called sons"—then come and hear: And it is said, "A seed of evil-doers, sons that deal corruptly." And should you say, "They are indeed called sons that act corruptly, but not good sons"—then come and hear: "And it is said, and it shall come to pass that in the place where it was said unto them, You are not My people, it shall be said unto them, You are sons of the living God."[31]

Rabbi Meir argues that the people of Israel are referred to as "sons" even when they violate the covenant and do not act as children. In contrast to Rabbi Judah, who maintains the unyielding conditional nature of God's relationship to Israel, Rabbi Meir indicates the unconditional endurance of the covenantal relationship irrespective of strict merit. Rabbi Judah focuses on the halakhic-legal pole; Rabbi Meir is prepared to admit a permanent relational pole.[32]

The unconditional feature of divine love in Rabbinic Judaism differs from a theology of grace in that it is conjoined with an all-demanding normative system. The permanence of the relationship with God is not antithetical to the halakhic demand; but divine acceptance mitigates the anxiety of failure and is a source of renewed effort in the event of failure. Moreover, consciousness of divine presence may act as a catalyst for *teshuvah*, the spiritual self-transformation that leads ultimately to a return to halakhic duties and tasks.

In explaining how Aaron "held the many back from iniquity" (Malachi 2:6), the midrash explains:

When Aaron would walk along the road and meet an evil or wicked man, he would greet him. On the morrow if that man sought to commit a transgression, he would think:

"Woe unto me! How shall I lift my eyes afterward and look upon Aaron? I should be ashamed before him, for he greeted me." And thus that man would refrain from transgression.[33]

Someone's relationship with another may be a source of strength and an influence on conduct. Similarly, God's enduring love is not so much atoning as inspiring. Grace acts as an impetus to action and renewal.[34]

We can bear the burden of enormous responsibility when the ground of our existence is permanent and secure. Halakha is legality and accountability; the God of the Torah commands and judges. Yet, for all that, we need not be crushed, for God's love and concern is independent of our performance. *Rachamim* makes it possible to live according to *din* without becoming paralyzed by inadequacy and guilt.[35]

Low Standards and Impure Motives: The Risks of Democratizing the Spiritual to Create a Community of Action

Religion is often regarded as essentially an activity of the individual. The movement of the "alone to the Alone" or "what one does with one's aloneness" are plausible definitions insofar as they focus on the common belief that ultimately the religious experience is the privilege of the solitary individual.[36] Such definitions are not wholly applicable to Judaism. The classical definitive relationship to God in Jewish history is the relationship between God and the people of Israel. The towering figures of the sacred past are prophets, that is, people mediating between the two main parties in the relationship, God and Israel. In a revealing midrashic account of Moses's forty-day encounter with God on the secluded heights of Mount Sinai, God "notices" the people's perversion around the golden calf and immediately interrupts Moses with the order: "Go down! All the greatness that I have given you is for the sake of Israel! And now that they have sinned, what need do I have of you?"[37] Divine revelation in Judaism is first and foremost the giving of the Torah to the people of Israel. "And I shall be sanctified in the midst of the people of Israel" (Leviticus 22:32).

The primacy of community accounts for the characteristic uniformity and standardization of halakhic practice. Responsibility for the spiritual welfare of an entire people comprising the prophet, the poet, "from woodchopper to water drawer" (Deuteronomy 29:10), sets into motion a process of democratizing the spiritual.[38] To enable a historical community to share in a common spiritual enterprise, halakha was compelled to develop a spiritual language that would cut across individual and generational differences.

As our thesis that "heaven does not grant halves" suggests, this process was not without serious risks. A selection of various sensitive areas of halakha will reveal the pros and cons of the influence of community on halakhic practice.

The challenge met by halakhic specifications is that of translating abstract vision into concrete action. Marriages often encounter their first crisis when the emotional "highs" of single-minded love meet the undramatic tasks of the everyday. In order to save Judaism from becoming an alienated domain of ineffectual fantasies and verbiage, halakhic Judaism translated the notion of the sanctity of all of creation on the Sabbath into "hands-off" restrictions, the freedom of the Exodus from Egypt into scrubbing one's house free of leaven, and the empathy of charity into rules and percentages.

Detailed specification, however, engenders spiritual risks. One risk is missing the forest for the trees. One can become so caught up in details that the point of the norm or practice in question can be lost. Fascination with legalistic detail can lead to a religiosity of compulsive normative conformity. To counter this risk, some have sought to explicate *ta'amei ha-mitzvot* (reasons for commandments). Whether we claim to uncover the reasons for the enactment of the commandments or simply to indicate reasons for fulfilling commandments in the present, we "loosen up" halakhic practice by keeping alive the connection between halakhic details and normative intent. Also, the integration of *aggadah* (story form of midrashic literature) with legal halakhic material in the midrash and Talmud helped retain the teleology of the system. General halakhic insights and goals, which are often best captured in dramatic story form, are an integral part of jurisprudential texts. *Aggadah* counteracts the tendency of law to become tight and humorless.[39]

Another consequence of the concern with developing a community of action was the legitimization of minimal standards of practice. For the sake of encouraging concrete action, halakha was prepared to accept action however impure the motives:

> One who says: "This *selah* is for charity so that my son will recover from sickness or so that I shall enter the world to come," behold this person is a perfectly righteous person.[40]

Halakha took the risk of praising deeds of questionable moral motivation in light of the fact that the act benefitted another. The good effects of the act, whatever the agent's reasons, are relevant to the halakhic response. Because community is so important, the Rabbis were willing to adjust the criteria of good actions to include such behavior.

Similarly, the halakhic principle "Mitzvot do not require *kavanah* [intention]," as formulated by Rava in the Talmud,[41] leads to the puzzling case where a person who had been *forced* to eat matzah during Passover is regarded as having fulfilled the commandment of eating unleavened bread. The absence of the intention to fulfill a religious norm and the presence of coercion notwithstanding, swallowing matzah on Passover meets the necessary conditions for fulfilling the legal norm of eating matzah on Passover.[42] This decision exposed Judaism to loneliness and ridicule for two thousand years; what sort of spiritual system can ascribe religious value to such an act?

Accordingly, Judaism has been attacked for being mechanical, compulsive, and legalistic and for ignoring inwardness and purity of soul. Halakha exposed itself to the great risk of this challenge because its task is to create a spiritual people. If a community is not only composed of prophets, it must create conditions for growth, however imperfect the starting point.

The willingness to validate acts resulting from imperfect motives is not only explained by the Rabbis' focusing on the good consequences of an act, but also reflects a deep-seated Rabbinic belief that action leads a person to higher levels of conduct. "From an act done not for its own sake, one comes to do the act for its own sake" reflects an important developmental hypothesis of halakhic Judaism.[43] Where an act could be regarded as the potential starting point in a process of spiritual growth, the Rabbis were prepared to risk being accused of mechanistic legalism. They even went so far as to encourage halakhic practice without proper belief in God.

> Rav Huna and Rabbi Jeremiah said in the name of Rabbi Hiyya bar Rabbi Abba: "It is written, 'They have forsaken me and have not kept My law' (Jeremiah 16:11)—that is, Would that they had forsaken Me but kept My law, since by occupying themselves therewith, the light which it contains would have led them back to the right path." Rav Huna said: "Study Torah even if it be not for its own sake, since even if not for its own sake at first, it will eventually be for its own sake."[44]

The validation of minimal conditions, however, was not a policy without detractors. The fear that people would be satisfied with the minimum conditions of fulfilling their duty and would not aspire to higher levels of practice led some to voice opposition to this approach.

> Rabbi Ammi said: "From these words of Rabbi Jose we learn that even though a man learns but one chapter in the morning and one chapter in the evening, he has thereby fulfilled the precept of, 'This book of the law shall not depart out of your mouth, but you shalt meditate therein day and night' (Joshua 1:8)."

> Rabbi Johanan said in the name of Rabbi Simeon ben Yohai: "Even though a man but reads the *Shema* ['Hear, O Israel ...'] morning and evening, he has thereby fulfilled the precept of ['This book of the law] shall not depart.' It is forbidden, however, to say this in the presence of *ammei ha-aretz*." But Rava said, "It is a mitzvah to say it in the presence of *ammei ha-aretz*."[45]

The juxtaposition of the scriptural prescription to meditate on Torah "day and night" and the halakhic specification of reciting several verses in the morning and in the night is a classic case of halakhic minimalization. The danger that common people (*ammei ha-aretz*) will consider such minimum conditions to be an adequate realization of the study of Torah led Rabbi Johanan, in the name of Rabbi Simeon ben Yohai, to oppose publicizing that halakhic decision. On the other hand, Rava's enthusiasm for publicizing the minimal requirements for fulfilling the norm may be explained by belief in the power of action to generate development. Feelings of achievement (fulfillment of halakhic duties) may generate either complacency or a hunger to intensify and broaden the range of one's service to God. Minimalization provides an opportunity for those who would otherwise be content to remain among the spiritually impoverished to taste the dignity of fulfilling a divine norm. The pious scholar who studies Torah day and night and the simple peddler who can hardly find time to recite the *Shema* once in the morning and once at night both fulfill the mitzvah of *talmud Torah* (studying the Torah). Halakha sought to bridge the gaps between social strata and weaken the barriers separating peddlers from scholars and saints.

Community Welfare and Personal Prayer: A Case Study in Halakhic Risk Taking

Another situation that reveals the problematics of the centrality of community in halakha is that of prayer. On one level, halakha includes statements affirming the spontaneous features of prayer.

Make not your prayer a fixed routine but [let it be] beseech-
ing and entreaty before God.[46]

And you shall serve Him with all your heart. (Deuteronomy
11:13)
　　What service is that of the heart? You must say that it
is prayer.[47]

On another level, halakha instituted fixed times and text and hence
formalized the "service of the heart." In his codification of Jewish
law, *Mishneh Torah*, Maimonides explains the historical factors that
moved the Rabbinic authorities to institutionalize prayer:

To pray daily is an affirmative duty, as it is said, "And you
shall serve the Lord your God" (Exodus 23:25). The service
here referred to, according to the teaching of tradition, is
prayer, as it is said, "And to serve Him with all your heart"
(Deuteronomy 11:13), on which the Sages commented,
"What may be described as service of the heart? Prayer." The
number of prayers is not prescribed in the Torah. No form
of prayer is prescribed in the Torah. Nor does the Torah prescribe a fixed time for prayer.... One who was fluent would
offer up many prayers and supplications. If one was slow of
speech, he would pray as he could and whether he pleased.
Thus also, the number of separate services depended on an
individual's ability. One would pray once daily; others, several times in the day.... When the people of Israel went
into exile in the days of the wicked Nebuchadnezzar, they
mingled with the Persians, Greeks, and other nations. In
those foreign countries, children were born to them whose
language was confused. Everyone's speech was a mixture of
many tongues. No one was able, when he spoke, to express
his thoughts adequately in any one language, otherwise than
incoherently, as it is said, "And their children spoke half in

the speech of Ashdod and they could not speak in the Jews' language, but according to the language of each people" (Nechemiah 13:24).

Consequently, when anyone of them prayed in Hebrew, he was unable adequately to express his needs or recount the praise of God, without mixing Hebrew with other languages. When Ezra and his council realized this condition, they ordained the Eighteen Benedictions in their present order.

The first three blessings consist of praises of God and the last three of thanksgiving to Him. The intermediate benedictions are petitions for the things that may stand as categories of all the desires of the individual and the needs of the community. The object aimed at was that these prayers should be in an orderly form in everyone's mouth, that all should learn them, and thus the prayer of those who were not expert in speech would be as perfect as that of those who had command of a chaste style. For the same reason, they arranged [in a fixed form] all the blessings and prayers for all the Jews so that the substance of every blessing should be familiar and current in the mouth of all.[48]

Formalized prayer answers the needs of a community that can no longer articulate prayers to its satisfaction. Whatever the accuracy of the historical facts referred to, the thrust of Maimonides's account is that the needs of the community led to the institutionalization of prayer. Were the needs of community beyond the scope of Jewish spirituality, prayer could have remained the spontaneous outpouring of each individual Jew, with its length, form, and time differing according to the needs and abilities of every individual.

The overriding constraint of community welfare led to the formulation of a fixed language; the philosopher, the poet, and the simple inarticulate Jew are bidden to stand before God at the same time and to address God with the same words. The undeniable risk of such standardization is that prayer will lose its immediacy and its inner feeling. Rabbinic teachers were fully awake to this danger.

In the Talmud, Rabbi Eliezer cautions that "if a man makes his prayers a fixed task, it is not a [genuine] supplication," and hence it is defective prayer. Rabba and Rabbi Joseph explicate Rabbi Eliezer's comment as referring to one "who is not able to insert something fresh [into his prayers]." At this point Rabbi Zera interjects, "I can insert something fresh, but I am afraid to do so for fear I should become confused," that is, for fear of losing his place.[49]

Rabbi Zera's fear of losing his place inhibits him from opening up and pouring out his soul. Institutionalized prayer can suffocate genuine prayer. The tragedy of human institutions is that they may work against the very activities they are meant to support and cultivate. Nevertheless, halakhic Judaism hazarded the potential consequences of formalized prayer. Rather than allowing prayer to become the possession of a spiritual elite and to be lost to the majority of the people of Israel, halakha made prayer a communal practice.

As in all the instances discussed above, the underlying hope was that the minimum standard would not become confused with the desired form of practice.[50] Action lacking proper intention was not the desired form of behavior; reciting one verse in the morning and in the evening and verbalizing the fixed formula of the liturgy were not meant to become final expressions of Torah study and prayer, respectively. Nevertheless, as "halves are not granted in heaven," the danger of such things happening became part of halakhic Judaism. Though minimalistic standards abound, there is room for individual excellence. Maimonides spent ten years writing the *Mishneh Torah* for the community, and he also devoted ten years to *Guide of the Perplexed*. The latter was addressed to a single student, in effect to interested individuals capable of ascending what Maimonides considered to be the solitary path of spiritual perfection. The tension between excellence and commitment to community lies at the very heart of halakhic Judaism.[51]

Overthrowing the Pharaohs of History: The Value of Community and the Risks of Contemporary Life

The revelation at Sinai differs from the mystic experience. The Torah does not present human beings with esoteric otherworldly mysteries, but with a clear task. God's disclosure is in the form of mitzvah. In contrast to the mystic urge to withdraw from the world and from human history, one who receives Torah is thrust into the affairs of humanity.[52] Revelation at Sinai is an encounter with a mission to sanctify the earth and to establish a covenantal community: "And I shall be sanctified in the midst of the people of Israel" (Leviticus 22:32).

Halakha anchors Jews in time and place; its very nature compels its embodiment in the social reality. History—that is, community—is the essential context of halakhic practice. While not dismissing the importance of the ahistorical domain of *olam haba* (the world to come; life after death), Rabbinic Judaism tolerated such paradoxical formulations as "Better is one hour of repentance and good deeds in this world than all the life to come; and better is one hour of calmness of spirit in the world to come than all the life of this world."[53]

The primary focus, however, was on this world.[54] Halakha focused on redemption that would make a noticeable difference to the material conditions of human society. The Hasidic story of the rebbe who, on being informed of the rumor that the Messiah had come, opened the window, looked out, and asserted, "Not yet,"— expresses the belief that redemption is not an inner spiritual event but a public, historical occurrence.[55] The paradigm of a redemptive act is not individual spiritual illumination, but the Exodus of a people from slavery.

The three events that shape Jewish spirituality and constitute models for understanding the conceptual dynamics of halakha are the Exodus from Egypt, the revelation at Sinai, and entering the Promised Land. The shared suffering and longing for liberation in

Egypt forged a collectivity with a common historical destiny, and the memory of this event is central to much of halakhic practice. The revelation at Sinai was considered by the tradition as consummating the liberation from Egypt.

The quest for freedom is not realized solely by overthrowing the pharaohs of history, but by building a community that embodies a disciplined normative existence. The mitzvah that emanates from Sinai is addressed to individuals organically linked to a community. Egypt is both temporally and conceptually prior to Sinai. And just as Sinai consummates Egypt, so too, the land is the consummation of Sinai. The Word at Sinai is addressed to a people who are challenged to realize divine law within the framework of a human society. Geographic space is necessary in order to concretize a way of life based upon mitzvah.

The Jewish community in modern history, however, is not organized according to these three elements (Egypt, Sinai, and the Land). The Zionist revolution that restored national self-determination to Jews in their ancient homeland has created a contemporary risk. The Zionist revolution was essentially secular. Many Zionists rejected the burden of Torah and halakha, which they regarded as obstacles on the path of Jewish renewal and self-determination. Israel was fashioned to a great extent by people seeking a way to rebuild Jewish communal existence without being committed to halakha (Sinai). Secular Zionism is at once rooted in the Jewish past and a revolt against its traditional way of life.

A not uncommon response of some groups within the Orthodox Jewish community is to retreat in the face of secularity and enclose themselves in protective isolation. Why expose your children to the risks of forming a community with those who have severed the vital connection with the chain of tradition? As opposed to the separatist response, others within the Orthodox community refuse to build spiritual life around a "Sinai" severed from "Egypt." The ringing echoes of past suffering annul any institutional arrangement where the shared destiny of all Jews is not a primary conviction. Because

Judaism is inconceivable without a community with a shared history, this group is prepared to work alongside those who define themselves as secularists, outside the domain of Torah.

The choice between these two approaches is not a simple one. Nor is either choice without risks. Whether you opt for community with those with whom you endured "slavery" or whether you elect to share community only with those who stand together at Sinai, you risk dangerous consequences.

The classical Talmudic account of Hillel and Shammai's confrontation with a person seeking to join the Jewish community shows striking similarities to the modern Jewish dilemma:

> A certain heathen once came before Shammai and asked him, "How many *Torot* have you?" "Two," he replied, "the Written Torah and the Oral Torah." "I believe you with respect to the Written, but not with respect to the Oral Torah; make me a proselyte on condition that you teach me the Written Torah [only]." [But Shammai] scolded and repulsed him in anger.
>
> When he went before Hillel, he accepted him as a proselyte. On the first day, he taught him *alef, bet, gimmel, dalet*; the following day he reversed (the order of the letters) to him. "But yesterday you did not teach them to me thus!" he protested. "Must you then not rely upon me? Then rely upon me with respect to the Oral [Torah] too."[56]

Shammai spoke the truth: Torah is composed of the Written and the Oral Law. Hillel, however, held back, hoping to overcome what he believed to be the obstacle on the path of the convert's accepting the oral tradition.

A statement in a written text is sometimes assigned authority in excess of its supporting evidence simply by virtue of its written form. And particularly where a faithful account of a divine revelation is sought, one becomes suspicious of a tradition that openly acknowledges the human medium of transmission. Hillel softened the convert's opposition by indicating the inescapability of trust in human beings as far as any human enterprise is concerned. If mastery of the rudiments of written language is inconceivable outside of a social matrix, then certainly no tradition can claim to transcend the need for trust in other human beings.

> On another occasion it happened that a certain heathen came before Shammai and said to him, "Make me a proselyte, on condition that you teach me the whole Torah while I stand on one foot." Thereupon [Shammai] repulsed him with the builder's cubit that was in his hand. When he went before Hillel, he said to him, "What is hateful to you, do not do to your neighbor: that is the whole Torah, while the rest is the commentary thereof; go and learn it."[57]

Again, Shammai's forthright honesty contrasts with Hillel's not telling the whole truth. Hillel, in contrast to Shammai, is willing to risk people's confusing Torah with ethical conduct alone, in order to enable a person to begin a spiritual process of growth. Shammai is not prepared to risk destroying what is in truth halakhic Judaism; Hillel cannot be certain that the person will not stop at the golden rule and ignore the essential unity of the various components of the halakha.

In general, Hillel yields and bends, rather than risk alienating others. While Shammai insists on sharp boundaries to demarcate genuine Judaism from spurious alternatives, Hillel risks blurring the borders. Hillel avoids definitive criteria for membership in his community. He appears tender-minded in contrast to Shammai's no-nonsense, uncompromising approach to what, in truth, is halakhic Judaism.

We may look at Shammai's response as insisting on consistency and the dignity of presenting one's way of life in one's own terms. That approach rejects Hillel's blurring of distinctions and cautions against the dangers of losing sight of the distinctive characteristics of one's way of life. As has often happened, we may regard Hillel's definition of Judaism as nothing more than "the golden rule." By ignoring the end, "Go and learn it," we can falsely associate Hillel's position with some type of Jewish ethical culture.

Yet, Shammai too risks a great deal; he risks losing the opportunity of building Torah with community. Guarding the purity of Torah becomes ludicrous if the price is the dissolution of the people of Israel. The Talmud mentions a number of converts saying to one another, "Shammai's impatience sought to drive us from the world, but Hillel's gentleness brought us under the wings of the *Shekhinah*."[58] Shammai may have had the truth, but he risked having no people; Hillel may have had people, but he risked losing Torah.

The path of halakha is fraught with risks and uncertainties. This, however, is the adventure of living by a Torah that is "not in heaven."[59]

4

EMBRACING COVENANTAL HISTORY

COMPASSION, RESPONSIBILITY, AND THE SPIRITUALITY OF THE EVERYDAY

> Hands off: neither the whole of truth nor the whole of good is revealed to any single observer, although each observer gains a partial superiority of insight from the peculiar position in which he stands.... It is enough to ask of each of us that he should be faithful to his own opportunities and make the most of his own blessings, without presuming to regulate the rest of the vast field.[1]
>
> —William James

I
The Modern Loss of History:
Existential and Religious Responses to Secularism

One of the salient characteristics of modern secular thinking is the loss of a connection to history. Modernity in many respects manifests "discontinuous consciousnesses": a lack of rootedness in and a sense of irreverence toward the past, the feeling that the moment in which one is engaged is not to be judged by any reality outside of itself. The present is an instant locked into itself, self-justifying and oblivious to claims or dreams of the past.

This modern attitude toward the past has yielded two dominant existential moods between which modern individuals, communities, and societies tend to oscillate:

1. The "triumphant" mood, in which attachment to the past is deemed unnecessary because of the belief that the solutions to your problems lie within yourself. One may argue plausibly that technological consciousness neutralizes the lessons derived from the past and makes it seem unnecessary. In this light, modernity represents immanence in time, devoid of any traces of transcendence.[2]

2. The "tragic" mood, which entails constant reflection on the failures of revolutionary dreams—indeed, on all the hopeful attempts at making radical, permanent change in sociopolitical conditions for great numbers of people. It is difficult to inspire faith in a new future that is recognizably different from what we have always known in view of repeated disillusionment with totalistic sociopolitical movements. Consequently, a modernity locked into itself lacks the resources to provide us with a vision of a future in which we can believe.

Modern formulations of traditional religions have attempted to provide various responses to what I will call the spiritual-historical dilemma of secularism: modern people who feel trapped between tragedy and triumph, in an incoherent present unanchored by past traditions or future hopes. One of the most popular religious responses to the loss of history has been to the leap into a mysticism that offers eternity in the present moment. This approach is exemplified by British historian of religion Robert Charles Zaehner, who first stridently critiques the "historical" God of the Hebrew Bible, whose only "valid defense ... is that he had to be represented in these terms to a primitive and savage people," before celebrating the demise of the "God of History" in the eyes of the West.

> The Western interest in Eastern religions is very largely a revulsion against this type of deity, the deity who is very involved in human affairs, what Protestants call the God of History. For if history—and religious history in particular— teaches us anything, it is that every single ideal, whether religious or secular, that man has ever had, is sooner or later utterly corrupted. We seem to be imprisoned in a cycle of *yin* and *yang*. The only answer for the individual, then, is to find eternity within himself.[3]

In other words, Zaehner argues that Judaism's attachment to history, by its very definition, leads to its self-destruction. The "only" religious response to the apparent frustration of God's dreams for people and to the recurring defeat of human attempts to establish God's kingdom on earth entails the quest for a religion of the private self where one abandons or "escapes" from both community and history. What is offered in place of the uncertainties of history is a personal refuge, religious life severed from the concrete structures of social reality. This religious outlook can offer meaning and spiritual fulfillment for an individual without requiring that its worldview be seen within the sociopolitical frameworks of society. We may characterize this religious option as an *escape response* to modern secular civilization.

Another response that has typified modern spirituality is perhaps best referred to as a *retreat response*. Rather than escape from history to the haven of the private self, this response retreats from the broad stage of history to the confines of community or sect.

In *Secularization and Moral Change*, Alasdair MacIntyre argues that industrialization and the development of technology inaugurated a new human reality. Moral and social change are not the consequences of the decline of religion. Rather, the causes of moral and social change lie in the same urbanization and industrialization that produced secularization. The efforts of the "death of God" theologians, or of Paul Tillich, Rudolf Bultmann, or Dietrich Bonhoffer, at translating religious language for a secular world are, for Macintyre, irrelevant, because modern social structures no longer mirror a religious worldview:

> For when theology is reinterpreted to make it relevant to the substantial secular life of the modern world, it always seems to lose any distinctive theological content and often, too, any logical consistency.[4]

MacIntyre speaks of the "religion of the enclave," the religion in which a remnant develops some form of earnest religious life within community.[5] We might call such a community a communion that prays together, or a fellowship that shares Sabbath together, but not a community that is responsible for a total collective existence. It is a mode of social involvement and spiritual intensity in isolation from the total rhythm of life, where the sacred is severed from the profane.

An example of this phenomenon might be the synagogue where people meet together on the Sabbath for a few, perhaps very concentrated, hours, but where the rest of the week has no relationship to what those few hours are about. In this context, the purpose of the synagogue and of the Sabbath is to provide moments of repose and tranquility for anxious, weary people. People seek some sort of lived community ("It's nice to come here; people know me by my name") or rest and peace ("It's a nice alternative to the golf course"). The synagogue can act as a corrective to the anxieties and pains of everyday life. Going to a house of worship can be a moral holiday, an oasis in a desert of busyness and anonymity, where people can escape the impersonality of the marketplace. There was a period in America when large synagogues were thought to be the sign of the Jews' entering modernity. Today there is reason to believe that large synagogues are failing and that people seek smaller congregations that allow for deeper interpersonal experiences.

Thus another religious response to secularization is to provide an alternative form of leisure. Religion's role, in this case, is to turn its back on the world and to provide a framework for the weary to rest. Religious institutions justify themselves by showing how religion can offer a form of leisure that secularism cannot. Indeed, religion as the "enclave" prospers by emphasizing its separation from the profane and by pointing out the failures of secular efforts. Sermons tend to harp on the ill-conceived consequences of technology, reveling in the moral failures of technological advance. The more the failures of secular society are emphasized, the more religious institutions can justify their place in the modern world.

The religion of the retreat is not the mystical escape in search of eternity within the self, but a framework for a religious community consciously alienated from society. The biblical God of History, intent on becoming manifest on earth, is given a day (the Sabbath) and a place (the synagogue).

A third, and not unrelated, response to secularism is the identification of religion with *"prophetic" social criticism.* Religion then moves to the margins of history, and from its aloof, isolated vantage point, safe from involvement with the material and social forces that shape life, it condemns and criticizes. In the role of relentless critic, religion can abandon its role in history. By giving to Caesar what is Caesar's, it in effect turns its back on the social collective world.

None of these modern religious formulations reflect what I understand as Judaism's attitude toward history or appropriate responses to the sense of its loss. The burden of the biblical tradition unequivocally is to be *in* history. For example, to use (as is often done) the biblical prophets to validate the type of "prophetic" alienation described above is a perversion of prophetic teachings and responsibility. The prophet's alienation and criticism of community are serious because of his charge to anoint kings and priests. The prophet is a messenger of a God seeking embodiment in all aspects of communal life. But the God of modern "prophets" remains transcendent and thereby fosters deep religious alienation. Transcendence is expressed in the inability to translate the spiritual vision into concrete involvement with the lived history of human beings.

The spiritual-historical dilemma of secularism, then, has often led to (1) the escapist religion of the mystic moment; (2) the divorce of the sacred from the profane, in the retreat to the enclave; or (3) the "prophetic" religious posture of pointing to the failures of human efforts.

II
Obligation and Empowerment:
A Covenantal Approach to History

These three religious orientations toward modernity's dominant existential moods are characteristic responses to the remarkable growth in human power in the modern world. Science and technology constitute the core of secular power insofar as they are the products of human knowledge and initiative and not of a divinely anchored revelation. Secular power is often viewed as a challenge to religion, with its tendency to produce feelings of human pride and self-sufficiency. But the responses discussed above share a common failure to cope with the success of secular power. Having accepted the loss of history as a given, each, in different ways, seeks to undermine the legitimacy of human effort and competence.

None of these approaches expresses what I understand to be Judaism's response to the loss of history. The Jewish covenant requires an active engagement with history—a key assumption of the covenant being that we are endowed with all the requisite capabilities to fulfill our responsibility to act as a redemptive force within it. Obligation and empowerment are, from this perspective, two sides of the same covenantal coin. Classical Judaism, extending this core biblical value, thus leads us to approach the spiritual-historical dilemma of secularism differently. Halakhic thought and practice suggest a religious orientation that carefully balances positions of human *adequacy* and *dependence.*

To gain a fuller understanding of the nature of these two countervailing forces, let us draw on, as a metaphor, the traditional conception of the relationship between the Sabbath and the other days of the week. Let us distinguish between the sacred and the profane (secular) within the framework of "Remember the Sabbath day and keep it holy. Six days you shall labor and do all your work, but the seventh day is a Sabbath of the Lord your God; you shall not do any work" (Exodus 20:8–10).

An analysis of the nature of the Sabbath, and of the Jewish approach to Creation, revelation, and redemption, will reveal a continuous theme: the preservation of the delicate balance between human power and ability, and human limitation and dependency.

The Spirituality of Secularism:
Creation and the Expanding Domain
of Human Responsibility

In Genesis, the biblical narrative begins with God creating for six days. The God of the Bible is a God who constantly manifests God's will by shaping the environment. In fashioning a finite being that is free, God creates a being in God's own image. Humanity's ability to structure the social and natural environments and create a human home in the midst of hostile or indifferent conditions are hallmarks of the dignity of the religious person conscious of having been created in the image of God. Passive acceptance or contemplation of nature is not the desideratum of the biblical tradition.

The religious significance of human activity in conquering and controlling nature has been articulated in great depth by Rabbi Joseph B. Soloveitchik. According to Soloveitchik, Creation is not simply a cosmological event but a model to be imitated by human beings.[6] As God is a Creator, so shalt thou be a creator. Creation (in its nontechnical sense) is not the exclusive prerogative of God. In other words, the biblical vision is not of a humanity programmed into passivity, guilt, and fear of self-expression.

One whose religious sensibilities have been nurtured by the biblical Creation model cannot sit passively and watch a child die of leukemia. We must reject the myth that hunger, sickness, and exploitation are the inevitable fate of a significant part of the population of the world. Biblically inspired human attitudes cannot tolerate the appeal to some divine immutable law to justify social or economic deprivation. Feelings of responsibility and the efficacy of human efforts characterize a central thrust of biblical anthropology.

In this light, we may argue that one of the profound *spiritual* implications of secular technological progress is the increase in the scope of human responsibility:

> The brute's existence is an undignified one because it is a helpless existence. Human existence is a dignified one because it is a glorious, majestic, powerful existence.… Dignity of man expressing itself in the awareness of being responsible and of being capable of discharging his responsibility cannot be realized as long as he has not gained mastery over his environment.… Man of old who could not fight disease and succumbed in multitudes to yellow fever or any other plague with degrading helplessness could not lay claim to dignity. Only the man who builds hospitals, discovers therapeutic techniques and saves lives is blessed with dignity.… Civilized man has gained limited control of nature and has become, in certain respects, her master, and with mastery, he has attained dignity, as well. His mastery has made it possible for him to act in accordance with his responsibility.[7]

In line with Soloveitchik's approach is the argument that technology expands human ability to affect the environment and thereby extends the range of human obligations. The exponential modern expansion of the scope covered by mass media, for example, no longer allows us to claim ignorance of suffering even in remote corners of the earth. Coupled with rapidly expanding scientific innovation, this expanded knowledge extends the range of human responsibility beyond our immediate environment. Technology disturbs the complacency of the private self; it truly universalizes moral obligation by confronting abstract pontification with concrete opportunities for action.

It is in this light that secularization—in the sense of the expansion of the domain of human responsibility—can be described as an instrument of God. God does not give humanity a mandate to establish the kingdom of heaven on earth without providing the human ability to fulfill this task. Technological consciousness takes the world seriously. In this sense, it may be regarded as an instrument of the willful God of History.

The Sabbath:
Healing Human Grandiosity

The weekly cycle alternating between the "six days of the week" (construed by the tradition as, essentially, a single unit) and the Sabbath expresses the dialectical relationship between emulating the Creator God and accepting our role as creatures *of* God.[8] The Sabbath, emphasizing our creature-hood, conveys the message that human power and assertion are gifts of God and not unrestricted, self-sufficient prerogatives.

Rabbi Hoshaya, in *Midrash Rabbah*, uses a metaphor to highlight the theological problematics of having been created in the image of God:

> When the Holy One, blessed be He, created Adam, the ministering angels mistook Adam for a divine being and wished to exclaim "Holy!" before him. What does this resemble? A king and a governor were riding together in a chariot. The king's subjects wished to greet their king with cries of "Sovereign!" but they did not know which the king was.

> What, then, did the king do? He pushed the governor out of the chariot, and thus the subjects knew who the king was. "Similarly," said Rabbi Hosyaha, "when God created Adam, the angels mistook him [for God]. What did the Holy One, blessed be He, do? He caused sleep to fall upon him and thus all knew he was a human being."[9]

This midrash addresses the problem of the danger of human deification, understood to be implicit in the creation of Adam. Because of the greatness of humankind, as manifest in willful control and power over the rest of nature, the gap between God and human beings might seem blurred, and humanity may turn to worship human power. Sleep, however, destroys the illusion of omnipotence and forces recognition of our vulnerability as creatures. Sleep symbolizes a state of consciousness in which human beings lose conscious or willful control of their existence.

The dialectic between adequacy and assertiveness on the one hand and passivity/vulnerability on the other characterizes the dialectical tension a religious person faces in the confrontation with advanced technological society. Because human beings are accorded such majesty and given so great a task in history, technology can correctly be perceived as being an invaluable extension of humanity's God-given charge. The danger is that this nobility and majesty may lead to our usurpation of the role of God.

Hence, immediately after God creates Adam and enjoins him to be like the Creator—to "fill the earth and master it" (Genesis 1:28)— God "blessed the seventh day and declared it holy, because on it God ceased from all the work of creation which He had done." On the Sabbath, the Creator God ceases to act as an independent will shaping a passive material. In like manner, on the Sabbath, a person may not stand over and against the universe as a Promethean figure against an alien world. On the Sabbath we are expected to adopt a relationship to the world not based on subject-object mastery. On the seventh day, we must become attuned to an existential rhythm in which human beings and the world participate harmoniously as equal creatures of God.

The halakhic notion of the holiness of the Sabbath aims at controlling the human need to be master, setting limits to our dominance of nature. Nature is transformed (to use Buber's helpful terminology) from an "It" into a "Thou"; the world is no longer exclusively an object of human gratification. Thus, the halakhic norms of the Sabbath affirm the value of existence outside of an anthropocentric perspective.

The setting of the sun on the eve of the Sabbath ushers in a unit of time in which the flowers of the field stand over and against human beings as equal members of the universe. I am prohibited to pluck the flower or to do with it as I please; at that sunset, the flower becomes a "Thou" to me with a right to existence irrespective of its possible value for me. I stand silently before nature as before a fellow creature of God and not as a potential object of my control. The Sabbath aims at healing the human grandiosity of technological society.

The halakhic connection between the onset of the Sabbath and the setting of the sun also holds theological significance. Dependence on the sun's rotation as an objective mechanism for the Sabbath's beginning is integral to the meaning of its sanctity—allowing us to experience dramatically our inability to control the holy. Human beings may not decide when the Sabbath is to begin. As I race against time on Friday afternoon and fight like Joshua to hold back the sun, striving to complete some unfinished work, I realize that, despite my efforts, I must respond to that which is outside my control. The sun's silent, inexorable descent announces a divine message: "You are no longer a creator; you are a creature."

The holiness of the Sabbath does not depend upon human sanctification. As the *Kiddush* blessing that inaugurates the day declares—"Blessed art Thou, O Lord, who hallowest the Sabbath"—Sabbath sanctity is independent of human initiative.[10]

This view of Creation and of the Sabbath describes a core human dynamic between will/assertion on the one hand and limitation/

vulnerability on the other. On the day of rest, we consider and experience the boundaries of an embodied, mortal life. The Sabbath brings peace by healing the need to manipulate and control. The "willful" person of the six weekdays accepts and expresses his or her finitude in the restful joy of "Sabbath sleep" (in the midrashic sense of a "sleep" that indicates human creatureliness).

Compassion and Judgment: An Essential Spiritual Dialectic

The dynamic tension between willful assertion and quiet receptivity exemplified by the Creation/Sabbath paradigm emerges as a central motif of both biblical spirituality and Rabbinic thought. Jewish tradition crystallizes this essential human dialectic into the terms *rachamim* (unconditional love/compassion) and *din* (judgment/justice). According to the midrash,[11] these two poles, and the tension between them, are "built in" to the very fabric of Creation. God, the midrash explains, first considered creating the world exclusively with the quality of *din*: strict reward and punishment, merit based upon an objective consideration of acts and facts. God soon realized, however, that the world could not endure according to *din* alone and in response introduced the balancing quality of *rachamim*, or unconditional love.

The total accountability implicit in *din* evokes the willful and the assertive aspects of human conduct, constructing a world in which human beings are responsible and accountable before an unequivocal, uncompromising God. *Din* describes a universe of human dignity in which we are considered adequate to shoulder responsibility for our behavior. Justice and responsibility (*din*) presuppose the capacity to act or to refrain from acting. In this sense, *din* embraces the principle of will and assertion.

The midrash understands that a universe based strictly upon *din* would end quickly and disastrously—and thus attributes to God the wisdom of intertwining it with the quality of *rachamim*, unconditional love/compassion. In order for the assertive, aggressive quality of *din* not to warp into a demonic, inhuman or antihuman force, there must exist a dimension of relationship that transcends considerations of strict "merit." *Rachamim* is required to create an awareness that there is something beyond responsibility and accountability, beyond what we can do with our hands, see with our eyes, or judge with our faculties of discernment. *Rachamim* expresses the sense of a benevolence built into the universe, a sense that we are not judged—and thus must not judge others—upon what we see alone. Tempering ultimate responsibility, it acts as a curb on the destructive aspects of human willfulness.

In other words, *rachamim* indicates an aspect of reality that extends beyond our mastery, responsibility, and will. Unfettered *din* cultivates a personality driven by the compulsive need to control every situation. If one party in a relationship feels the need to control all the variables and to elicit all the desired responses, sooner or later the relationship will become empty and lifeless. We must receive that which is given freely, as a gift, in order to experience genuine acceptance and confirmation. Only a free response of love can satisfy the universal need for confirmation by another. The fear that unless we manipulate situations we will be ignored leads to a self-defeating pattern of constantly inducing the responses of others.

Hence the emergence of *rachamim*. Unbounded compassion, or grace, comes with the realization and acceptance that we are incapable of bearing limitless, objective responsibility for our conduct. The helpless child would not survive but for the unconditional care of its parent, and there are aspects of mature relationships as well in which this quality becomes indispensable. These two qualities come together to form an essential unit of human spiritual DNA.

Revelation:
The Acceptance of Failure and
the Embrace of History

The interplay between *din* and *rachamim* plays a defining role in the central event of Jewish spiritual history: divine revelation.

The giving of the Torah at Sinai is presented in both biblical and Rabbinic tradition as something very different from the classic mystic experience of communion with the Divine. The Torah does not immerse human beings in esoteric mysteries, but rather presents them with a clear task: God's disclosure comes in the form of the mitzvah (commandment). In contrast to the mystic urge to withdraw from the world and from human history, the receiver of Torah feels thrust into the affairs of humanity. Revelation at Sinai is an encounter with a mission to sanctify the earth and to construct a covenantal community upon it: "And I will be sanctified in the midst of the people of Israel" (Leviticus 22:32).[12]

The law-giving nature of revelation implies an important corollary: the possibility of failure. The task of implementing the Torah is specified in a system of norms, and norms *qua* commands or laws generally presuppose the possibility of non-obedience. Both biblical and Rabbinic Judaism reveal the burden of the Sinaitic covenant, together with an appreciation of the reasons for human failure to live up to the task.

Sinai is not a romantic conception of humanity; Sinai points to real people who are vulnerable and weak.[13] The Torah was given in the desert where people, unprotected by externalized symbols of social order, are exposed to failure and defeat. In the desert, people are prepared to give up their freedom and their sacred destiny to satisfy their momentary desire for bread and water.

Jewish tradition acknowledges this possibility of (sometimes epic) failure and accepts it as the price of the original divine decision to seek to be revealed *within history*. The mystery of the biblical tradition is the belief that God chose community and history as the domains in which to be revealed. Unlike the God of Aristotle, who is wrapped in blissful self-contemplation, or the God of the mystics, for whom history is illusion, the God of the covenant forgoes the serenity of self-sufficient perfection and weds God's fate to the vicissitudes of human history. God chooses to be involved with human society, even while understanding that human beings may fail.

Sinai thus reveals a God who is present with humankind no matter what their failures and shortcomings. In the Talmud, Rabbi Meir argues that the people of Israel are referred to as "children" of God even when they violate the covenant and do not act as God's children.[14] Contradicting an opinion that God's relationship to Israel is ultimately conditional, Rabbi Meir indicates the unconditional endurance of the covenantal relationship irrespective of strict merit. Obligation and responsibility are again intertwined with love and acceptance. *Din* and *rachamim* are thus not only ontological principles—they permeate our relationship to Torah and history.

Prophecy and Repentance: Persevering in History

The prophet, as the carrier of further divine revelation, fulfills a dual role that embodies the synthesis of these two qualities. The prophet speaks to human beings in the name of God and transmits the uncompromising demands (*din*) of the Almighty. Yet at other times, the prophet approaches God on behalf of humanity and tries to temper divine judgment and anger at human failure (*rachamim*).

For example, the midrash elaborates on Moses's confrontation with the people at the golden calf immediately after his descent from Mount Sinai. In accordance with the metaphor of the revelation at Sinai as a wedding ceremony, the golden calf incident is perceived by Moses as Israel's engaging in adulterous intercourse right under the wedding canopy. As the intermediary carrying the marriage contract (the tablets of the law), what did Moses do? Notwithstanding his clear, objective judgment of the situation (*din*), he tore up the contract (smashed the tablets) so as to destroy evidence of the date of the wedding—a powerful act of *rachamim*.[15]

Rather than turn cynical or reject the people as being hopeless, Moses, the archetypal prophet, intercedes on their behalf and protects them from divine fury. The Bible and the midrash contain numerous similar narratives of prophets defending the people in the face of divine demands for justified retribution.

On one level, the prophet protects his fellow human beings and engages the Almighty in dialogue on their behalf, countering divine *din* with *rachamim*. Yet, vis-à-vis the people, the prophet never becomes patronizing. Unbending in his demands, he refuses to become their vicarious agent or to assume the role of all-protective parent—relentlessly holding the mirror of justice and human accountability to their face. At the same time, he communicates love and *rachamim*, encouraging people to continue despite failures and setbacks. His love is: "The gates of *teshuvah* [return] are never closed. One can begin anew." His justice is: "The covenant continues. Your choices make a difference!"[16]

The classic response of Rabbinic Judaism to failure and suffering—what the biblical prophets are constantly calling for— is *teshuvah* (repentance): a return, a new beginning.[17] Often, self-appointed religious "prophets" (of the "social criticism" model described above) cite moral failures in technological society, chastising contemporary culture for its hubris and concluding that human beings cannot succeed without God.

Rather than make homiletical capital out of technological society's setbacks, religious people, at least in the covenantal mode, should feel personally pained by human failure. The religious response should not be discouragement or disengagement but, on the contrary, encouragement to try again—in other words, a *teshuvah* response. Applied to history, the covenantal notion of *teshuvah* might be expressed in the following way: *Perseverance in the historical struggle to extend human responsibility by eliminating sources of suffering and chaos is the religious response called for by the biblical halakhic tradition.*

Approaching Redemption: A Jewish Approach to Historical Progress

The dialectic between *din* and *rachamim* as core dynamics in our relationship to history shapes Jewish concepts of hope and redemption. In the Talmud, *Sanhedrin* 97b, two views of the conditions for historical redemption are presented. Shmuel maintains that "it is sufficient for the mourner to persevere in his mourning," that is, human beings have no role in bringing about redemption in history other than to passively endure historical suffering. This perspective relies exclusively upon divine *rachamim*: redemption will "erupt" unpredictably, irrespective of human involvement or, for that matter, merit. In contrast, Rav and Rabbi Eliezer make *teshuvah* (repentance) a condition of redemption (*ge'ulah*). Human adequacy, responsibility, initiative, and will (*din*) define this approach to historical progress.[18]

Maimonides synthesizes these opposing Talmudic orientations toward history into a formulation that subtly balances the qualities of *rachamim* and *din*. Like Rav, Maimonides holds that redemption depends upon human initiative and the will to self-transformation, that is, *teshuvah*. Yet he makes a critical addition to the Talmudic version, declaring that the Torah implies a divine promise: "In the end," all people will, in fact, do *teshuvah*.

The notion of a divine promise of ultimate redemption is clearly drawn from the world of *rachamim*. Yet the unyielding insistence upon human accountability (*teshuvah*) retains a key element of *din*. Even when describing a divine guarantee, Maimonides refuses to countenance a passive apocalyptic eschatology.[19] Maimonides would have Jews nurture messianic hopes and aspirations and apply these hopes and aspirations to a sense of accountability with respect to the world in which they live.

Creative Partners:
The Interdependence of the Holy and the Profane

Maimonides's synthesis of *din* and *rachamim* into a prescription for an active, optimistic, and ultimately redemptive relationship to history has important implications for how we understand what constitutes the "holy" and the "secular/profane" within traditional Jewish thought. These two concept pairs are highly related: secular notions of ultimate human responsibility clearly map onto the traditional conception of *din* (as the negative connotation of "profane" implies an excess of human willfulness and self-reliance), while unbounded compassion and grace irrespective of merit (*rachamim*) resonate strongly with conventional ideas of the holy.

What emerges from this discussion, however, is the inherent interdependence of these paradigms—within the fabric of created life, within the human spirit. In the language of dialectics, there is a productive interaction between the opposing elements. Like *din* and *rachamim*, the holy and secular/profane require each other, just as humanity requires them both—requires living in the dynamic tension between them—in order to maintain a healthy spiritual outlook upon the potentials and limitations of our involvement in history.

In traditional Jewish thinking, the weekdays do not bear distinct names but are referred to as successive units in a progression leading to the Sabbath: "the first day to the Sabbath ... the second day to the Sabbath ... the third...." Secular/profane/"normal" time—the time emphasizing human accountability and initiative—is not a closed collection of discrete units resisting or opposing the holy, but a continuity continually directing our awareness toward it.[20]

The Sabbath introduces anticipation and aspiration into the struggles of each weekday. The liturgy pronounces, "This is the song of the day of the Sabbath"—the song that indicates what the world will be like according to the vision of the Sabbath. The Sabbath, then, with its vision and experience of holy *rachamim*, can influence and inspire the way in which we carry out our "secular" obligations and interactions in the weekday sphere of *din*.

Moreover, the sphere of the holy does not stand in abstract antithesis to the secular/profane. Holiness too may bear the dignity of human assertion and initiative. This dimension of the *din/rachamim* synthesis emerges in the distinction between the *Kiddush* that inaugurates the Sabbath and that which is recited on festivals. As discussed above, the blessing "Blessed art Thou, O Lord, who hallowest the Sabbath" suggests that the holiness of the day is independent of human initiative. The blessing recited on the festivals, however—"Blessed art Thou, O Lord, who sanctifies *Israel and the festivals*"—emphasizes *Israel's* agency in sanctifying the holy time of the festivals.[21] For natural, creature-conscious humanity, the Sabbath offers holiness as a gift from outside; for covenantal, historical humanity who engages in assertive cooperation with God, holiness can become the product of deliberate human action. Embedded in the concept of a holy people is the capacity and responsibility to become a copartner in the sanctification of the world.

Concreteness:
The Spiritual Significance of the Everyday

In stark contrast with the religious responses to the spiritual-historical dilemma of secularism described above—the escape into mysticism, the retreat to the insular enclave, the detachment of "prophetic" social criticism—for traditional Judaism, holiness is not achieved in withdrawal from reality. To the contrary, sanctity is expressed in our interaction with the everyday. An authentically "Jewish" experience of the holy comes only in concert with an expanded awareness of the spiritual opportunities inherent in the "secular" weekdays. "Six days you shall labor and do all your work" (Exodus 20:9) has far-reaching *spiritual* significance for the cultivation of Jewish historical consciousness.

Jews have often lived on the margins of history. There are Jews who feel most comfortable as protesters or outcasts. It is easy to be the conscience of the world while ignoring the difficulty of how ideals might actually, concretely be implemented within the limitations of reality. But Jewish tradition, through the concepts of *din* and *rachamim*, speaks insistently within the concreteness of life.

In Leviticus 2:32, God says, "I will be sanctified in the midst of the people of Israel," only after warning the people not to profane God's holy Name. The decision to sanctify God (*kiddush ha-shem*) in the midst of community exposes one to the dangers of failure and profanation (*chillul ha-shem*). The concrete confirms and bears witness either to the truths of the spirit or to the grandiose illusions of the imagination.

The challenge facing contemporary Jews is either to choose a Jerusalem of heaven, which is entered only in our Sabbath prayers, or to build a Jerusalem on earth, in which we are responsible for relating the spirit of the Sabbath to all seven days of the week. In conclusion, let us ask: Where is God to dwell? In mystic rapture, in the marginal enclave, in prophetic detachment—or in a living community committed to bringing sanctification to ever-expanding dimensions of our concrete experience in history, leading hopefully, incrementally, to redemption?

5

CREATING A SHARED SPIRITUAL LANGUAGE

THE URGENCY OF COMMUNITY AND THE HALAKHIC ROOTS OF PLURALISM

> Sound the great shofar for our freedom, and raise the banner to gather in our exiles, and gather us, God, from the four corners of the earth.
>
> —The *Amidah*

Zionist Dreams and Israeli Realities: Is There a Common Jewish People?

The dream of Zionism was to gather Jews from all over the world into a cohesive unity, a nation—to bring us safely from the ends of the earth and lead us in dignity to our holy land. For religious Zionists, this aspiration represented a fulfillment of the prayer spoken every morning as part of the *Shacharit* service, "Bring us in peace from the four corners of the earth, and walk us upright into our land." Beyond the practical goal of mass immigration, the theme of the unification of the Jewish people was part of the Zionist dream: that there will be a moment in history when Jews, finally gathered in after millennia of dispersal, will form a unified society.

91

In retrospect, Zionism proved overly sanguine about how the ingathering of large, diverse Jewish communities with widely divergent values, sensibilities, and traditions within a small, emerging nation would actually be accomplished. Taking for granted that the common Jewishness of these groups would provide sufficient cultural and political common ground to serve as the basis of a unified society has been proved by history as a shortsighted and naïve approach. What framework of Jewish meaning and identity might help catalyze this type of unity? This question was not asked and frankly has never been given the serious, sustained attention that is so clearly called for.

Paradoxically—though perhaps inevitably—it is through our very ingathering that we have discovered we are a much more divided people than we thought. The gaps among our sensibilities and values are much wider than the diaspora reality ever forced us to confront. Confusingly, we found that once brought together, the different branches of the family are not able to speak with each other—they lack a common language. Not only between religious and secular, but also within and among the various religious and secular communities, we found an ingathering of people who cannot understand or respect each other—who do not seem to share, or at least acknowledge, common values and thus common aspirations.

Within the symbolic world of Zionism, exile represented divisiveness itself, the ravaging and inevitable divisiveness of geographic dispersion. The very fact of the diaspora implied a nagging anxiety: Is there a common Jewish people? What holds them together? Israel was the axiomatic remedy to the diasporic condition, for Israel would represent national unity as a living fact. Zionism, in short, thought it had ended the exile.

National Jewish unity in Israel has proved a futile dream thus far because it never has been grounded in a shared understanding of what ostensibly binds us together in the first place: Judaism. Is the essence of our peoplehood to be found in religious rituals or ethical aspirations, in a love of the Torah or a love of the land? The only area in which the question of what might bind us together was seriously considered was in the agreement that Hebrew would be the common language of the Jewish state. The next obvious questions—Once the literal language barrier had been overcome, what would be its content? How would people speak with each other, and what would they have to say to each other?—have been given scant attention.

Many members of the Jewish family have returned to the ancestral homeland to find that they are unable to speak with many of their relatives. What is our unity of purpose? What are some of the values that inspire our collective sense of Jewishness? The great surge of "we" consciousness that was exhibited in establishing the State of Israel soon faded into self-interested factionalism. As long as there was an outside enemy and an immediate existential threat, there was a semblance of unity; but when that ceased to be the dominant national focus, the hollowness of communal Jewish life exposed itself. The arguments about "Who is a Jew?" became pervasive.

What is the relationship between a Jew living in Mea Shearim (an ultra-Orthodox neighborhood in Jerusalem) and a Jew living in Tel Aviv, much less a Jew living in Tel Aviv and one living in Manhattan? Are they part of a common people—do they share a common destiny, make claims on each other to uphold certain fundamental values? This is the condition of a country with a fundamental anxiety as to whether there truly is a nation called "Jews" living within it. It is a country that cannot politically organize itself in a way that yields anything close to a majority with shared values, leading to the perennial political paralysis of the fragmented coalition. Where are we going—and who are the "we"? Can I consider the *haredi* (ultra-Orthodox) man to be my brother when he throws stones at me as I drive on Shabbat? When he makes violent public protests against me for wanting to be able to park my car when I visit Jerusalem on the Sabbath?

With the *Amidah*, we say, "Gather us, God, from the four corners of the earth." And then what? Given the country's long history of internecine warfare, the miracle is that we have achieved anything at all. The will to survive has exerted a powerful influence in helping us establish the things that survival requires: a strong military, an exceptional health-care system. But the survival effort also allowed us, for too long, to sweep our great differences under the rug of communal life. The need for a shared understanding of each other—not necessarily agreement or common commitments, but a shared sense of what constitutes Jewish history and peoplehood—is greater than ever. This chapter is an attempt to show that these divisions might be overcome by a deeper understanding of what it is we value as Jews.

There is a powerfully telling midrash celebrating the exilic dispersion as an expression of divine benevolence. God showed kindness to Israel by dispersing us, the midrash asserts, for if we find ourselves persecuted in one part of the world, we can simply move to another. This pessimistic calculus typifies the ethos of "*galut* (diaspora) identity"—in terms of basic odds for survival in a hostile world, dispersal is good for the Jews. Returning to Israel, to political sovereignty in our homeland, we aspire to a deeper level of identity, fulfilling a deep ancient dream of coming home to live together as one nation. But that dream will continue to be proved a fantasy unless we can formulate a framework of mutual respect and some sense of shared purpose to our ingathering: a community of meaning.

"A Covenant of Purpose": Is It Possible to Create a Community of Shared Meaning?

Rabbi Joseph Ber Soloveitchik, in his article "Kol Dodi Dofek," utilizes traditional covenantal categories to illuminate the religious significance of a community forged by a common political destiny.[1] Soloveitchik views the resurgence of Jewish political autonomy in Israel as a contemporary resurgence of *berit goral*, covenantal destiny—the national or "familial" relationship shared by all Jews, manifested initially in the common identity-forging experience of slavery in Egypt.

This attempt of a great halakhist to understand the Zionist revolution and the State of Israel in traditional, covenantal categories indicates how deeply Israel's political existence has permeated the spiritual consciousness of contemporary Jews. But Soloveitchik is not satisfied merely with community based upon *berit goral*, a common historical and political fate. He argues that the Jewish people should again strive to become, as they were in the past, a community of shared spiritual goals. His article reflects the hope that beyond shared political destiny, the soil of the Israeli reality may nurture a widespread renewal of *berit ye'ud*, covenantal purpose—the experience of normative Jewish values through the way of life infused with traditional Jewish practice—for the Jewish people as a whole.[2]

We can appreciate the pathos of Soloveitchik's yearning that *berit goral* be consummated with *berit ye'ud*. But while the shared values of a Jewish society were quite clear during long periods of history, today, unfortunately, there is no consensus on how the Jewish people should give expression to *berit ye'ud*.[3] Given the contemporary breakdown of traditional Jewish society, is it possible to create a shared community of shared spiritual aspirations?

We may understandably question how any community of meaning is possible between Jews who subscribe to the normative structure of halakha, however understood, and those who do not feel bound to organize their pattern of living by those norms. Can those who seek to live within the halakhic framework understand and spiritually appreciate lifestyles whose values are not grounded in revelation and traditional halakhic authority?

Encountering the Other:
Intellectual Openness and the Spiritual Value of Doubt

To be sure, the project of creating a community of meaning among contemporary Jews is fraught with challenges. To begin with, any creative encounter changes all those who are involved. The "other" invades our sense of self. Our previous position must be reevaluated in light of new awareness and insights. In his introduction to *Guide of the Perplexed*, Maimonides is fully conscious of the fact that once his student—it is often forgotten that the *Guide* is framed as an address to a single, searching student—has encountered other philosophical positions, he cannot maintain a vital relationship to the tradition while ignoring the challenges they present to Judaism. Intellectual repression is not conducive to spiritual health.[4]

In encouraging an open theological dialogue among those who follow various lifestyles and become intellectually involved with different value systems, we are aware that we will be deeply affected by the encounter. The certainty that comes with maintaining a singular point of view—the believe that truth itself is singular—is shattered. We will not emerge without doubts and questions. We will be forced to rethink previously accepted certainties. A monolithic worldview has lost its power in the encounter; we live now in an open universe of competing values.

What spiritual-intellectual approach will best equip us to put uncertainty and doubt to constructive use within a religiously committed person? What insights might most usefully help us conceptualize the nature and significance of these types of inner turmoil? How can we sensitize ourselves to the understanding that our most painful doubts often contain the seeds of new insights that, rather than indicating some inner spiritual blemish, illuminate untapped depths of the tradition?[5]

Subjective Mitzvot and the Varieties of Halakhic Experience

We must begin with the principle that insulation from differing views and experiences does not, of necessity, characterize the spiritual life of those who ground their faith in the Jewish tradition. It is essential to emphasize the ways in which the spiritual heroes of our tradition confronted, and often welcomed, challenges that forced them to rethink their own beliefs and practices. Instead of viewing the tradition as immune to novelty, we must appreciate the profound dialectic between continuity and change that is present within it. In the form of commentary, masters of the halakhic tradition respectfully expressed their intense loyalty to the past while exploring the new insights made available by their own generation. Gershom Scholem's two essays, "Religious Authority and Mysticism" and "Revelation and Tradition as Religious Categories in Judaism," brilliantly illuminate the orientation of a traditional mind to novelty. These essays reveal that intellectual boldness is not antithetical to taking revelation seriously.[6]

A community that is prepared to grapple with significant intellectual challenges and grow spiritually within a society that is often indifferent to its deepest commitments must be provided with models that exemplify the creative possibilities that can emerge out of doubt and uncertainty. Too frequently in traditional religious culture, people of religious convictions are portrayed as models of dedicated, unquestioning simple faith. Too seldom do we dwell upon the dark nights of the soul that often precede the illuminating certainty of faith. Can one, however, imagine Maimonides's *Guide of the Perplexed* written other than by a sensitive spirit who had struggled with profound religious issues? It is inconceivable to think that his *Guide* was written only for others and not for himself. One cannot illuminate the perplexed without having first tasted the pain of doubt oneself. The price we pay for our neglect to show how religious people struggled with their faith is very heavy indeed.

Similarly, we must correct the mistaken perception that religious people of the past were of one cloth. We must give due recognition to the variety of religious sensibilities expressed in the tradition. Our community, therefore, should be exposed not only to the formal patterns of halakhic practice, but to the vital, inner spiritual life of the halakhic personality as well.

What is the personal meaning of a mitzvah—how does it affect one's awareness and development, and what are the different goals people have in performing them? Our community should accept, and reflect, the varied approaches to *ta'amei ha-mitzvot* (reasons for commandments) that are reflected in the tradition. We hold an incomplete understanding of the nature of halakhic practice if we divorce the *description* of an action from its *inner significance* for the actor. The observer who has access only to the external features of an act lacks a proper understanding of what he or she is observing. In the eyes of the observer, the kabbalists and Maimonides are performing the same mitzvah. However, a person who understands their respective approaches to *ta'amei ha-mitzvot* cannot continue to believe, in the fullest sense, that they are really doing the same thing. To do so is to reduce the observance of mitzvah to external mechanical behaviorism.[7]

Exposure to the multiple aggadic approaches to mitzvot lends emphasis to the important traditional concept that although the Torah was *given* once, it is *received* differently in each generation.[8] Those who create their own *aggadah* within the discipline of a common halakha give expression to their individual religious sensibilities.

What happens when a community emphasizes the variety of spiritual options expressed within the tradition? Its members become aware that the tradition asks for more than shared practice and behavioral obedience. It also encourages them to seek personal meaning and spiritual depth within the formal practices of halakha.

A community that encourages its members to confront the variety of rhythms present in modern society will have to face the reality that those it educates will not necessarily be of one cloth. Its leaders must present a broad range of authentic religious models with which their communities can identify. The multiplicity of models provides breathing space for the variety of psychological and intellectual sensibilities present among their members.

The variety of *ta'amei ha-mitzvot* brings to light that Jewish people never have been a monolithic community. Their spiritual hunger has always been diverse, and the way they integrated outside values with halakhic practice has never been uniform. Rabbi Soloveitchik's halakhic outlook was shaped in no small part by his university training in Berlin, through which he appropriated a new type of significance for the mitzvot. A sensibility of loyalty to the tradition confronts compelling values from the broader intellectual discourse, and new *ta'amei ha-mitzvot* result. Rabbi Samson Raphael Hirsch has a different set of *ta'amei ha-mitzvot* that reflect how deeply the Kantian ethical sensibility shaped his life. Many great religious spirits lived without Kant—some preferred the larger canvas of history that Hegel provided, and there are those, like Soloveitchik, who felt an intimate affinity with Kierkegaard.

Indeed, throughout Jewish history there have always been those willing to engage with the outside world, and others who felt that doing so was the only way to build a healthy people. Maimonides, perhaps the greatest example of a sweeping Judaic appropriation from another culture, showed that Aristotelian ethics can be integrated within halakhic tradition. While formally the two may seem very different—a system based solely on reason versus one based on revelation and authority—Maimonides showed that on a deeper level, they share a common perspective on the health of the soul, as well as similar appreciations of virtue.

Through the searching religious spirit of Maimonides, we find that Aristotle, a pagan, could live within our community. Though he does not believe in our God, he shares with us a common search for decency, an appreciation of what a civilized life looks like. Emphasizing these shared goals and sensibilities makes it possible for our community to live with diverse opinions, different approaches to the ethical, different foundations of what is required for the creation of a decent society. We discover that we're not as strange to each other if we look beyond the formal practices and the authority structures and focus instead on the substantial features of what other worldviews value and aspire to.

Some might argue (as many have) that bringing Aristotle into the Jewish tradition could only undermine the notion of the revealed tradition as the sole ground of absolute truth. I refer to this as the "You're not as unique as you thought you were" argument. And indeed, in his appropriation of Aristotle, Maimonides seems to demonstrate that there is a world "out there"—outside the parameters of received tradition—that is worthy of attention and respect. For some, dismayed at no longer having unique and exclusive access to the ultimate source of meaning, this may create a profound sense of insecurity. On the other hand, what an enormous awakening to realize that what we might have thought were exclusively Jewish values are actually valued by any society interested in cultivating a healthy foundation of decency and mutual respect.

In an attempt to achieve religious certainty, however, contemporary halakhic communities tend to emphasize one model of authenticity to the exclusion of all others. It attempts to gloss over and harmonize the teeming variety of religious sensibilities and approaches contained in our tradition. The religious security that a monolithic approach hopes to achieve is often hollow and atrophying. Religious monism excuses the person committed to halakha from developing his or her own *ta'amei ha-mitzvot*, a responsibility we must shoulder even in a system that has a detailed legal code. A community that ignores the complex emotional dimensions of spirituality inhibits the growth of a religious personality capable of engaging seriously and totally in the creative adventure of discovering new-yet-old vistas in religious life.

When we are exposed to the playful mythic imagination of the mystics, the sober, rational passion of Maimonides, the love of imagery in Judah Halevi, we recognize that the tradition is able to accommodate many different spiritual sensibilities. In the tradition, aggadic teleology was never normative.[9] A fuller understanding of Judaism must, therefore, contain an appreciation of the interaction between pluralistic *aggadot* and uniform halakhic practice. It must reflect the interplay between obedience and conformity to imposed authority on the one hand and a spontaneous, personal, freely chosen spiritual teleology on the other.

Emphasis on the subjective elements within halakha helps mitigate the monistic harshness that frequently accompanies a well-ordered and objective spiritual system. The mistaken claim that the goal of halakha is to provide objective certainty and religious security will be corrected when we realize that we cannot understand halakhic practice without appreciating the inner experience of the mitzvah.[10]

Those whose understanding of halakha contains an awareness of the variety of *ta'amei ha-mitzvot* will be educated to find security in their spiritual life even as they recognize that others will draw meaning for their halakhic practice from different spiritual sources.

"These and These Are the Words of the Living God": Pluralism and the Impossibility of Halakhic Certainty

Thus far I have suggested how important it is to show that halakha never freed the individual from the need to develop one's own spiritual worldview. Emphasis on the broad aggadic options available within the tradition may be helpful in developing a pluralistic sensibility; a person who is secure in his or her approach to religious practice, while recognizing that there are other perceptions of halakha, is well on the way to developing an appreciation of religious pluralism.

I would now like to indicate briefly how such a sensibility may also be nurtured by the study of the logic of halakhic argumentation.[11]

What is the relationship of halakhic argumentation to revelation? What are the logical tools needed to understand the rational basis for legal disagreement in the Talmud? How can two opposing views both be considered "the words of the living God"? What is the cognitive status of minority opinion? Is divine truth revealed in the opinion of the majority, or is majority rule merely a procedural, juridical principle that in no way claims exclusive identification with the truth?

Midrashic writers were fully aware of the diversity of opinions that exist within the tradition and wondered how revelation could lead to such disagreements:

> Rabbi Yannai said: "The words of Torah were not given as clear-cut decisions. For with every word that the Holy One, blessed be He, spoke to Moses, He offered him forty-nine arguments by which a thing may be proved clean, and forty-nine other arguments by which it may be proved unclean. When Moses asked: Master of the universe, in what way

shall we know the true sense of a law? God replied: The majority is to be followed: when a majority says it is unclean, it is unclean; when a majority says it is clean, it is clean."[12]

In order to reconcile diversity with revelation, the midrashic writers offered a new approach to how we understand revelation—claiming that implicit in revelation is diversity and that God seeks that the community develop multiple opinions in multiple directions. The only thing Sinai offers is that we choose on the basis of majority rule. But majority rule doesn't deny that there are competing points of view; in the very acts of divine revelation, God encourages the community to seek alternative possibilities to singular revelation—a procedural principle that allows the inherent integrity of diverse opinions to stand. Revelation, for Rabbi Yannai, encourages deep disagreements between Hillel and Shammai and others. This is how commentators understood the principle "These and these are the words of the living God."[13] Such words are fraught with disagreement and a celebration of multiplicity.

A serious study of these crucial questions may lead to the realization that halakhic argumentation never provided the cognitive certainty of a deductive syllogism. Legal decisions are not necessary inferences drawn from premises. Appreciation of the facts and the context in which we wish to apply the law do not flow necessarily from the law itself. Decision making in a legal system is not a mechanical process.[14] The emphasis placed on certain principles, the weight given to specific values, and the appreciation of the historical situation and its needs are all constitutive elements of a halakhic decision. In applying the law to a living situation, the judge gives expression to an entire philosophy of life. Judges, as distinct from logicians, are *responsible for their decisions*.[15]

A traditional understanding of revelation cannot be divorced from the way in which Talmudic scholars applied Torah to life. The halakhic process clearly shows that there was more than one road that led from belief in a literal revelation to halakhic decision making.

Those who have a deep appreciation of the logic of the halakhic system can never be certain that their actions represent the only possible cognitive response to the Torah of God. Alternate ways of practice are present in a system that applies *Torah mi-Sinai* to its everyday life. "These and these are the words of the living God" is an enduring description of halakhic thinking. Halakhic masters did not confuse the absoluteness of law grounded in revelation with the claim that halakhic decisions reflect the only logical response to divine law.[16] In the tradition, the ultimate source of halakhic authority is God; the application of halakha to life is multiple and human. *Keneset Yisrael* always was, and will remain, responsible for the way of life it developed.

Awareness that halakhic practice is never based, logically, upon the cognitive claim to certainty contributes a rational foundation for the development of a pluralistic sensibility. For pluralism, as distinct from tolerance, cannot be achieved unless our epistemology provides a cognitive basis for validating multiple ways of practice. Both the halakhic and the aggadic components of the tradition can help us find support for the possible development of a pluralistic spiritual sensibility. Total commitment and passion for action need not be grounded in an epistemology that provides absolute certainty. Halakhic practice should not be emphasized at the expense of denying the rich adventure of being exposed to multiple points of view. Those who are encouraged to practice a common halakha should use study texts that inspire them to choose their own *aggadah*. This is crucial to a religious system that wishes to sustain itself and grow within the complexities of the modern world.

"A Wise and Understanding People": The Argument for Intelligibility, against "A*kedah* Consciousness"

Let us now consider ways in which a shared language may be achieved between halakhic and non-halakhic society. Any discussion between two parties requires agreed-upon criteria of meaning, as well as shared values that provide a common universe of discourse. With reference to our discussion, we must explore the question of whether halakha and religious faith of necessity create a private world of meaning that is unintelligible to those who do not understand or share the presuppositions of the tradition. Is it possible to translate a way of life based upon belief in revelation into categories intelligible to those who do not share this belief?

What approach to understanding the mitzvot can effect such a translation? A mystic, theocentric orientation immediately rules out any common language between a believer and a nonbeliever. An approach that insists that duty to God's law must be the sole motivation for observance of the commandments similarly creates an insurmountable barrier to dialogue. The statement "I do this solely because I believe" usually blocks discussion between believer and nonbeliever. However, the tradition provides other approaches to halakhic practice that open up possibilities for a shared language of appreciation between individuals who do not participate in a common halakha. One approach is suggested by Maimonides in the *Guide*:

> There is a group of human beings who consider it a grievous thing that causes should be given for any law; what would please them most is that the intellect would not find a meaning for the commandments and prohibitions. What compels them to feel thus is a sickness that they find in their souls, a sickness to which they are unable to give utterance and of which they cannot furnish a satisfactory account. For they think that if those laws were useful in this existence and had been given to us for this or that reason, it would be as if they derived from the reflection and the understanding of some intelligent being. If, however, there is a thing for which the intellect could not find any meaning at all and that does not lead to something useful, it indubitably derives from God; for the reflection of man would not lead to such a thing. It is as if, according to these people of weak intellects, man

were more perfect than his Maker; for man speaks and acts in a manner that leads to some intended end, whereas the Deity does not act thus, but commands us to do things that are useful to us and forbids us to do things that are harmful to us. But he is far exalted above this; the contrary is the case—the whole purpose consisting in what is useful for us, as we have explained on the basis of its dictum: "For our good always, that He might preserve us alive, as it is at this day" (Deuteronomy 6:24). And it says: "Which shall hear all these statutes [*chukkim*] and say: 'Surely this great community is a wise and understanding people'" (Deuteronomy 4:6). Thus it states explicitly that even all the "statutes" [*chukkim*] will show to all the nations that they have been given "with wisdom and understanding".[17]

In this chapter, Maimonides argues against an approach to the commandments that insists that religious passion must be nurtured by a private language. According to this worldview, mitzvot *must* isolate us cognitively from those who do not believe in revelation. Without this sense of isolation, we do not appreciate the unique significance of mitzvot. The greater the separation of ourselves from nonbelievers, the more deeply do we experience the full meaning of halakha.

We may call this insular religious sensibility the "*Akedah* consciousness." For an important element of the *Akedah* is its total unintelligibility.[18] If the *Akedah* model symbolizes the highest rung of spiritual development, then those mitzvot that make our actions unintelligible to others will be seen as the supreme expression of our religious faith. No shared language is possible if the nonrational and the sense of isolation feed the religious passion.

Maimonides sought to correct this religious "sickness." He insisted that belief in revelation does not require us to dissociate ourselves from rationally communicating the values of our religious life to others who are not committed to *Torah mi-Sinai*. Maimonides uses the proof-text "for it is your wisdom and your understanding in the sight of the peoples" (ki hi chokhmatkhem u-vinatkhem l'einei ha'amim; Deuteronomy 4:6) to demonstrate that the Torah informs us that other nations can recognize the wisdom of a way of life that they themselves do not obey. Appreciation by others, however, is only possible if we are able to explain the purpose of our actions in categories that can be generally comprehended. Maimonides seeks to cast particularist halakhic Jews into the world and informs them that he can explain their spiritual life to others. He offers his reader universal criteria for understanding the purpose of halakha.

> Rather things are indubitably as we have mentioned: every commandment from among these six hundred and thirteen commandments exists either with a view to communicating a rule of justice, or to warding off an injustice, or to endowing men with a noble moral quality, or to warning them against an evil moral quality. Thus all [the commandments] are bound up with three things: opinions, moral qualities, and political civic actions.[19]

Given these criteria that are universally intelligible, a halakhic Jew can begin to communicate with others. In Helek, Maimonides again uses the proof-text quoted above with regard to the cognitive claims of the tradition.[20] Here he argues against those who do not subject the truth claims of aggadic teachers to universal criteria of rationality. The knowledge claims of aggadah and the behavior patterns of halakha need not isolate us from participating within a universal culture. To Maimonides, commitment to tradition is not fed only by nonrational leaps of faith. Cognitive isolation need not be the price we pay for commitment to a particular way of life.

The implications of Maimonides's orientation to religious experience are of utmost importance to communal policy. Such a community would not allow its members to revel in distinctiveness and separation from the world. They would be taught to discover *ta'amei ha-mitzvot* that are grounded in values that can be understood by all. They would find it valuable and necessary to construct a teleology of their own system that could be appreciated by others. They would be trained to speak intelligibly without having to validate the significance of their actions solely by an appeal to faith. Exclusive reliance on faith, *emunah*, can easily serve as a moral escape for a person who does not want to be troubled to consider the human implications of his or her way of life.

The comfortable security that habit provides and the psychological and intellectual support gained from living only with those who think and behave similarly are shaken when we recognize the important spiritual orientation that Maimonides applies to the commandments. We must constantly oscillate between two powerful poles, the universal and the particular, always striving to find a way of integrating both claims upon our life. We must evaluate our spiritual growth not in terms of the *Akedah* model, but in terms of Abraham's passionate prayer for the people of Sodom. Abraham demands that God make God's words intelligible within universal criteria of morality. The model of Abraham at Sodom corrects the one-sided notion that religion creates a private language. At Sodom, God does not demand that Abraham sacrifice his sense of morality.

Finding Community in Shared Aspirations

In exploring the possibility of a shared language for believer and nonbeliever, we must also consider the following serious question: can halakhic Jews recognize in non-halakhic behavior those aspirations that their own system is attempting to realize? If they could do so, they could share with non-halakhic Jews a common teleology. Again, let us turn to Maimonides.

Before discussing the teleology of many halakhic rulings, Maimonides begins chapter 4 of *Shemonah Perakim* with a discussion of the ethical theory of Aristotle. He indicates the nature of virtue based on moderation, the relationship between action and the formation of character, and then shows that halakha aims at realizing those virtues that are also present in the Aristotelian system. Aristotelian ethics and the halakhic system share a common approach to the nature of virtue. Although the two systems do not have a common halakha, Maimonides indicates that, to a great extent, they do share a common teleology.[21]

We find the same approach in chapter 1 of *Mishneh Torah*, "Laws of Moral Disposition and Ethical Conduct." Maimonides again follows the pattern he set in *Shemonah Perakim*. He begins by establishing the concept of virtue based on moderation, but again, he does not derive this approach from any authoritative source within the Judaic tradition:

> To cultivate either extreme in any class of dispositions is not the right course nor is it proper for any person to follow or learn it. If a man finds that his nature tends or is disposed to one of these extremes, or if one has acquired and become habituated to it, he should turn back and improve so as to walk in the way of good people, which is the right way. The right way is the mean in each group of dispositions common to humanity, namely, that disposition that is equally distant from the two extremes in its class, not being nearer to the one than to the other.[22]

In *Shemonah Perakim*, Maimonides shows how the specific details of halakha aim at the formation of healthy character traits. In "Laws of Moral Disposition and Ethical Conduct," he identifies God's attributes—being merciful, gracious, and so on—with the virtuous actions of a healthy soul:

> We are bidden to walk in the middle paths that are the right and proper ways, as it is said, "and you shall walk in His ways" (Deuteronomy 28:9).
>
>   In explanation of the text just quoted, the Sages taught, "Even as God is called gracious, you be gracious; even as He

is called merciful, so you be merciful; even as He is called Holy, so you be holy." Thus too the prophets described the Almighty by all the various attributes "long-suffering and abounding in kindness, righteous and upright, perfect, mighty and powerful," and so forth to teach us that these qualities are good and right and that a human being should cultivate them, and thus imitate God, as far as he can.... And as the Creator is called by these attributes, which constitute the middle path in which we are to walk, this path is called the Way of God and this is what the patriarch Abraham taught his children.[23]

In Judaism, we arrive at the ideal of a healthy soul through halakhic prescription or by imitating the moral attributes of God.

What is important for our purpose is that in both *Shemonah Perakim* and "Laws of Moral Disposition and Ethical Conduct," Maimonides enables the halakhically committed person to recognize many similarities between the goals of his or her religious practices and the teleology of other systems. Halakha and the imitation of God aim to develop character. These goals are perceived to be religious commandments by the halakhic Jew. But that perception does not prevent Maimonides from making halakhic practice intelligible within categories that are not grounded in revelation and mitzvah.

If we follow in the spirit of Maimonides, it would be correct to show that individuals can share halakhic *aspirations* even though these are not concretized through halakhic *guidelines*. A student trained in this perspective will find it possible to participate meaningfully with others who do not share the presuppositions upon which his or her own lifestyle is based.

Many claim, even at this still-early moment in the history of the Israeli state, that national unity predicated on anything other than basic survival is a lost cause. They may be right—if they are, it should be acknowledged that another central facet of the Zionist vision has been relegated to the status of a pipe dream. In my own view, while nothing about the present—much less the future—is divinely assured, it always remains within our hands which elements of our tradition to appropriate and amplify in our personal and collective lives.

My claim is that if the more traditionalist branches of the family that has come to live together in the ancestral homeland were to prioritize not only the reactive unity of survival but also proactively cultivate a community of meaning with the rest of their Jewish family, then they would have plenty of resources from within the tradition upon which to draw. By opening ourselves to the intellectual openness and diversity of religious models found within Judaic tradition, emphasizing the impossibility of certainty and the live religious possibilities of intelligibility built into the halakhic enterprise, and focusing on the tradition's essential values and goals, its telos, to find community in shared aspirations with those espousing other value systems and practicing alternate forms of religious and secular life—in these ways, we might at least begin to lay the groundwork for a shared community of meaning.

6

CONQUERING MODERN IDOLATRY

BUILDING COMMUNITIES OF MEANING AROUND SHARED ASPIRATIONS

The Dream of Unity and the Divisiveness of "God Talk"

At the conclusion of the previous chapter I described the ways in which cultivating a sense of common aspirations might be useful in forging a path toward a shared spiritual language among groups with differing orientations toward Judaism. While I believe that this approach is conducive to increased dialogue and mutual respect, I am also aware of the reality of such conversations when the topic turns to central theological motifs like God and revelation. Although shared language is possible in certain ethical areas of life, when it comes to "God talk," the walls of separation grow higher, and alienation returns with its ominous sense that we can't really make it together as a unified Jewish nation. While halakhic practice need not isolate one from sharing common goals with those not committed to the behavioral prescriptions of the halakha, a much more difficult question is whether a shared theological language is possible between the believer and the agnostic or atheist.

For some groups God language is critical to any authentic Jewish identity. For others it is an enemy of human progress.

111

When national dialogue begins to turn around belief in God and the authority of revelation becomes a central motif, opposing voices draw lines in the sand: we don't want to build a society around faith in revelation or the authority of halakha. We can't understand you and we can't travel with you, because the God from which you derive all your meaning does not, as far as we are concerned, exist. Moreover, we will only be a free and healthy nation when we rid ourselves of this traditional frame of reference, with its emphasis on divine will and providence. Jewish society will flourish only when we unburden ourselves from the biblical God and Talmudic notions of authority.

By definition, these theological differences lead to opposing perspectives on history. One group sees events as expressions of divine providence whose religious interpretations should drive all political discourse and action. The other views history as a naturalist evolution reflecting human development as it emerges from amid the complex structures of history, independent of "external" notions like chosenness or providence. One group feels it possesses the truth in history according to the will of God as expressed in the Bible and interpreted for our time by traditional authorities. The other wants a Bible, and a history, without God. (Indeed, there were those within Israeli society at the time the state was founded who wanted to remove God's name from the Bible. They blocked all overt mention of God in the Declaration of Independence, substituting the more naturalistic-sounding term "Rock of Israel" [Tzur Yisrael].) One group sees atheism and atheists as destroying the future of the Jewish people; the other sees the ultra-Orthodox as undermining human responsibility and freedom. Let us be a normal nation, proclaim the secularists, without building our value system upon irrational leaps of faith.

Is this division ultimate? Can these barriers of language be overcome? Let us again look into the vast sea of Jewish tradition to see if it can provide us with any guidance about how to share God talk. In fact, I believe the tradition contains resources that may enable us to overcome this seemingly inevitable and deeply ingrained sense of mutual alienation, estrangement, and mistrust. I find the potential for this type of discourse in a clear understanding of what constitutes, in modern terms, the battle against the seductive powers of *avodah zarah*, "idolatry."

Conquering Idolatry: The Unifying Power of Negation

I use the evocative term "seductive" intentionally, to indicate that the rejection of idolatry is important only if what is rejected has a luring power.[1] To negate can be a moving experience and be deeply meaningful if what is negated has a powerful attraction. Our convictions gain vitality when we understand what is not compatible with them. The negative illuminates the force of the positive. If our belief in God sometimes appears to be a hollow and superficial gesture, it may be due to our limited understanding of what constitutes modern idolatry.

Idolatry was the fundamental enemy of Jewish history, conquering it the fundamental shared mission of the Jewish people. In a Talmudic discussion on why Mordechai was called *yehudi* (which would suggest that he belonged to the tribe of Judah) when he came from the tribe of Benjamin, Rabbi Johanan answers: He was called a Jew because he rejected idolatry. "For anyone who repudiates idolatry is called a Jew."[2]

Elsewhere the Talmud declares, "The person who negates idolatry fulfills the entire Torah." And after asking, "Which is the commandment that is as weighty as all other commandments?" it confidently concludes, "Surely, it is that concerning idolatry."[3]

Can we speak to each other as soldiers in the battle against idolatry? Can we unite in that struggle?

Abraham as the iconoclast of history is a weak figure, I would suggest, if the only idols he smashes are the ones found in his father's shop. Indeed, Maimonides sees the rejection of idolatry as one of the primary goals of halakha:

The precept relating to idolatry is equal in importance
to all the other precepts put together, as it is said, "And
when you shall err and not observe all these commandments" (Numbers 15:22). This text has traditionally been
interpreted as alluding to idolatry; hence the inference
that acceptance of idolatry is tantamount to repudiating
the whole Torah, the prophets and everything that they
were commanded, from Adam to the end of time, as it
is said, "From the day that the Lord gave commandment
and onward, throughout your generations" (Numbers
15:23). And whoever denies idolatry confesses his faith
in the whole Torah, in all the prophets and all that the
prophets were commanded, from Adam to the end of
time. And this is the fundamental principle of all the
commandments.[4]

If our communities are to appreciate their role as iconoclasts in
history, it is important that we educate them to understand how the
yetzer hara (evil inclination) of idolatry is still alive.[5]

In his book *The Morality of Law*,[6] Lon L. Fuller considers the
question of whether we can know what is bad without knowing
the perfectly good. Fuller argues that we *can* know what is plainly
unjust without committing ourselves to declare with finality what
perfect justice would be like. In terms of our concern, we can
ask whether rejection of idolatry is possible without a positive
affirmation of God.[7] If we can assume that it is possible for
individuals to agree on what they reject, without acknowledging
what they affirm, we may be able to create a shared theology of
the repudiation of idolatry, without demanding a clearly defined
commitment to belief in God. The believer can share common
aspirations with the atheist and the agnostic if all three strive to
reject idolatry. This striving can have great significance and far-
ranging consequences if the idolatry that is combated is luring and
constitutes a vital problem to be eradicated.

Emperor Worship and the Idolatry
of Absolute Power

Ephraim Urbach, in his article "The Rabbinical Laws of Idolatry," develops insights that can be helpful to our discussion.[8] He notes that although the Talmud records differing approaches to idolatry, "one thing is certain—neither the *Tannaim* of the second century nor the *Amoraim* of the third showed any tendency to compromise or to concede to anything connected with emperor worship." Evidently the worship of idols was not luring to the Jews of the period, but the worship of the emperor had a power of attraction that had to be combated as forcefully as possible. Urbach writes:

> According to the Jerusalem Talmud, the *Tannaim* were divided in their opinions about the generality of images, but if it was certain that they were images of kings, all agreed in forbidding them.... In the ancient world there were—on the evidence of Pliny—more gods than human beings ... but in that same world, there was only one emperor whose sovereignty and power were felt daily.

The power of Rome, as distinct from pagan idolatry, impinged upon the daily life of the community. It was a felt reality. Emperor worship had to be combated because its attractiveness and power could lure a person away from religious commitment.

As Urbach develops his thesis, he notes that from the time of Antonines onward, the cult of the emperor became "the religion of absolute political power. It was not an individual that was worshipped, but the more than human power of which he was the personification.... Everything connected with this cult was absolutely forbidden [by the Sages]."

The idolatry of absolute power has not been destroyed. The urge for political power and control present in the twenty-first century is a flagrant rejection of the sovereignty of God. The demand for total and uncritical allegiance to a political state is idolatrous. Any political figure or party that considers itself beyond criticism has, in a very important sense, denied the reality of God. Insisting on criticism, demanding accountability, limiting the dangerous hunger for power, and building political structures that create balances of power may be important ways to implement the halakhic struggle against idolatry.

"As One Who Worships Idols": Anger, Arrogance, and Idolatrous Behavior

The *yetzer hara* of idolatry need not, however, manifest itself solely in the political longing for absolute power. Its seductiveness may also be evident in the personal realm. It is interesting to observe the Rabbis' use of the term "as one who worships idols," *ke'ilu oved avodah zarah*, and similar references to idolatry, with regard to specific behavioral traits:

> Rabbi Johanan said in the name of Rabbi Simeon ben Yohai: "Every man in whom is haughtiness of spirit is as though he worships idols." ... Rabbi Johanan himself said: "He is as though he had denied the existence of God, as it is said, 'Your heart be lifted up and you forget the Lord your God' (Deuteronomy 8:14)."[9]
>
> Rabbi Elazar also said: "Every man in whom is haughtiness of spirit is fit to be hewn down like an *asherah* [an object of idolatrous worship]."[10]
>
> Rav Hisda said, and according to another version it was Mar Ukba: "Every man in whom is haughtiness of spirit, the Holy One blessed be He declares, I and he cannot both dwell in the world."
>
> Rabbi Simeon ben Elazar said in the name of Halfa ben Agra in Rabbi Johanan ben Nuri's name: "He who rends his garments in his anger, he who breaks his vessels in his anger, and he who scatters his money in his anger, regard him as an idolater, because such are the wiles of the

Tempter: Today he says to him, 'Do this,' tomorrow he tells him, 'Do that,' until he bids him, 'Go and serve idols,' and he goes and serves [them]." Rabbi Abin observed: "What verse [intimates this]? 'There shall be no strange god in you; neither shalt you worship any strange god' (Psalm 81:10); who is the strange god that resides in man himself? Say, that is the Tempter."[11]

We may claim that there is no actual relationship between idolatry and arrogance and uncontrolled anger. We may argue that the Rabbis' evocative language is simply pedagogical, a way of educating their constituents about the spiritual seriousness of these destructive personal traits. Perhaps in order to stress the importance of guarding oneself against arrogance and the loss of temper, the Rabbis used such phrases as "I and he cannot both dwell in the world" and "as though he had denied the existence of God." This may be true. However, the choice of these terms, with all their associations and overtones, may be *literally* significant and indicate a goal far more profound. Perhaps the Rabbis wished to suggest that we may perceive the ugliness of idolatry in the character structure of people. Perhaps our Sages sought to educate us to recognize that the person who is subject to rage so intense that he or she loses self-control or the person who is swollen with arrogance manifests character traits that are incompatible with the worship of God.

The capacity for self-transcendence is an essential element in the faith experience. The believer is conscious of his or her creatureliness and finitude when he or she stands before the Infinite. This awareness should enable one to appreciate the dignity of others and be responsive to realities beyond one's own self. The person who says, wholeheartedly, "Blessed are You," *Barukh atah*, is a human being who has broken out of the prison of egocentricity. In the stages of rage, however, the person is trapped within his or her own hate. In moments of arrogance, the individual is imprisoned within his or her own inflated sense of self. Arrogance and rage prevent the full appreciation and confirmation of a reality beyond oneself; they inhibit a person from transcending him- or herself, a condition that is essential for the encounter with God.

In this sense, there is an important similarity between these character traits and the longing for absolute power in the political realm. Hunger for power, arrogance, and rage all prevent the individual from seeing and appreciating the dignity of others. Not to respond to others as persons is, in fact, a denial of one's creature consciousness. Arrogance and the urge for absolute power are states of consciousness in which the individual does not recognize the human implications of God's dwelling in the world.

The translation of idolatry into behavior patterns and character traits is a mode of thought inherent to the spirit of normative Judaism. The halakhic person always translates belief into behavior.[12] Just as the Rabbis recognized that an acceptance of the kingdom of heaven is incomplete if it does not lead to the acceptance of the commandments, they may also have recognized that belief in God is void of significance if it does not lead to the shaping of character.[13]

A Shared Language of Idolatry

The insistence that faith be expressed in behavior patterns and the shaping of character creates a realm of common categories that makes possible a fruitful discussion between a believer and a nonbeliever. The importance that Judaism ascribes to practice makes possible the creation of a shared language. If faith alone were the major focus of the spiritual life in Judaism, this attempt at translation would be far more difficult.[14]

If our communities would emphasize the character traits that emerge from faith in God and educate toward a full appreciation of what constitutes the contemporary struggle against idolatry, we might alleviate the sense of value isolation that frequently oppresses the person committed to faith in the revealed word of God and begin to create a theological language that is intelligible and usable by broad sectors of the community.

The Urgency of Community:
Mitzvah and the Battle against Idolatry

The significance given to practice within Judaism not only makes the creation of a shared language around idolatry a rational possibility, but also provides the sense of urgency to make that attempt. Mitzvah illuminates the *centrality of community* within Judaism. Halakha is a way of life of a community and serves to develop a collective consciousness within the individual Jew. Systems of thought in which the individual is dominant cannot do justice to a worldview where law, which is vital to community, plays a central role. Existentialism, which focuses primarily on individual self-realization, cannot illuminate sufficiently the communal depths of halakhic Judaism. Halakha can best be understood through the categories of political philosophy, for example, law, community, and authority.

Maimonides, the master halakhist, perceived the halakhic system in political terms.[15] For Maimonides, the legal category of mitzvah did not exist prior to Moses. Only after the Exodus from Egypt, with the formation of a community, did halakha become the dominant and organizing principle within Judaism. Abraham is described by Maimonides as a teacher who convinces through rational argumentation. Moses, who brings the law to the people, addresses the community in the name of God's legislative authority.[16]

Prior to Sinai, humanity sought God through reflection upon God's power and wisdom, as revealed in nature. That spiritual way, based upon philosophy, is individualistic. The authority of mitzvah becomes central to Judaism only when the collective community stands before God at Sinai. Halakha, therefore, guides the individual to realize his or her longing for God within the context of community. As the "I" becomes a "we" consciousness through the collective covenant, it must seek a communal language: the language of mitzvah.

According to Maimonides, the halakhic Jew who has traveled the individual road of philosophy never abandons his or her collective consciousness. Community and practice are central even for the Jew who seeks contemplative love of God.[17] The profound longing for community is intrinsic to a worldview in which halakha is the dominant organizing principle. Halakha cannot respond to humanity's yearning for self-realization if we do not first feel the urgency of building a covenantal community.

Unfortunately, however, rather than serving as a catalyst for the building of the community, halakha is often used as an instrument for divisiveness, subtle aggression, and spiritual isolation. Instead of mitzvah awakening the individual to embrace *kelal Yisrael*, it is often, and mistakenly, viewed as calling for the isolation of the individual from the community. The performance of the mitzvah becomes exclusively an expression of a striving for personal excellence.

One who hears a collective call in mitzvah is pained by the sectarian isolationism prevalent today. One who seeks to receive the Torah every day *within community* feels the urgency to build shared spiritual meanings within our society. Maimonides describes the transition in Jewish history from the individualistic, philosophical spirituality of Abraham to the collective, mitzvah-based spirituality of Moses specifically as a necessary evolution in the core religious battle against idolatry. While Abraham had certainly created something new in the world—"a nation that knew God"—the "long days" of oppression and suffering of Egypt wore them down until finally they (with the exception of the tribe of Levi) yielded to the influence of the idolatrous culture in which they had become immersed. "And they regressed and learned from [the Egyptians'] practices and to serve idolatry … and all was almost lost, and the principle that Abraham planted nearly uprooted." It was precisely the need to create a system that could resist this kind of cultural pressure—to create not only a pious nation devoted to its God but also a religious community unified around collective norms—that led to the emergence of Moses and mitzvah. "Until from His love of us, and in observance of His oath to Abraham our Father, He made Moses our Teacher, and the teacher of all the prophets, and sent him." In his summary of this historical sea change, Maimonides reaffirms the aspiration that brought it about: "When Moses our Teacher prophesied, and God chose Israel as an inheritance, He crowned them with mitzvot and informed them in the path of His service—the judgment of idolatry and all those who stray after it."[18]

Can a religion of philosophical individualism withstand idolatry? Maimonides describes the failure of Abraham's philosophical community in precisely these terms, and it was this failure that in turn necessitated a new strategy better designed to assist humanity in resistance against the seductive powers of idolatry: the strategy— the category—of mitzvah. The community built on philosophy could not alone maintain sufficient resistance to the pervasive pagan culture. The battle against idolatry in the believer's world is able to resist such cultural influence only through mitzvah and halakha, thinking of Judaism as a political system with legal authority. All the details about how halakha emerges comes from the idea that an alternative community must be created for this battle to be taken seriously. Moses's political-halakhic community is the response to the failure of Abraham's philosophical community.

The Halakhic Process:
Educating against Idolatry

For Maimonides, then, the central purpose and thrust of halakha is to turn a community of idolatry into a community of faith. The method through which halakha attempted to achieve this collective goal was by, in effect, "co-opting" pagan idolatry through the sacrifices. For in Egypt, as idolators, the people's form of worship was sacrifice. To free the community from its attachment to pagan idolatry, the Torah appropriated pagan forms of worship and brought them within the culture of Judaism, albeit in a highly restricted way. Thus absorbed, pagan impulses were disciplined and transformed, rechanneled through a monotheistic lens.

This description of Jewish intellectual history illustrates how a community of faith might begin to speak to a community of nonbelievers: not by invalidating them wholesale, but to the contrary, by allowing their values to enter into the Judaic tradition. Maimonides sees the passion of idolatry as having been integrated into the passion of Judaism. He is willing to make the bold move of seeing halakha not only as a political framework but also as an educational process of incrementally weaning the community away from idolatry. He does not take a rejectionist stance. He is not frightened from allowing halakhic Judaism to absorb and incrementally transform pagan practices, because he knows that a sudden transition is impossible and that meaningful communal change must be gradual. Indeed, he outlines this process explicitly in the *Guide of the Perplexed*:

> For a sudden transition from one opposite to another is impossible. And therefore man, according to his nature, is not capable of abandoning suddenly all to which he was accustomed.... At that time the way of life generally accepted and customary in the whole world and the universal service upon which we were brought up consisted in offering various species of living beings in the temples in which images were set up, in worshipping the latter, and in burning incense before them—the pious ones and the ascetics being at that time, as we have explained, the people who were devoted to the service of the temples consecrated to the stars. His wisdom, may He be exalted, and His gracious ruse, which is manifest in regard to all His creatures, did not require that He give us a Law prescribing the rejection, abandonment, and abolition of all these kinds of worship. For one could not then conceive the acceptance of [such a Law], considering the nature of man, which always likes that to which it is accustomed. At that time this would have been similar to the appearance of a prophet in these times who, calling upon the people to worship God, would say: "God has given you a Law forbidding you to pray to Him, to

fast, to call upon Him for help in misfortune. Your worship should consist solely in meditation without any works at all." Therefore He, may He be exalted, suffered the above-mentioned kinds of worship to remain, but transferred them from created or imaginary and unreal things to His own name, may He be exalted, commanding us to practice them with regard to Him, may He be exalted.... What was there to prevent Him, may He be exalted, from giving us a Law in accordance with His first intention and from procuring us the capacity to accept this?... The text of the Torah tells us a quite similar story, namely in its dictum: "God led them not by the way of the Philistines, although it was near," and so on. "But God led the people about, by the way of the wilderness of the Red Sea" (Exodus 13:17). Just as God perplexed them in anticipation of what their bodies were naturally incapable of hearing—turning them away from the high road toward which they had been going, toward another road so that the first intention should be achieved—so did He in anticipation of what the soul is naturally incapable of receiving, prescribe the laws that we have mentioned so that the first intention should be achieved, namely, the apprehension of Him, may He be exalted, and the rejection of idolatry. For just as it is not in the nature of man that, after having been brought up in slavish service occupied with clay, bricks, and similar things, he should all of a sudden wash off from his hands the dirt deriving from them and proceed immediately to fight the children of Anak, so it is also not in his nature that, after having been brought up upon very many modes of worship and of customary practices, which the souls find so agreeable that they become as it were a primary notion, he should abandon them all of a sudden ... so did this group of laws derive from a Divine grace, so that they should be left with the kind of practices to which they were accustomed and so that consequently the belief, which constitutes the first intention, should be validated in them.... What was to prevent Him from causing the inclination to accomplish the acts of obedience willed by Him and to avoid the acts of disobedience abhorred by Him, to be a natural disposition fixed in us?

There is one and the same general answer to all these three questions and to all the others that belong to the same class: Though all miracles change the nature of some individual being, God does not change at all the nature of human individuals by means of miracles. Because of this great principle it says: "O that they had such a heart as this" (Deuteronomy 5:26), and so on. It is because of this that there are commandments and prohibitions, rewards and punishments. We have already explained this fundamental principle by giving its proofs in a number of passages in our compilations. We do not say this because we believe that the changing of nature of any human individual is difficult for Him, may He be exalted. Rather it is possible and fully within capacity. But according to the foundations of the Law, of the Torah, He has never willed to do it, nor shall He ever will it. For if it were His will that the nature of any human individual should be changed because of what He, may He be exalted, wills from that individual, sending of prophets and all giving of a Law would have been useless.[19]

One must not forget that the master halakhic judge of the *Mishneh Torah* perceived and understood revelation and sacrificial service within these profound educational categories. Halakha, as understood by Maimonides, expresses the sober passion of a wise teacher who begins the spiritual process from where his or her students stand. A teacher who has internalized the power and strength that tradition and knowledge provide should manifest the loving patience reflected in Maimonides's theory of the relationship between history and revelation.

A contemporary theology following this spirit will seek to develop in its adherents patience and an ability to listen and respond to the other in terms of his or her worldview—in other words, it will educate us to imitate the divine qualities that God exhibited at Sinai.

Israel:
Historic Opportunity for a Covenant of Meaning

There are dangers in suggesting that religious education deal with issues that may weaken the halakhic person's loyalty to the halakhic tradition. There are risks in encouraging intellectual openness, in exposing the halakhic community to views and lifestyles that do not conform to or confirm its pattern in life. This is why we are invariably greeted with words of extreme caution when suggesting that we encourage religious communities to confront the modern world. We are told that we must wait until filled sufficiently with *lechem ubasar*, "the knowledge of what is permitted and what is forbidden," before entering into such a potentially dangerous enterprise.[20] But how are we to judge when we are sufficiently strong and learned to withstand the challenge of new ideas?

There is an attractive simplicity in the isolationist approach to religious education, but we must also recognize the very severe risks involved in waiting to be sufficiently strong before engaging in encounter. We may find that when we are ready to speak, there is no community willing to listen.

The opportunity to begin the process of creating a collective covenant of meaning does not come often in history. The presence of a living Jewish society in Israel, with its dedication to a covenant of national political destiny, constitutes a fruitful soil for the creation of such a community of meaning. The danger in a separatist religious philosophy today is that Judaism may turn into a sect and cease being a way of life for the total community. A philosophy that ignores the challenge of the present opportunity takes a great risk indeed. Single-minded concern with saving the

Torah for the few may entail losing the people as a whole. *This should not be the response of a halakhic Jew to history.* The centrality of mitzvah demands that we feel the urgency of concretizing norms within the public domain of the Jewish collective, *kelal Yisrael.*

7

LEARNING TO HOPE

A HALAKHIC APPROACH TO HISTORY AND REDEMPTION

The Potentialities of the Present: Finding Hope in Memory

Hope is a category of transcendence that expands our sense of the possible beyond what we sense and experience directly. It is the belief or conviction that present reality (what I see) does not exhaust the *potentialities* of the status quo. Hope opens the present to the future; it enables us to look ahead, to break the fixity of what we observe, and thus to perceive the world as open-textured. The categories of possibility and transcendence interweave a closely stitched psychological and spiritual fabric; hope says that tomorrow can be better than today.

Hope, however, is not merely a perspective that draws its nourishment in the present from the future. Often the roots of hope lie in memory. Thus, the greatest potential for transcending the despair that often accompanies the seeming fixity of the present may be found by directing our attention to both the future and the past. Memories of certain moments or events may provide a key for expanding the present beyond its sense of givenness and escort us past empirical reality. Indeed, upon reflection the extent to which future expectancy is tied to one's memories—how memories define our eschatology and our orientation toward hope—begins to seem obvious.[1]

To seek an understanding of hope is not necessarily to desire an interlude of romanticism. We need only consider the reality of the twentieth century—in which the Jewish people have, with faith and expectancy, demonstrated a profound, practical will to emerge from the abyss of human brutalization and depravity and build an ancient society anew—to gain a grounded appreciation of the indispensable role of hope in our individual and collective survival.

I
Two Types of Hope

To begin, it is important to identify two significant types, or dimensions, of hope: (1) the courage to bear human responsibility, to persevere in partial solutions, and to accept the burden of living and building within contexts of uncertainty; and (2) the expectancy of a future resolution to all human problems. The former, as I will show, might aptly be described as "halakhic" hope; the second, "radical" hope.

Halakhic hope liberates action, for it provides a means by which to overcome the paralysis of dejection. Where our outlook is thoroughly hopeless, notions like progress and duty become meaningless, and our capacity to act is severely impaired. A prospect of attainment, on the other hand, helps generate the strength required to act. Expectancy that something new and good may occur often creates the very impetus necessary to implement one's goals.[2]

Radical hope need not address itself to action. It is a mode of anticipation, a faith that ultimately redemption will come, in its appointed time, irrespective of what we do or don't do. It is not expressed through action, but through inaction, a sustained waiting that in mystical thinking is intimately associated with the messianic concept. Indeed, according to Gershom Scholem, the mystic's hope is by definition radical and apocalyptic:

> This redemption ... is in no causal sense a result of previous history.... It is not the product of immanent developments such as we find in modern Western reinterpretations of Messianism since the Enlightenment where, secularized as the belief in progress, Messianism still displayed unbroken and immense vigor. It is rather transcendence breaking in upon history, an intrusion in which history itself perishes, transformed in its ruin.... The apocalyptists' optimism, their hope, is not directed to what history will bring forth but to that which will arise in its ruin, free at last and undisguised.[3]

Scholem contrasts this "utopian" model of hope against what he calls the "restorative" secular messianism[4] of the post-Enlightenment West. In fact, both sides of this dichotomy are presented as legitimate expressions of messianic hope in a Talmudic discussion[5] regarding redemption. Rav declares, "All the appointed times of redemption are over, and the matter depends wholly upon repentance and good deeds." History, in other words, will not be redeemed of necessity: redemption is contingent on human action and efforts. In response, Samuel states, "It is sufficient for the mourner to remain in his mourning." It is enough for Israel to sustain herself in history, for redemption is not dependent on successful moral renewal.

This Talmudic debate parallels an earlier one. "If Israel repents," claims Rabbi Eliezer, "they will be redeemed; if not, they will not be saved." Rabbi Joshua answers, "If they do not repent, they will not be redeemed? But what will happen? God will send a wicked king, one whose decrees will be as Haman's, and then Israel will do *teshuvah* [turning, repentance]."[6]

Is redemption ultimately dependent upon human choice? Rabbi Eliezer proposes a vision of hope centered around human freedom of choice and the will to change. Rabbi Joshua argues that God will enter the process of history. While perhaps not freeing humanity from the need to change, God will create conditions compelling people to respond in *teshuvah*. In Talmudic thought, oppression and suffering were considered to be catalysts for moral change. God can intervene in history, then, by fashioning circumstances impelling the Jewish people to repent.

Reconsidering Redemption: Hope, History, and Halakha

It should be noted that both of the above schools of thought stipulate some sort of divine provision for deliverance—for without God's promise of salvation, there would be no certainty that even repentance would bring redemption. Nevertheless, they do differ significantly in their interpretations of hope, human redemption, and ultimately of our relationship to history itself. Samuel and Rabbi Joshua view national salvation as an inevitable process: history as we know it will eventually be transformed by a force that transcends human agency. Rav and Rabbi Eliezer, to the contrary, understand history as an open-ended set of possibilities dependent upon human choice and action.

It is in large part due to the security of its built-in fail-safe—a reassuring "escape clause" from the seemingly interminable rigors of history—that so many religious frameworks are structured around and animated by some form of radical hope. This is why Scholem, above, identifies progressive, "restorative" hope with modern, secular trends of thought. Thus it seems natural to ask, is it possible to construct a viable religious approach without the certainty of redemption? What might such an approach look like?

I find a compelling answer to this question suggested in the approach to hope voiced by Rav and Rabbi Eliezer, which gives rise to a kind of religious faith emphasizing progressive, restorative hope. This, I suggest, is the type of hope—and consequently the orientation toward our role in history—that halakhic Judaism primarily expresses and seeks to cultivate. When Rav asserts that redemption is dependent on *teshuvah*, he believes with absolute certainty its eventual realization; he feels the certainty of deliverance. But this confidence in redemption sets into motion a liberating dynamic that expresses itself in deeds. "Halakhic hope," the school of thought represented by Rav and Rabbi Eliezer, thus enhances our practical capacity to act in history.

To proponents of "radical" hope, however, salvation is not a process in history, but a cataclysm shattering the natural order. A Mishnaic passage reflecting this orientation paints a sobering picture of the time when the Messiah will come. Human arrogance will become great. Prices in the marketplace will soar. Vines will yield fruit, but wine will be costly. Heathens will be converted to heresy, and there will be no dissenting voice. Houses of worship will become brothels. Groups of people will wander from town to town, and none shall show them compassion. The wisdom of the scribes will become decadent, and the morally upright will be despised. The young will shame their elders. "The face of the generation shall be like the face of a dog." Father and son together will visit the same prostitute. "On whom then shall we lean?" asks the Mishnah. "On our Father who is in heaven," is the response.[7] A later Talmudic statement claims that the Messiah will come in a generation that is either all meritorious or thoroughly guilty.[8]

Thus, proponents of radical hope find signs of redemption not in the evolution of better social conditions but in utter darkness and despair. Apocalyptic notions of redemption do not encourage action toward realistic social goals, for they incorporate the essential premise that no matter how miserable life will be, God will not abandon humanity.

II
Two Visions of the Messianic Era

These two dimensions of hope, with their implications for history, human responsibility, and redemption, are further developed in the approaches of two major medieval Jewish thinkers, Maimonides and Nachmanides. The former "normalized" the radical, apocalyptic vision of messianic expectancy, depicting a vision of the messianic era brought about and sustained by what I refer to as halakhic hope:

Do not think that King Messiah will have to perform signs and wonders, bring anything new into being.... Rather, this Law of ours ... is for ever and all eternity; it is not to be added to or taken away from....

Let no one think that in the days of the Messiah any of the laws of nature will be set aside.... The world will follow its normal course. Said the Rabbis: "The sole difference between the present and the messianic days is delivery from the servitude to foreign powers" (BT *Sanhedrin* 91b).... In that era there will be neither famine nor war.... The one preoccupation of the whole world will be to know the Lord. Hence Israelites will be very wise (Isaiah 11:9).[9]

Human nature will not change, says Maimonides. Isaiah's picture of the lamb and the lion is only allegorical.[10] Torah and halakha will be as binding in the messianic period as before; the Torah will be needed then, as now, to guide and discipline human conduct. There will be neither a new law nor a new human nature. The distinction between the messianic and the pre-messianic period lies within the political domain. The novelty of the messianic age will consist in the intensification of spiritual seeking among a large part of the population, and this will result from the political and economic security of the times.[11]

In contrast, Nachmanides envisions a messianic era characterized by a miraculous transformation of the human heart, obviating the need for mitzvot. Interpreting the verse "God will circumcise your heart" (Deuteronomy 30:6), he writes:

But in the days of the Messiah, the choice of ... men's genuine good will be natural; the heart will not desire the improper.... There will be no evil desire in man but he will naturally perform the proper deeds and therefore there will be neither merit nor guilt in them, for merit and guilt are dependent upon desire.[12]

Nachmanides builds upon Jeremiah's vision (31:30–32) of a divine dispensation: the Torah will be inscribed in the human heart. A thirst to do good will dominate human nature. Deliberation between good and evil, and the struggle between reason and inclination, will be eliminated. The coming "complete redemption" will bring about a new evolution in human consciousness.[13]

For Maimonides, however, the open-endedness of human choices will remain even during the messianic age. His vision of hope incorporates uncertainty; the human condition is not transcended, and moral struggle remains an abiding feature of history.

Repentance versus Rupture:
Will Redemption Come from Above or Below?

While recognizing how Maimonides neutralized the apocalyptic strands of messianism, Gershom Scholem claims that there is, nevertheless, a radical "rupture" element in the Maimonidean eschatology:

> Maimonides nowhere recognizes a causal relationship between the coming of the Messiah and human conduct. It is not Israel's repentance which brings about redemption; rather, because the eruption of redemption is to occur by divine decree, at the last moment there also erupts a movement of repentance in Israel itself. The Messianic restoration, which is tied to no idea of progress toward the redemption, is and remains a miracle—though of course not a miracle that occurs outside of nature and her laws, but a miracle because it has been previously announced by the prophets to affirm God's dominion in the world. The Messianic age is a free-will gift of God, but it is a gift which has been promised, and that raises its beginnings above the level of nature, even if they do occur under natural conditions. Maimonides did not attempt a purely philosophical justification of the Messianic idea on the basis of his ontology or ethics.[14]

According to Scholem, the rationalism of Maimonides's description of the messianic era is circumscribed by a certainty that the mass religious revival that it will bring about is itself the eruption of "a gift which has been promised," a product of a force "above the level of nature." As will be shown below, anticipating ruptures in history is out of tone with the Maimonidean spirit of translating "vertical" decrees into "horizontal" naturalism. There is no compelling reason to maintain, as Scholem does, that Maimonides reverted to an eschatology of sudden divine intervention. Scholem is not sufficiently radical in his treatment of the "rationalism" of Maimonidean Messianism—a claim supported by further examination of Maimonides's description of *teshuvah* and redemption.

Scholem treats redemption and the occurrence of *teshuvah* as events that will "erupt," that is, as events independent of the chain of natural historical connections. A key text to which Scholem's position may appeal is the following statement in *Mishneh Torah*:

> All the prophets charged the people concerning repentance. Only through repentance will Israel be redeemed, and the Torah promised that in the end, at the end of their exile, Israel will repent and immediately they will be redeemed.[15]

The two elements in the above quotation that support Scholem's position are (1) the prophetic *promise* regarding repentance and the eventual realization of the messianic age, and (2) the notion of an *end*, that is, a time that will constitute the end of ordinary history and the commencement of the messianic era.

While it is true that Maimonides's philosophy of Judaism did include belief in miracles and nonrational doctrines, it is also true that he went to great lengths to negate any conception of history relegating humanity to the role of passive participant in a drama dominated by God. Wherever possible he naturalizes the miraculous, argues for human freedom and responsibility while concurrently denying historical inevitability, and rejects the notion of an end to history where the world as we know it is replaced by a "new heaven and a new earth." These positions lead to an interpretation of the promise of ultimate repentance that are far more aligned with Maimonidean rationalism than Scholem acknowledges, leaving little room for the type of historical rupture he claims as inherent to the Maimonidean concept of redemption.

Neutralizing Miracles, Naturalizing History: Reward, Punishment, and Prayer

In his *Treatise on Resurrection*, Maimonides writes of the many pious Jews whose most beloved activity is to thrust a wedge between Torah and reason by emphasizing the biblical and Talmudic texts that seem to contradict the natural order. He goes on to explain that his own agenda is to offer interpretations of these passages that demonstrate the Torah's compatibility with the order of nature. Only when such an approach does violence to the explicit sense of certain biblical statements does he feel compelled to admit the occurrence of direct divine intervention in history, that is, a miracle.[16]

A Talmudic principle suggests that God intervenes in history by rewarding or punishing humanity in accordance with the nature of their deeds: "By the standard with which a man measures, with it shall he be measured."[17] Maimonides does not reject the principle; instead, he categorically transforms it with a rational, naturalistic interpretation:

> This is a matter that is apparent to the inner eye in every time, in every period, and in every place—that everyone who will do evil and devise forms of wrongdoing and vices, he himself will be injured by those evil deeds themselves that he devised, for he taught the art that will do harm to him and to someone else. Thus, whoever teaches virtue that brings into being any manner of good act, he will attain the benefit of that act, for he taught the matter that will do good to him and to someone else. The words of Scripture pertaining to this are excellent: he [Job] said, "The work of a man

will He requite unto him (and according to the way of a man will He cause him to find)" (Job 34:11).[18]

Maimonides understands the language of reward and punishment in terms of the social consequences of human action; it need not imply divine miraculous intervention. This method of naturalizing texts that appear to suggest miraculous, supernatural occurrences can further be detected in his discussion of prayers for grace:

> What is meant by David's utterance, "Good and upright is the Lord; therefore does He instruct sinners in the way. He guides the humble in justice; and He teaches the humble His way" (Psalm 25:8–9)? It refers to the fact that God sent them prophets to teach them the ways of the Lord and bring them back in repentance; furthermore, that He endowed them with the capacity of learning and understanding. For it is characteristic of every human being that, when his interest is engaged in the ways of wisdom and righteousness, he longs for these ways and is eager to follow them. Thus the Sages say, "Whoever comes to purify himself receives aid"; that is, he will find himself helped in his endeavor.[19]

Petitional prayers for divine guidance can be understood within the horizontal structure of given reality. We can interpret God's response to petitional prayers for divine guidance as a consequence of the heightened spiritual engagement and moral agency that such prayers both reflect and help intensify.

Another Rabbinic principle—"All is in the hands of heaven except the fear of heaven"[20]—also seems to suggest a direct and near-comprehensive divine governance of human affairs. Again, Maimonides offers a naturalistic interpretation:

> By the word "all," the Rabbis meant to designate only natural phenomena which are not influenced by the will of man, as

whether a person is tall or short, whether it is rainy or dry, whether the air is pure or impure, and all other such things that happen in the world, and which have no connection with man's conduct.[21]

Faced with a tradition that seems to enlarge the scope of divine intervention in human affairs, Maimonides offers an interpretation that relegates such involvement to the natural sphere alone, where it can have no impact upon human agency.

Of course, the Bible itself seems to depict many instances of divine action that impinges on human affairs, painting God as the true mover of historical events (for example, Joseph's stated reason for forgiving the brothers who sold him into slavery: "It was not you who sent me here but God" [Genesis 45:8]). The preponderance of such events in the book of Genesis alone led one biblical critic to claim that "ultimately, man is but the unwary and unwitting tool in the hands of the Supreme Power who charts the course of the universe."[22]

Challenging this concept of biblical history, with its emphasis on divine agency and human impotence, Maimonides offers a sweeping exegetical principle:

> It is very clear that everything that is produced in time must necessarily have a proximate cause, which has produced it. In its turn that cause has a cause and so forth till finally one comes to the First Cause of all things, I mean God's will and free choice. For this reason, all those intermediate causes are sometimes omitted in the dicta of the prophets, and an individual act produced in time is ascribed to God, it being said that He, may He be exalted, has done it. All this is known. We and other men from among those who study true reality have spoken about it, and this is the opinion of all the people adhering to our Law.
>
> After this introduction, listen to what I shall explain this chapter and consider it with particular attention, with

an attention exceeding the attention with which you consider the other chapters of this treatise. This is the matter
that I shall make clear to you. Know that all proximate causes
through which is produced in time, regardless of whether
these causes are essential and natural, or voluntary, or accidental and fortuitous—I mean by the voluntary cause of
that particular thing produced in time, the free choice of a
man—and even if the cause consists in the volition of an
animal other than man: that all these causes are ascribed in
the books of the prophets to God, may He be exalted. And
according to their manner of expressing themselves, it said
of such and such an act that God did it or commanded it or
said it. For all these things the expressions to say, to speak,
to command, to call, and to send are used.[23]

Acts are attributed to God by virtue of God being the ultimate, and
not the direct or proximate, cause in a chain of causal connections.
God, in other words, does not usurp human volition; the "free
choice" of people remains alive and well.

The theory ... that man's sitting and rising, and in fact all
of his movements, are governed by the will and desire of
God ... is true only in one respect.... For instance, when
a stone is thrown into the air and falls to the ground, it is
correct to say that the stone fell in accordance with the will
of God, for it is true that God decreed that the earth should
be the centre of attraction, so that when any part of it is
thrown into the air, it is attracted back to the centre.... But
it is wrong to suppose that when a certain part of the earth
is thrown upward God wills at that very moment that it
should fall.... The Divine Will ordained everything at creation, and ... all things, at all times, are regulated by the
laws of nature, and run their natural course, in accordance
with what Solomon said, "As it was, so it will ever be, as it

was made so it continues, and there is nothing new under the sun" (Ecclesiastes 1:9).[24]

Maimonides thus takes pains to undermine any interpretation of the Torah that subverts human freedom in favor of divine omnipotent will. Clearly he found unacceptable any concept of history as determined by a fixed divine blueprint. He applies this principle of divine actions in history even to biblical-historical events that are explicitly depicted as having been preordained by God. Rather than understanding these events as a product of divine decree, he presents an image of God as a perceptive prognosticator of human events:

> But is it not written in the Torah, "And they shall be enslaved and oppressed" (Genesis 15:13)? Did not then the Almighty decree that the Egyptians should do evil? It is also written, "This people will thereupon go astray after the alien gods in their midst" (Deuteronomy 31:16). Did He not decree that Israel should worship idols? Why then did He punish them? The answer is that He did not decree concerning any particular individual that the individual should be the one to go astray. Any one of those who went astray and worshiped idols, had he not desired to commit idolatry, need not have done so. The Creator only instructed Moses as to what the future course of history would be, as one might say, "This people will have among them righteous and wicked persons." A wicked man has no right, on that account, to say that it had been decreed that he should be wicked, because the Almighty had informed Moses that among Israel there would be wicked men, just as the text, "For there will never cease to be needy ones in your land" (Deuteronomy 15:11) does not imply that any particular individual is destined to be poor.[25]

Maimonides gives a similar treatment to the biblical description of Pharaoh. The narrative of God repeatedly "hardening" Pharaoh's heart suggests that he was divested of free will. Maimonides, however, interprets these verses in a way that protects human freedom from such nonrational intrusions of the vertical will of God. No one, not even Pharaoh, is a lifeless tool in the hands of an omnipotent will:

> To sum up, God did not decree that Pharaoh should ill-treat Israel, or Sihon corrupt his land, or that the Canaanites should commit abominations, or that Israel should worship idols. All of them sinned by their own volition; and all accordingly incurred the penalty that repentance should be withheld from them.[26]

Maimonides's approach to history maximizes the significance and impact of human freedom. In doing so, it also removes the theological security characteristic of belief in a fixed divine historical plan. This open-ended approach to the flow of history was flatly opposed by (among others) Nachmanides—who, for example, discounts Maimonides's claim that God's prophecy to Abraham was not precise and did not concern particular individuals. The Egyptians, moreover, were punished because they exceeded the divine mandate of enslaving Jews; they attempted to exterminate them and were judged for their presumptuousness. Finally, Nachmanides argues that if a person is inscribed and sealed by God for violent death, bandits who freely murder that person are not considered to be guiltless unless they do the deed out of deliberate and sincere obedience to a specific prophecy. According to this theology, had the Egyptians enslaved the Jews out of this pure motivation, and only enslaved them, they should have been lauded for carrying out God's will and considered blameless of any crime.

Eternity versus Creation: "The Foundation of the Entire Law"

Is the universe eternal, or was it created at a fixed moment in time? This was a central philosophical issue of Maimonides's day, one upon which the validity of the Torah itself seemed to hang. "If the philosophers would succeed in demonstrating eternity as Aristotle understands it, the Law as a whole would become void."[27] Creation implies will: nothing exists because of some eternal necessity; existence requires a God who brings it into being. Maimonides thus argues that the key indemonstrable (but also irrefutable) revealed tradition that a Jew must accept is belief in Creation:

> Know that our shunning the affirmation of the eternity of the world is not due to a text figuring in the Torah according to which the world has been produced in time. For the texts indicating that the world has been produced in time are not more numerous than those indicating the deity is a body. Nor are the gates of figurative interpretation shut in our faces…. We could interpret them as figurative, as we have done when denying His corporeality….
>
> In fact the belief in eternity [of the universe] … destroys the Law in its principle…. It might be said: Why did God give prophetic revelation to this one and not to that? Why did God give this Law to this particular nation, and why did … He legislate at this particular time?… Why did He not, if such was His purpose, put the accomplishment of the commandments … into our nature?… The answer to all these questions … is: He wanted it this way; or His wisdom required it this way…. We do not know His will or the exigency of His wisdom that caused all the matters … posed above…. If, however, someone says that the world is as it is in virtue of necessity, it would be … obligatory to ask all those questions; and there would be no way out of them except through a recourse to unseemly answers in which there would be … annulment of all the external meanings of the Law with regard to which no intelligent man has any doubt that they are to be taken in their external meaning. It is then because of this and because of the absence of

all proof that this opinion of the eternality of the world is
shunned....[28]

The giving of the Law and the intervention of God in history would
be impossible if we accepted a metaphysic of eternal necessity. The
doctrine of Creation makes the particular covenant at Sinai possible.

While insisting on a closed past, Maimonides also argues that
the future is open. Just because there was one Creation event does
not mean there will be another—that the world as we know it will
be destroyed and superseded by a new one.

> The belief in the production of the world is necessarily the
> foundation of the entire Law. However, the belief in its pass-
> ing away after it has come into being and been generated is
> not, in our opinion, in any respect a foundation of the Law,
> and none of our beliefs would be hurt through the belief in
> its permanent duration.[29]

What emerges is a picture of history with a fixed beginning and no end:

> We agree with Aristotle with regard to one half of his opin-
> ion and we believe that what exists is eternal *a parte post* and
> will last forever with that nature that He ... has willed....
>
> However, that which exists has had a beginning, and at
> first nothing at all existed except God. His wisdom required
> that He should bring Creation into existence at the time
> when He did do it, and that what He brought into existence
> should not be annihilated nor any of its nature changed
> except in certain particulars that He willed to change.[30]

This understanding of history clearly has profound consequences for
how we might conceptualize the messianic era. While often referred
to as "the end of history," it would be more consistent with the spirit
of Maimonides's writings to propose a messianic vision that is not

the end of ordinary human history at all ("what He brought into existence should not be annihilated nor any of its nature changed"). What we are left with is instead a description of a historical period in which political and social conditions make the demands of Sinai more fully realizable.[31] The yearning for the messianic era, moreover, emerges from an ever clearer recognition of the impact of spiritual and moral striving upon the material conditions of history.[32]

> When one is troubled here on earth with diseases, war, or famine, he does not occupy himself with the acquisition of wisdom or the performance of religious precepts by which life hereafter is gained.
>
> Hence, all Israelites, their prophets and sages, longed for the advent of messianic times, that they might have relief from the wicked tyranny that does not permit them properly to occupy themselves with the study of the Torah and the observance of the commandments.[33]

Nachmanides describes the messianic age in terms of a permanent resolution of human uncertainty. For Maimonides, freedom and human choice will endure, and the human "instinct for evil" will persist, even then. The Messiah will not create a new human nature. Consequently, messianism does not supersede the legal obligations of Sinai but should rather be seen as a return to, and fulfillment of, the full scope of the Sinaitic covenant.

Maimonides's historical realism and his restriction of miraculous divine intervention in history are inseparable from his understanding of the nature of Torah and halakha. Internalizing the worldview of Torah, Maimonides accepted not only a set of norms and beliefs but also a philosophy of history and of human action. Divine eruptions into history to create anew or unilaterally to impose God's will in human history are foreign to the spirit and the essential nature of the halakhic conceptual framework. Maimonides's messianism is but an extrapolation of his philosophy of halakha.

The "Promise" of Repentance and the Possibility of Multiple Messianic Eras

What, then, is the meaning of the prophetic "promise" that in the end Israel will repent? One possible interpretation is that the Torah makes such a promise because living according to Torah motivates us constantly to assess our nature and improve our behavior. Torah fashions a person who is always in the process of transforming him- or herself through *teshuvah*. A person who lives by the Law organizes his or her life around the imperative of continual self-transformation. The Law energizes us to enlarge our scope of responsibility. Torah eschews despondency and feelings of futility by always pointing to human tasks and potential achievements.[34]

The Talmud enjoins, "If a person sees that painful suffering visits him, let him examine his conduct and do *teshuvah*."[35] Torah trains us to recognize the power of *teshuvah* to alter our political and economic condition by reminding us that our communal, material life is determined by our normative behavior:

> A positive scriptural commandment prescribes prayer and the sounding of an alarm with trumpets whenever trouble befalls the community. For when Scripture says, "Against the adversary that oppresses you, you shall sound an alarm with the trumpets" (Numbers 10:9), the meaning is: Cry out in prayer and sound an alarm against whatsoever is oppressing you, be it famine, pestilence, locusts, or the like.
>
> This procedure is one of the roads to repentance, for as the community cries out in prayer and sounds an alarm when overtaken by trouble, everyone is bound to realize that evil has come upon him as a consequence of his own evil deeds, as it is written, "Your iniquities have turned away these things, and your sins have withheld good from you" (Jeremiah 5:25), and that his repentance will cause the trouble to be removed.
>
> If, on the other hand, the people do not cry out in prayer and do not sound an alarm, but merely say that it is

the way of the world for such a thing to happen to them, and that their trouble is a matter of pure chance, they have chosen a cruel path that will cause them to persevere in their evil deeds and thus bring additional troubles upon them.[36]

Fatalism, accident, the belief in historical inevitability—these are all alien to halakhic activism. So, too, the concept of the suffering servant, where the pain of one person is redemptive for another's sinfulness, is outside the framework of halakhic sensibility. Halakha does not admit spiritual incapacity. Those who live by God's law experience renewal not through vicarious relationship or passive acceptance, but through seeking and discovering within themselves new capacities for moral change. Central to Maimonides's philosophy of history and concept of hope is the belief that we can always do *teshuvah*.[37]

Based on the four central thrusts of Maimonides's thinking described above—(1) the naturalization of miracles, (2) understanding the novelty of the messianic era in political terms, (3) the claim that human nature is unchanging and thus the Law will be perpetually necessary, and (4) the rejection of an end to human history—it seems reasonable to conclude that the possibility of a repeated loss and reattainment of a messianic age is consistent with his overall approach to God, halakha, and history. Once we assent to eternity *a parte post*, then worldly time is everlasting, and there may be innumerable moments in which humanity creates conditions generating new spiritual hungers. The possibility of losing or of regaining messianic social and political conditions is a perennial feature of history.

Maimonides does use the word "permanence" to describe the Messiah's kingdom:

With regard to the permanence of the King that is the Messiah, and to Israel's kingdom not being destroyed after that, he [Isaiah] says: "Your sun shall no more go down" (60:20), and so on.[38]

However, he then explains the meaning of this extended duration naturalistically, invoking the principle, for example, that when good things are established they usually endure:

> But the Messiah will die, and his son and son's son will reign in his stead. God has clearly declared his death in the words "He shall not fail nor be discouraged, till he has set judgment in the earth" (Isaiah 42:4). His kingdom will endure a very long time and the lives of men will be long also, because longevity is a consequence of the removal of sorrows and cares. Let not the fact of the duration of his kingdom for thousands of years seem strange to you, for the Sages have said that when a number of good things come together it is not an easy thing for them to separate again.[39]

The promise of Israel's ultimate repentance emerges from the prophetic certainty that a people living according to the Torah will do *teshuvah*. This process of self-transformation will bring about a messianic era of political security, peace, and prosperity, which will in turn make possible the unprecedented flowering of human spiritual potentialities.[40] Messianism is not a final resolution to the struggles of human history,[41] but the cultivation of a society in which the Torah may be most fully received and implemented.

III
Collective Memories and Constitutive Moments: Exodus versus Sinai

Every tradition provides us with a set of collective memories upon which to draw. To organize and understand our experience through the lens of our traditions, we select from this store of memories those events that can serve as principles of integration. At different times and in various circumstances of our histories, different events may be chosen as especially relevant in helping us make sense of the world we find ourselves in, the particular challenges we face. Indeed, phenomenologically speaking, religious practical systems are often tied more intimately to collective memories than to metaphysical beliefs. Those memories that we choose to emphasize are elevated in status, deemed constitutive or essential to the nature of the religious system our traditions frame and endorse.

We have thus far presented two different approaches to hope and messianism: one that anticipates final resolution, the emergence of a new type of human and a new type of history, awaiting redemption irrespective of human action; and another that insists upon *teshuvah*, that expects the enrichment of human spiritual possibilities, but that guarantees no final resolution. These divergent approaches to redemption and hope may have their roots in two distinct historic memories. One attitude may emerge from consideration of the redemption of Israel at the Exodus; the other, from remembrance of the revelation of the Torah at Sinai. The former would seem to undergird a radical, "rupture" concept of history; the latter, a halakhic, covenantal concept of history.

"Let There Be a Jewish People": Exodus and Apocalyptic Hope

One of the dominant theological motifs found in the biblical account of the Exodus from Egypt suggests that human beings are basically helpless before God. The Children of Israel do nothing to warrant their redemption, nor do they cooperate prominently in their deliverance. In this model, God suddenly breaks into history and, from a non-people, creates an elected community.

For the Jewish slaves in Egypt, the given reality was totally bleak and indicated no ground for hope, dream, or redemptive expectation. The empirically given, however, in no way defined the historically possible—and this indeed seems to be one of the story's dominant themes. The Exodus narrative dramatizes a historical novelty; something totally new balloons, unforeseen and unexpected, into human experience. Nothing in the observable process of history would have led one to anticipate this unprecedented redemptive moment. God takes decisive action in history again and again, even as the objects of God's grace continue to founder and fail to recognize, much less receive, the great gift being bestowed upon them. They are paralyzed and in one moment seem literally unable to understand what Moses is speaking about as he attempts to exhort them into embracing their liberation (Exodus 6:9)—a potent illustration of an entire society whose members have lost the image of themselves as free people.

The historical rupture occasioned by the Exodus parallels the Creation story of Genesis. God breaks into chaos and says, "Let there be light" (Genesis 1:3); transcendence rends the void. The Egyptian experience is that of God exploding into the historical status quo to transform a chaotic horde of slaves into a light unto the nations of the world: "Let there be a Jewish people."

What would a historical philosophy based on the Exodus model—that takes this model as constitutive of the Jewish approach to history—look like? It would elevate the divine rupture into human affairs to the level of a central preoccupation, defining hope for the future as intrinsically connected to the expectation of a new creation, the product of an external Will. It would likely, in the spirit of the Talmudic sage Samuel, conceive of a redemption that comes through suffering alone: "It is sufficient for the mourner to persevere in his sorrow."[42] As God promised Abraham (Genesis 15:13–14), the oppression of God's people would, in the unknowable appointed time, instigate God's avenging intrusion into history: "God heard their moaning, and God remembered His covenant with Abraham and Isaac and Jacob" (Exodus 2:24).

Thus, apocalyptic messianism finds a compelling, constitutive source in the rupture paradigm of the Exodus from Egypt. At the Passover Seder, which begins with the phrase "We were slaves in Egypt," the participants are instructed, "In every generation each person must feel as though he himself came out of Egypt." The linking of past salvation with future redemption is made explicit in the blessing recited before drinking the second cup of wine. The two motifs are joined together, linking the past ("who redeemed us") immediately to the future ("bring us to other festivals … happy in the building of Your city … where we shall eat of the sacrifices and paschal offerings … and we shall give thanks to You with a new song").

Whenever the Passover was celebrated, it brought hope, and so the Exodus became a crucial element in Jewish communal experience. As the tradition vividly evoked the memory of the miraculous deliverance from Egypt, it inspired the certainty of a parallel future redemption. Empirical conditions need not define the possible as long as the Exodus memory is alive. The Seder begins with the story of the Exodus from Egypt and concludes with *Le-shanah ha-ba'ah be-Yerushalayim* (Next year in Jerusalem)—expressing the radical messianic hope that in the meantime a divine hand will pluck us from our beds and finally bring us home.

The Covenantal Optimism of Sinai

The story of Sinai suggests a very different model of history and nurtures a very different type of hope than that of the Exodus.

> Then [Moses] took the record of the covenant and read it aloud to the people. And they said, "All that the Lord has spoken will we do and obey." Moses took the blood and dashed it on the people and said, "This is the blood of the covenant that the Lord now makes with you concerning all these commands."
>
> (Exodus 24:7–8)

The giving and acceptance of the Torah does not present a picture of God's single-handed redemption of powerless slaves, nor of unilateral divine fiat ordering primal chaos. Sinai is rather an experience of mutuality in which God speaks and humanity listens, decides, and responds.[43] The Law implies God's enduring confidence in humanity to carry and live out a divine vision for the world, notwithstanding the shortsightedness and weakness Israel showed in the desert. Indeed, Sinai inscribes divine acceptance of human limitation: it signifies God's move from a Creator-Redeemer to a Teacher who is prepared to educate, guide, and engage in a covenantal relationship in which failure or success depends upon human agency and will. It says that humanity has the capacity to implement right behavior in its individual and collective lives.

A sense of hope emerges from the memory of the command to become holy that is very different from the hope of the Exodus. Despite human limitations, weaknesses, perversities, and ugliness, we are charged with responsibility for bringing about our own redemption by living out the values of the Torah.[44]

In contrast to certain Greek notions of self-sufficiency, the revelation at Sinai proclaims that perfection is to be realized in relationships. The covenantal God of the Bible chose interaction with human beings. The Lord of history, as opposed to an impersonal ground of being, pronounces that interdependency is an ultimate datum of reality. History and community, therefore, are central to a tradition in which perfection is grounded in relationship.[45]

The hope of Sinai need not be fueled by romantic dreams; it can be nurtured by feelings of adequacy to bear the responsibility of becoming a spiritual person. The very giving of commandments is a source of confidence. The Torah, the eternal command, binds hope, indeed optimism, into its essential gesture of mutual obligation.[46] In contrast, the vision of Ezekiel and the burden of Jeremiah—the apocalyptic hope for a new creation, a new human with a new heart—must be recognized as expressions of black pessimism.[47] When the Law fails, when humanity sinks back into chaos, God must start all over again with a new human and a new world.

One might raise the challenge that a Sinai model, with its emphasis on human responsibility and self-sufficiency, risks diluting the spiritual vitality often inspired by a theology of ultimate dependence upon divine intervention. In response, however, we might invoke Maimonides, the greatest explicator and advocate of halakhic hope, whose writings reveal a depth of love for God that bordered on mystic yearning. His passionate spiritual striving was sparked by an image of God not as parent or protector, but as the ultimate source of life's meaning. The model of Sinai has the potential to promulgate a more mature, and no less intense, relationship with the Divine. God provides the world with ultimate significance, even though God's presence offers covenantal challenge rather than eschatological certitude.

Sifting through our tradition's storehouse of collective memories, we often find ourselves faced with choices. When paradigmatic events, such as Exodus and Sinai, present distinct and opposing perspectives, which do we choose to embrace as constitutive of Jewish tradition? Which theological frameworks best equip us to face the world as we find it? Should we emulate the eschatological hope that emerges from the memory of the Exodus, or the model of revelation and repentance, of redemption through human agency, set into motion at Sinai? When we align ourselves with Sinai, the end of history is not as crucial as present action. In a Maimonidean framework of halakhic hope, the range of human responsibility is extensive. At the same time, the trust implicit in the covenantal charge yields a relationship of greater maturity, mutuality, and dignity.

Philosophies of history founded upon apocalyptic utopian outlooks have often led to distressing consequences. Viewing redemption as a divine eruption into history categorically diminishes the value of reason itself—to say nothing of morality and ethics—in this world. What value are they if in the end we will be saved by a divine will that transcends reason, irrespective of what we do or do not do to ourselves, others, and the world? This religious perspective has led to many reckless, tragic chapters of human history.

Disciples of a rupture view of history can revel in the failures of modernity, focus on the futility of human endeavor, and rest securely in a radical redemptive hope with no relationship to human effort and progress. Alternatively, they might reverse this dialectic: instead of ordaining futility and despair as the basis of a jaded, introspective quietism, they might leap into the hubris of secular or religious utopianism, imagining that through their own efforts they will bring about a new city, a totally novel world. Revolutionaries are often prepared to risk a great deal because they believe their violent actions will indeed herald redemption. The destruction of twenty million human beings may be a small price to pay for endless future generations of tranquility.

In contrast, a Maimonidean orientation offers a sober conception of hope. Those who live with an awareness that the human condition will never be transcended are more likely to tread with greater caution and commit themselves to its protection and improvement. Moreover, modern technology that expands the range of human power is not perceived as a threat to this religious sensibility, but a welcome expansion of human moral responsibility.[48] We are encouraged to bear ever greater levels of responsibility, without being promised that this will solve, once and for all, every difficulty of the human condition.

Choosing Memories in Context: Catastrophic Failures, Grandiose Visions, and Passionate Sobriety

Of course, it is possible to integrate the Exodus model, with its theology of divine intervention in history, with the Sinai model of responsibility, adequacy, and progress. Indeed, Exodus preceded Sinai; God's rescue of Israel predicated the revelation. When the Sinai model breaks down in the face of disillusioning historical events, we may fall back on the memory of the Exodus and plead for God's intervention. At a different time, we may neutralize the memory of Egypt and call upon another memory to carry us through another experience.

While these two models may be seen to coexist and in some ways complement one another, we are still left with the question of which to rely upon as the dominant, constitutive paradigm of our relationship to history and to hope. It may be overly sanguine to overlook their essential distinctions. Given their radically divergent implications and consequences, discussed above, we would appear to do so at our peril.

The choice of which memory or memories to view as constitutive depends to a large extent on collective historical, as well as personal, context. Perhaps prisoners and other victims of despair need Egypt to cling to as a source of hope. We may legitimately doubt whether Sinai alone can provide the strength to persevere in the face of humanity's continual and often catastrophic failures.[49] Perhaps we need the spiritual energy provided by mighty myths and grandiose visions. Perhaps it is not enough to tell a person that he or she can become a little better and that, as the situation improves, new goals will be possible. Given how daunting and futile the realistic prospect of human progress often seems, the "passionate sobriety" of Maimonides may sometimes appear, ironically, the more radical, utopian goal.

Can spiritual strength be nourished by widening the range of human responsibility, by continually attempting to begin again, by the prospect of incremental progress? Can we center our recollections on Sinai, where the impetus, the human beginning, is decisive? Or must aspiration be nurtured by a vision of the conclusion, a longing for final *ge'ulah* (redemption)?

When we marry, do we know how long it will last? When we have a child, can we foresee his or her future? The fragile quality of human love may mirror the enduring mystery of our relationship to God. If Maimonides is right, then the comfort provided by religious hope need not be based on discontinuous ruptures in history. Humanity bears witness to God's presence in history by persevering in the struggle for justice.

Part II

Abraham's Argument

Reclaiming Judaism's
Moral Tradition

8

ABRAHAM'S ARGUMENT

EMPOWERMENT, DEFEAT,
AND THE RELIGIOUS PERSONALITY

A "Great Thing":
Understanding Our Stories and Ourselves

As members of the Jewish people, our understanding of ourselves and of our relationship to God grows out of the narratives most fundamental to our collective identity. The Creation, Exodus, and Sinai narratives shape our conceptions of who we are and who we can become: first and most foremost as human beings (Creation); as a distinct people, bound to a God who took us out of Egypt (Exodus); and as a spiritual-political collective (Sinai). Yet Jews have never been literalists. We can read these narratives and cherish the collective consciousness they symbolize, but the question that must always remain forefront in our minds is, how do we use these narratives? How do they contribute to our conceptions of what is demanded of us and what our potential is? How do the biblical accounts that are most central to our identity help us gain a deeper sense of ourselves and of what Judaism is about?

The ways in which we interpret our inherited narratives constitute a critical piece toward understanding what it means to be a Jew living in the world today. As a student of Judaism, I understand the role of

Jewish philosophy as offering a different perspective on the central narratives that have shaped—and continue to shape—our collective self-understanding. In the philosophical quest for a deeper sense of ourselves and our roles vis-à-vis a Jewish God, Maimonides is both my greatest teacher and my guide. Following his example, I don't claim to be the holder of the "true" Jewish philosophy, nor do I make the claim to have the only authentic interpretation of the Bible. Rather, I hope to offer what Jewish philosophers have always offered: another perspective with which to make sense of our narratives. Maimonides's greatest contribution, in my opinion, was to reestablish the centrality of philosophy in the Jewish tradition, to in some way take us away from the world of pure legalism and admit that philosophy and philosophical thought are an integral part of the narratives we share.

As the author of the *Mishneh Torah*, Maimonides was unquestionably the greatest halakhist of all time. Yet the greatest halakhist of all time understood the purpose of halakha, and the practice of ritual in general, as a gateway through which we might immerse ourselves in the larger questions of humanity's true purpose. Even in the *Mishneh Torah* itself, Maimonides refers to halakha as *davar katan*, a "minor thing," in comparison to the "great thing" of metaphysics and philosophy. It is not that Maimonides dismisses halakha; on the contrary, he sees its role as vital and necessary in constructing an ordered political community. It is, in his view, the psychological and moral discipline that halakha provides that enables us to enter into the realm of philosophical exploration. For Maimonides, halakha is an instrument through which to reach God, but it is nevertheless merely an instrument: it must ultimately find its complete expression in the philosophical yearning for the Divine.

It is crucial to understand, then, that this master of Jewish law made the decision that the law is not primary. It is a largely forgotten footnote of Jewish history that the codifier of the *Mishneh Torah*, which remains the foundational pillar for authoritarian halakha, is the very thinker who recognized its limitations. For Maimonides, and for me, it is only through examining the larger philosophical implications of our shared stories that we reach our true purpose in longing for the Divine.

Sodom and the A*kedah*: Two Models of Relating to God or Abraham's Paradox

It is against this backdrop that I propose looking at two of our narratives, which while not generally considered archetypal in the same sense as the Creation, Exodus, or Sinai stories, constitute for me the two paradigmatic approaches to Jewish consciousness and character. Both stories are found in the book of Genesis in the life of Abraham.

The first of these narratives is the binding of Isaac, known in the Hebrew parlance as the *Akedah*. While Isaac is not ultimately sacrificed by his father in the most literal sense, the theological implications of a God who would issue such an order to his most loyal servant—and furthermore that Abraham would, in turn, seemingly eagerly obey the command—present us with one of the most morally and psychologically confounding episodes in the entire Bible. The Abraham of this story is a passive figure, quietly acquiescing to God's demands, in full acceptance of his role as a finite human, incapable of questioning or deciphering God's omniscience.

The second of these narratives is Abraham's argument with God regarding the fate of the inhabitants of Sodom and Gomorrah. In this story, God is not an issuer of command but a solicitor of human opinion. Upon considering the destruction of the city of Sodom, God asks, "Shall I hide from Abraham what I am about to do?" (Genesis 18:17). This is the rhetorical question of a God who has conceived of God's creations as full partners and to whom God considers Godself accountable. When God informs Abraham of God's plan to destroy the city, Abraham responds, "What if there should be fifty innocent within the city?" (Genesis 18:24). He continues to challenge God, as the number of theoretically righteous dwindles, finally, to ten. In Abraham's challenge to God, "Shall not the Judge of all the earth deal justly?" (Genesis 18:25), Abraham reveals himself not only as a man of faith but also as an *empowered* man of faith, for whom insistence on his own moral intuition is as vital as his belief in a monotheistic God.

These two narratives, Abraham at the *Akedah*, and Abraham at Sodom, present us with two very different portraits of what it means to be in relationship with God. Although the account of Sodom precedes that of the *Akedah* in the biblical sequence of events, it is not chronology that interests me, but what the narratives represent. The *Akedah* seems to posit obedience as the highest level of relationship; what does the binding of Isaac come to teach us, after all, if not that loyalty and submission are the pinnacle of religious life? The story of Abraham arguing with God about destroying the city of Sodom, on the other hand, holds up the concept of moral challenge as the highest level of relationship. In this model, which is utterly and completely antithetical to the *Akedah* model, Abraham not only confronts God based on his own moral intuition, but he also maintains a sustained insistence on the validity of his claims, ultimately arguing with God for the sake of just ten human lives.

These stories, seen side by side, present us with the paradox that is Abraham. The forefather of the great monotheistic traditions contained within him two incompatible realities: one of heroic self-affirmation, and one of self-denial. In one story, the protagonist maintains the ability to render an independent moral awareness, to know what he knows. He is an actor with full authority over his own moral universe. In the other story, he is unable to recognize even his most primal paternal instinct. In one story, he acts; in the other, he simply obeys. The fact that two such dichotomous approaches are embodied by the very same person only highlights the polarity of these two narratives—both of which, it is important to note, are read on Rosh Hashanah, the Jewish New Year.

The accounts of Sodom and the *Akedah* represent two very different religious anthropologies; how you relate to God is going to be determined by these two stories. Which story is constitutive of Judaism? Which story reflects our tradition's deepest depths: the narrative of sacrificial self-surrender or the narrative of assertive moral challenge? These stories represent two distinct views of religion; two distinct views of living according to halakha; two distinct views of what it means to stand before God in prayer.

How do we live with these two stories?

Self-Defeat as Redemption: Soloveitchik and Paradoxical Heroism

Is self-denial, even the complete negation of the self, the peak of religious consciousness? Joseph B. Soloveitchik, the revered Rosh Yeshiva of Yeshiva University, and my teacher, believed, essentially, that it is. In his essay "Catharsis," he tells the story of a young bride and groom, passionately in love, who, on their wedding night, are suddenly prohibited from having sex when the woman discovers a spot of blood that renders her in a state of *niddah*, ritual impurity. For Soloveitchik, the acceptance of self-defeat in the midst of passion is a moment of great religious vitality. Without that precept, writes Soloveitchik, sex becomes a brutal, unredeemed—and unredeemable—reality of life. He writes:

> What does man cherish more than his intellect around which his dignity is centered? Precisely because of the supremacy of the intellect in human life, the Torah requires at times the suspension of the authority logos. Man defeats himself by accepting norms that the intellect cannot assimilate into its normative system. The Judaic concept of *chok* represents human surrender and human defeat. Man, an intellectual being, ignores the logos and burdens himself with laws whose rational motif he cannot grasp. He withdraws from the rationalist position, in a word, withdrawal is required in all areas of human experience and endeavors, whatever is most significant, whatever attracts man the most, must be given up. What happens after man makes his movement

of recoil and retreat? God may instruct him to resume his march to victory and move onward in conquest and triumph. Movement of recoil redeems the forward movement and readiness to accept defeat purges the uncontrollable lust for victory. Once man has listened and retreated, he may further be instructed to march straight to victory.

How does man purge himself in this realm? By engaging in a dialectical movement by withdrawing at the moment when passion reaches its peak. The stronger the grip of the psychological drive is felt by man and the more intoxicating and bewildering the prospect of hedonic gratification, the greater the redemptive capacity of the dialectical catharsis of the movement of recoil.[1]

Soloveitchik quotes a midrash:

Bride and groom are young, physically strong, and passionately in love with each other. Both have patiently waited for this rendezvous to take place. Just one more step and their love would have been fulfilled. A vision realized. Suddenly the bride and groom make a movement of recoil. He gallantly like a chivalrous knight exhibits paradoxical heroism. He takes his own defeat. There is no glamour attached to the withdrawal. The latter is not a spectacular gesture since there are no witnesses to admire and to laud him. The heroic act did not take place in the presence of a jubilating crowd, no bards will sing of these two modest, humble young people. It happened in the sheltered privacy of their home. In the still of the night, the young man like Jacob of old makes an about-face, he retreats at the moment when fulfillment seems assured.[2]

In Soloveitchik's theology, the will to self-denial is the will to redemption. And it is this idea that, for Soloveitchik, represents the key distinction between the Greek model of heroism, which is public, and the Jewish model of heroism, which is experienced in the intimacies of one's life. For Soloveitchik, this is the heroic moment, the moment when we are faced with a choice—with an intimate, personal choice—and we say no to what we want most. I don't like Soloveitchik's story; I cry with the young bride and groom. I'd like to say to them, "Why not keep quiet and enjoy your wedding night?" I cannot accept that model—the model of self-denial, self-negation, self-defeat—as reflective of the highest level of religious consciousness, nor as the most authentic interpretation of our tradition's teachings.

The *Akedah* represents the submissive unconditional surrender in which sacrifice is seen as the highest spiritual achievement. In some very elemental sense, then, Soloveitchik chooses the *Akedah*; I choose Sodom. This does not mean that I believe that Judaism does not require sacrifice. *Every* relationship requires sacrifice. There's no marriage without sacrifice. You certainly can't have children if you're not prepared to sacrifice. What concerns me is the form that sacrifice takes. Soloveitchik believes in a kind of catharsis that comes from self-negation. But, in my experience, this approach leads to a reality in which we celebrate pain, suffering, and death as though it were an expression of our deepest faith.

I believe there can be a kind of sacrifice in which we choose to give something up, but we choose with our moral consciousness and self-awareness intact. For me, that is the difference between sacrifice and self-negation. In Judaism, there is a concept called *mesirat nefesh*, literally "giving of breath" or "giving of soul": this is a kind of giving, of sacrificing, that doesn't betray you to yourself, that doesn't ask you to abandon your God-given human intellect and intuition. This is the sacrifice of a father who works long hours so that he can afford to send his children to school; it's not the disregarding of a person's rational mind or the crushing of the spontaneous joyful moments of self.

It is not enough to inherit both these stories; we must choose between them. When the contradiction between value systems is so diametrically opposed, we must choose. The ultimate question for me, then, is which story do we embrace? Which Abraham presents the truest picture of what it means to be a person and a Jew?

Akedah:
Submission and the Silencing of Conscience

I don't love the God of the *Akedah*. This God is very strange to me, playing with human beings like puppets. You feel, from the very first words here, that something is wrong, that the text is leading with violence. It is hard for me to love this God. But the Abraham of this story is no easier to take. Some people say that the Abraham of the *Akedah* is a man who can pray for other people but can't pray for his own son, like the rabbi who worries about all the families in his congregation but his own. That's one way to read this text. How we live with the *Akedah*, how we live with the God of the *Akedah*, is something we'll explore at much greater depth later in this chapter.

> Some time afterward, God put Abraham to the test. He said to him, "Abraham." And he answered, "Here I am." And He said, "Take your son, your favorite one, Isaac, whom you love, and go to the land of Moriah, and offer him there as a burnt offering on one of the heights that I will point out to you." So early next morning, Abraham saddled his ass and took with him two of his servants and his son Isaac. He split the wood for the burnt offering, and he set out for the place of which God had told him. On the third day Abraham looked up and saw the place from afar. Then Abraham said to his servants, "You stay here with the ass. The boy and I will go up there; we will worship and we will return to you."
>
> (GENESIS 22:1–5)

Abraham got up early in the morning: I remember this is how I was taught about Abraham when I was a child. This is the Abraham that everyone loves, the Abraham who wakes up early (read: eagerly) to kill his son. How could Abraham go? How did he get up in the morning? The text tells us that the journey to the mountain took three days; the midrash uses this point to assure us that despite his initial haste, Abraham had had time to think about this. He wasn't overwhelmed with the rush of the moment; he went coolly, reflectively, to murder his son. Early in the morning, without confusion, with several days to think it through, and with clarity of purpose, Abraham goes to murder his son.

What type of test is this? Is this a test? There are some Hasidic commentators who say that the test was to see whether Abraham would heed God's command, and that Abraham, in obeying God, failed the test. This is a comforting way to make peace with Abraham's actions, but this reading does not ultimately hold up against the rest of the story.

> Abraham took the wood for the burnt offering and put it on his son Isaac. He himself took the firestone and the knife; and the two walked off together. Then Isaac said to his father Abraham, "Father!" And he answered, "Yes, my son." And he said, "Here are the firestone and the wood; but where is the sheep for the burnt offering?" And Abraham said, "God will see to the sheep for His burnt offering, my son." And the two of them walked on together. They arrived at the place of which God had told him. Abraham built an altar there; he laid out the wood; he bound his son Isaac; he laid him on the altar, on top of the wood. And Abraham picked up the knife to slay his son. Then an angel of the Lord called to him from heaven: "Abraham! Abraham!" And he answered, "Here I am." And He said, "Do not raise your hand against the boy, or do anything to him. For now I know that you fear God, since you have not withheld your son, your favored one, from Me." When Abraham looked up, his eye fell upon a ram, caught in the thicket by its horns. So Abraham went and took the ram and offered it up

as a burnt offering in place of his son. And Abraham named
that site Adonai-yireh, whence the present saying, "On the
mount of the Lord there is vision." The angel of the Lord
called to Abraham a second time from heaven, and said, "By
Myself I swear, the Lord declares: Because you have done
this and have not withheld your son, your favored one, I
will bestow My blessing upon you and make your descen-
dants as numerous as the stars of heaven and the sands on
the seashore."

(Genesis 22:6–17)

How can we possibly understand this story with the tools we have
at our disposal? Here is a story about a father who tells his son that
they are going on a pilgrimage to worship but fails to mention that
that worship is in fact a premeditated murder. Who is the most
problematic figure in this problematic story? In some basic way,
it is God, who, after all, instructs Abraham to kill his beloved son.

But the Isaac of this story is not a child; he is a grown man
(thirty, according to the midrash), so why is he just standing there?
He can see the knife, he can see that there's no animal to slaughter,
so why doesn't he run away? Where is his personal agency? The
midrash understands the phrase "they walked together" to mean
that Isaac was aware of God's instruction to his father, that he knew
what was happening, that he and his father were of one mind. But
even if we understand the Isaac of the *Akedah* to be, like his father,
a man of faith, we still must ask of Isaac, did he—could he—truly
know what was about to happen? Kierkegaard asks that question.
Can the knight of faith communicate his faith, or must it remain
permanently with him alone?

Although my understanding of the *Akedah* is based primarily
on my reading of Abraham's actions, it is worth pausing to examine
the character of Isaac in this narrative. Many commentators see the
Akedah as the crucible for the formation of Isaac's identity. But for
me, that is a very problematic way of reading this story. Why must

death and suffering mark Isaac's passage to maturity? I do not accept a reading of this text that says it is only through the knife and the blood that Isaac reaches the highest levels of spiritual authenticity.

Why can't Isaac's spiritual authenticity derive from an experience of joy or spontaneity? I maintain that a more authentic reading of the text presents the *Akedah* not as a moment of great spiritual achievement for Isaac, but as a moment of lost opportunity for him. I reject a reading of the *Akedah* that negates the importance our tradition places on personal freedom and celebration. We often forget that we are commanded, *Ivdu et Hashem b'simchah*, to worship God with joy. I do not believe in submission and surrender as the faculties that make Judaism vital; for me, personal expression and individual agency are the values that are most constitutive of Judaism.

That is the reason I cannot read the *Akedah* as the formative religious experience of Isaac's life. I maintain, rather, that the story of the *Akedah* is primarily a story about Abraham that, when contrasted with the account of Sodom, presents us with a critical key toward understanding his personality and spiritual development.

The Abraham of the *Akedah* doesn't say a word. He doesn't utter a single syllable of protest against a God who commands him to murder. Who is this Abraham that swallows his own voice, who silences his own conscience? Is this an Abraham that embodies our most deeply held Jewish values? How can we reconcile this Abraham with the Abraham that appears at Sodom?

Sodom:
Empowerment, Responsibility, and Freedom

The men set out from there and looked down toward Sodom, Abraham walking with them to see them off. Now the Lord had said, "Shall I hide from Abraham what I am about to do, since Abraham is to become a great and populous nation and all the nations of the earth are to bless themselves by him? For I have singled him out, that he may instruct his children and his posterity to keep the way of the Lord by doing what is just and right, in order that the Lord may bring about for Abraham what He has promised him." Then the Lord said, "The outrage of Sodom and Gomorrah is so great and their sin so grave! I will go down to see whether they have acted altogether according to the outcry that has reached Me. If not, I will take note." The men went on from there to Sodom, while Abraham remained standing before the Lord. Abraham came forward and said, "Will You sweep away the innocent along with the guilty? What if there should be fifty innocent within the city; will You then wipe out the place and not forgive it for the sake of the innocent fifty who are in it? Far be it from You to do such a thing, to bring death upon the innocent as well as the guilty, so that innocent and guilty fare alike. Far be it from You! Should not the Judge of all the earth deal justly?"

(GENESIS 18:16–25)

We can see here that Abraham is essentially asking God, "What type of God are you?" It's a question that encompasses at least two appeals: first, that God should not destroy the righteous people of the city of Sodom, and second, that on the merit of those righteous people, God should forgive the entire city. In other words, Abraham is demanding from God not only justice but also compassion. A God who would destroy the righteous would be unjust; a God who would punish an entire city would lack compassion. There is a name for what Abraham is doing: it's called prayer.

The text continues, as Abraham pleads for forty-five, then forty, thirty, twenty, even just ten righteous people.

"Far be it from You! Shall not the Judge of all the earth deal justly?" And the Lord answered, "If I find within the city of Sodom fifty innocent ones, I will forgive the whole place for their sake." Abraham spoke up, saying, "Here I venture to speak to my Lord, I who am but dust and ashes: What if the fifty innocent should lack five? Will You destroy the city for

want of the five?" And He answered, "I will not destroy it if
I find forty-five there." But he spoke to Him again, and said,
"What if forty should be found there?" And He answered, "I
will not do it, for the sake of the forty." And He said, "Let
not my Lord be angry if I go on: What if thirty should be
found there?"

(Genesis 18:25–30)

In the midst of his protest, Abraham remains humble. He does not
approach God with arrogance; he acknowledges he's just dust and
ashes. He seems to approach God with the attitude of someone
saying, "I agree with you, God, that I'm nothing, but I can't help
but speak. Please forgive me for being so bold …"

And he doesn't stop. That's the most important thing about
his prayer: he doesn't stop. Perhaps God wants him to stop, and
the God of the Bible certainly could have made him stop, but God
allows Abraham to continue. In Abraham's argument—and in God's
acceptance of his argument—I imagine God is saying to Abraham,
"I love you for challenging Me. I want to hear you challenge Me
more. Don't give in too quickly."

On what basis did Abraham bring his moral challenge to God?
We see from the text that God baits him to continue, even seduces
him to continue. God understands that in questioning God's justice,
Abraham is offering a prayer. And God, in some way, loves this
prayer—loves humanity questioning God's justice. The God in the
story of Sodom is a God who feels responsible to Abraham.

I celebrate the God who asks, "Shall I hide from Abraham what
I am about to do?" (Genesis 18:17). Rashi, the famous medieval
commentator, brings in a midrash in which God elaborates on this
question; "Before Abraham, I was the God of the world," says God.
"After Abraham, he's the God of the earth and I'm the God of the
heavens." God, in other words, decides it is not possible to act
without asking permission from Abraham. This is the moment when
God decides to no longer demand total obedience from human

beings but will allow them to assume responsibility, to become empowered through their relationship with God.

"Shall I hide from Abraham what I am about to do?" is one of the most powerful verses in the Torah. In posing this rhetorical question, God, as the Creator of the world, gives up unilateral authority over history and articulates the essential model of covenantal morality: that God can no longer act unilaterally. This is the covenant. And this, for me, is the paradigm for how to approach our understanding of a Jewish God.

It's important to remember that Abraham did not succeed in saving the city of Sodom. His argument with God—however theologically important—in the end failed. At the end of the story, God destroys the city of Sodom. That's God's final answer. Strangely, it is the submissive narrative (the *Akedah*) that ends with mercy, and the non-submissive narrative (Sodom) that ends in tragedy. Not all's well that ends well. But the endings of these stories need not be the guides by which to read them. All is not measured by literal success. What is valuable about the story of Sodom is Abraham's *process*. God ultimately destroys Sodom because God doesn't find enough righteous people. That doesn't interest me as much as the fact that Abraham felt he had the legitimacy to ask God not to do it. And that God felt obliged to respond to Abraham's demands.

There are essentially two ways to view our relationship with God: One approach says I'm nothing; only in my relationship to God am I something. In the other approach, an individual's relationship to God makes him or her feel enhanced, enriched, empowered. Covenantal spirituality moves us toward self-expansion. It endows us with the ability to trust our own moral intuition, our own moral sensibility, our whole spiritual hunger. One problem in the Jewish religious world today is the abdication of the language of personal moral agency to secular humanists. I would like to suggest that giving strength to that inner moral voice is in itself not only very deeply religious but also very deeply rooted in the tradition. It's not just a liberal perspective; it is fundamental to the God relationship that we not abandon our moral integrity.

I don't celebrate the *Akedah*. I don't celebrate submission. For me, the ultimate expression of Jewish spirituality is the celebration of life, of human powers, of human moral dignity. I don't choose to see submission, pain, suffering, and death as a reflection of our deepest faith.

But if the account of Sodom is our paradigm for relationship with God, what do we do with the story of the *Akedah*? If we embrace the Abraham who is unafraid to approach the Divine with his covenantal claims, how can we understand the Abraham who acquiesces to God's most incomprehensible command?

The *Akedah*:
A Moment at the Edge of the Intelligible

When we read the account of Abraham going to sacrifice his son, we must ask ourselves, is the *Akedah* constitutive of the religious experience, or is it a moment in the context of a broader religious worldview? I maintain that the *Akedah* is not constitutive of Judaism. It is a moment in a religious life, but it is just that: a moment. It is not the organizing framework for how to live. For me, the *Akedah* is the moment when we come to the edge of the intelligible, when we meet suffering or tragedy, or any experience that we cannot make sense of with our rational minds.

There are moments when the life of faith requires submission or silence. Sometimes even empowered people meet a situation in which they are overwhelmed. Sometimes even Abraham is at a loss for an adequate response to the divine will. Eventually, we all reach a moment in our lives when we feel the world is absurd, when we wonder why we should continue. The *Akedah* means we acknowledge—and allow a place for—resignation as a moment in the spiritual life. The *Akedah* represents our *encounter* with the unintelligible—not our willingness to allow that encounter to destroy any possibility for a new future.

Yet, for me, the *Akedah* is also the moment when we say *Kaddish*. At the very time when we feel that life has lost its meaning, we affirm our commitment to stay in the covenant. *Yitgadal ve-yitkadash shemei raba*, "May Your name be glorified in history." *Kaddish* means we say, "I'm not leaving because of a tragic moment. I'm going to remain in history." *Kaddish* is not a blessing of theodicy. In proclaiming our will to go on, to affirm life and maintain the covenant, *Kaddish* articulates an answer to the question of how we retain dignity in an unpredictable world.

The *Akedah* is the moment when we find ourselves living in the midst of an unintelligible universe. But it is not the defining moment. The most authentic religious reality is not lived through tragedy, though tragedy itself is inescapable. So what do we do? We sustain ourselves by asserting our desire to continue in the covenant.

The *Akedah* is a critical juncture in spiritual consciousness because we can never completely evade the tragic aspects of life. The absurd follows us. When we see a child with leukemia, when we hear of a bride and groom killed in a car accident coming home from their wedding, how does our tradition inform our response? First and foremost, we do not offer convenient theological explanations. The *Akedah* instructs us to be quiet and to go on. From the *Akedah* we learn that there is a nonrational feature to reality. We don't have to be able to explain why a bus with children on it was blown up, and the effort to do so is a symptom of vulgar spirituality. The *Akedah* instructs us on the limitations of facile spiritual answers. It teaches us that the incomprehensible is part of our reality; we cannot always understand.

That's the reason why, according to Jewish law, we do not speak when we visit a mourner until the mourner engages us in conversation. Silence shows a great deal of respect. That's what I call refined spirituality before the tragic. There is no explanation for unfathomable loss—the loss of a child, of a spouse, of a sibling; the *Akedah* teaches us not to offer one.

Choosing Sodom:
Revelation, Responsibility, and Covenant

Given that the Bible presents Sodom and the *Akedah* on equal footing, as it were, providing no explicit basis for privileging one over the other, how, we might ask, can I justify doing just that? My view of the *Akedah* as a moment of religious experience—rather than its apex—is predicated first and foremost on my understanding of revelation. The very concept of revelation indicates that God wants us, in some way, to understand the world. If we were incapable of understanding, why would God bother commanding us? Intelligibility is the sine qua non of any relationship. The very notion of revelation implies that we *can* understand.

Of course, we sometimes live in a world in which we don't understand what's happening. Sometimes we live in a universe that invades us, that pushes us, that confronts us with the unimaginable. Other times we live in a universe of clarity and purpose; we are able to look around and see a world filled with beauty and meaning. Or we see decency beginning to show itself. Life moves in more than one direction. A dynamic and spiritually vital religious life means embracing both strands of reality.

That is, in part, one of the lessons that our modern-day history teaches us. The story of the establishment of the State of Israel is a story of great significance and also a story of great suffering. History is not a story of harmony and goodwill. I want to believe that kindness is constitutive of humanity, yet violence and murder seem to be an ineradicable part of the human experience. The world cannot be distilled down to a single essence.

This is what it means to live with Sodom, to live with the *Akedah*. It means balancing all of these moments in our lives, trying to understand all the different strands of reality. Life, everyone seems to notice, is a struggle. The first task that falls to us is to learn to struggle within; that is what it means to live with Sodom, to live with the *Akedah*. Without learning how to struggle within, we cannot hope to have the strength to carry us through the darkest moments.

The *Akedah* represents the darkness of the human experience, the times when we stand before the Divine in silence or resignation. But the defining metaphor for us must remain the image of Abraham standing before God—not in submission—but in empowerment. The Abraham that we look to must be the Abraham who is unafraid to argue with God: to demand that God act with justice, to beseech God toward compassion. The measure of a human being—the very *genuineness* of a human being—is his or her capacity for compassion. In his prayer to God, Abraham is only asking that God act in accordance with God's own value system. This is the Abraham of the covenant, the covenant that is a call to responsibility, on all levels.

Today, as we struggle to understand the meaning of Jewish spiritual consciousness, we would be wise to look to our biblical narratives for models of religious expression. As we see in the case of Abraham, our biblical forebears did not limit themselves to a single mode of spiritual engagement. Abraham shows us—with his silent resignation at the *Akedah* and with his empowered argument at Sodom—that an authentic relationship with the Divine requires different responses at different moments. At the *Akedah*, Abraham responded with silence and self-denial, as the moment demanded. At Sodom, he responded with heroic self-affirmation, acting in the fullness of his moral conviction.

It is important to note that it is not my intention to glorify the Abraham of Sodom; as we know from the biblical text, his argument ultimately had no effect on God's decree. Yet because Abraham's argument with God was consensual—because Abraham sensed, in that moment, that God would be receptive to his claims—this is the Abraham that I look to as a model for relating to the Divine. Abraham demonstrates not only that there is room for dialogue in the human-God relationship but also that it is the defining characteristic of the covenantal bond. At the same time, I want to be clear that I do not disown the *Akedah* narrative, nor do I disparage the qualities of character that Abraham exhibited there. The *Akedah* reminds us that at some point in our lives, we all must face the dark night of the soul—but that we do not permit that darkness to eclipse our commitment to life. Covenantal consciousness means we admit that the darkness is present—but it is present as episodes in human history; it can never be allowed to wipe out our hope for a covenantal future.

9

A COVENANT OF EMPOWERMENT

DIVINE WITHDRAWAL AND HUMAN RESPONSIBILITY

The central motivating principle that has characterized my whole theology is the covenant. For most people, the covenant is God's promise to watch over Israel and Israel's promise to be obedient to God's law. That's the last chapter in Leviticus:

> If you follow My laws and faithfully observe My command-ments, I will grant your rains in their season, so that the earth shall yield its produce, and the trees of the field their fruit.... I will look with favor upon you, and make you fertile and multiply you; and I will maintain My covenant with you.
>
> (LEVITICUS 26:3, 26:9)

Many people have written about the covenant as a set of if-then causalities. I propose looking at covenant in a different way: as a category of empowerment. I claim that it is the very essence of the covenant to empower us, to allow us to trust our own moral convictions—and to trust our ability to act. The covenantal relationship places the responsibility for the development of self and the development of history on human beings. The covenant with Abraham empowers him to take responsibility for his own moral future, just as the covenant at Sinai empowers the people of Israel to take responsibility for their future as a nation.

The covenant is about the liberation of human beings in all their powers—morally, but also intellectually and creatively. For me, the true meaning and purpose of the covenant are that human beings, by entering into the reality and presence of God, access the ability to discover themselves and their abilities.

Divine Failure and the Three Stages of the Covenant

As I have written elsewhere in this book, my understanding of the Jewish people's relationship to God grows out of the narratives most fundamental to our collective identity. The Creation, Exodus, and Sinai accounts inform our conceptions of who we are and how we can shape our collective future. These relational moments are what nurture Jewish self-awareness and consciousness and are the source of what I call covenantal theology, a framework I outlined in my earlier book, *A Heart of Many Rooms*. In that book I provided the groundwork for a theological framework based on the paradoxical idea of divine self-limitation, which unfolds in three stages: biblical, Talmudic, and ongoing.

The covenant is not only about the empowerment of human beings; it is also about the withdrawal of God's control. God's shift from the model of a singular will to the model of the covenant reflects a critical change in the way God relates to the world. God initiates Creation, revelation, and the movement of history; then God calls upon human beings to complete the task and take responsibility for areas of life once within God's purview. God presents us with the normative founding moment for building an ordered moral world and then steps back so that we can step forward, an act that can be understood as a manifestation of divine love.

Stage One:
Individual Responsibility

The God first introduced to us in the book of Genesis is the God of Creation—the God on whom human beings are entirely dependent. Omniscient and omnipresent, the God of Creation need only say, "Let there be …," and reality springs to life. This all-powerful God is the God who creates humanity with the intention that it reflect the divine image:

> And God said, "Let us make man in our image, after our likeness. They shall rule the fish of the sea, the birds of the sky, the cattle, the whole earth, and all the creeping things that creep on earth." And God created man in His image, in the image of God He created him.
>
> (GENESIS 1:26–27)

The Garden of Eden, for all its splendor, was a place where man—and then woman—possessed no agency of his or her own, no chance to establish a consciousness independent from that of the Divine. Yet it is only a few chapters later in the biblical narrative that humankind, once entirely subsumed by the will of God of Creation, has turned to corruption and cruelty. It is only because God is so invested in God's human creation, so invested that human beings reflect divine goodness and compassion, that God's response is so punishing when they fail to meet God's expectations.

> The Lord saw how great was man's wickedness on earth, and how every plan devised by his mind was nothing but evil all the time. And the Lord regretted that He had made man on earth, and His heart was saddened. The Lord said, "I will blot out from the earth the men whom I have created—men together with beasts, creeping things, and birds of the sky; for I regret that I made them."
>
> (GENESIS 6:5–8)

In this moment, God feels deep regret for ever creating human beings. And so God's response to Creation is a destruction of the world. It is only through Noah that God retains a thread of hope in the potential for a future humanity:

> God said to Noah, "I have decided to put an end to all flesh, for the earth is filled with lawlessness because of them: I am about to destroy them with the earth. Make yourself an ark of golfer wood...."
>
> (GENESIS 6:13–14)

It's very important to distinguish between the covenant with Noah and the covenant with Abraham. There is no real covenant with Noah in my view, because Noah is not an empowered person. God tells him to build an ark, because the whole world is going to be destroyed, so Noah buys some lumber and starts hammering in nails. Noah does not respond to God with any argument or challenge, because he and God do not share the sense of mutual accountability that defines the covenantal relationship.

Yet after the flood, God begins to rethink not just God's relationship with Noah, but also God's relationship with humanity in general. The first glimpse of the covenant enters into the story of Genesis after the flood, when God decides it is destructive to continue to meet human frailty with such severity and decides instead that it is necessary to empower human beings to become accountable for their own behavior:

> And God said to Noah and to his sons with him, "I now establish My covenant with you and your offspring to come, and with every living thing that is with you—birds, cattle, and every wild beast as well—all have come out of the ark, every living thing on earth. I will maintain My covenant with you: never again shall all flesh be cut off by the waters of a flood, never again shall there be a flood to destroy the earth."

> God further said, "This is the sign that I set for the covenant
> between Me and you, and every living creature with you, for
> all ages to come. I have set My bow in the clouds, and it shall
> serve as a sign of the covenant between Me and the earth."
>
> (GENESIS 9:8–13)

As I wrote in *A Heart of Many Rooms*, the post-flood covenant, symbolized by the rainbow, is the first sign of a process of divine self-education that culminates in revelation. The "rainbow covenant," in this sense, foreshadows the covenant with Abraham and the covenant at Sinai.

It is not until Abraham is introduced into the biblical narrative that the God of Creation becomes the God of the covenant. It is only upon entering into a covenantal relationship with Abraham that God begins to change the way God deals with human failure. As I wrote in *A Heart of Many Rooms*, it is only through God's relationship with Abraham that God "admits" that it is not possible to become the God of History without making room for human responsibility. Thus, God's presence in the world becomes conditional in a deep sense on human beings sharing the burden of history. Instead of a total welfare state, God decides to allow people to become responsible for themselves and for each other on a volunteer basis. Covenantal theology is defined by humanity's assumption of moral responsibility, encapsulated in the following famous passage in Deuteronomy: "I have put before you life and death, blessing and curse. Choose life" (Deuteronomy 30:19).

Uvacharta, "You must choose," is the a priori commandment, the mitzvah that, in a sense, informs all others. Choosing life is the precondition upon which rests the observance of all other commandments. In asserting the most basic value of human life and dignity, *Uvacharta* reflects the first stage of the covenantal relationship in which we are responsible for implementing the mitzvot.

Stage Two:
Interpretation and Partnership

If the first stage of the covenant is about performing the commandments, then the second stage is about interpreting their meaning. In the second stage of the covenant, we assume responsibility for implementing the Torah in our time, as we understand it. God exits the picture as the giver of the Torah and hands over the task of its interpretation and application to human beings. In the first stage of the covenant, God recognizes humanity as an equal partner; in the second stage, humanity takes on the mantle of that partnership. This is the stage at which human beings become the shapers of revelation.

In taking responsibility for the implementation of Jewish law, we follow the Talmudic precedent *Lo ba-shamayim hi*, that the Torah is not in heaven, but in the hands of human beings.[1] Historically, the Jewish people have always taken responsibility for how they understand what it means to live by the Torah. There are many instances where the Torah appears to take a clear stance on a particular legal issue, but we learn from Rabbinic sources that it was interpreted differently by the actual community. On the face of it, the Bible seems to celebrate capital punishment, for example. Countless times, the Bible informs us that the punishment for a given sin is *Mot yumat*, "He should surely be killed." Yet the Mishnah states, in unequivocal terms, that a court that orders capital punishment once every seventy years is considered a "murderous court."[2] How can we explain the dissonance between the written text and the way in which that text was interpreted and carried out—or, in this case, not carried out?

The answer is that the Rabbis developed a rigorously codified legal system in which the implementation of capital punishment would be virtually impossible. They developed a long list of highly specific criteria necessary for a capital conviction: no circumstantial evidence is allowed, there must be eyewitnesses to the crime, those witnesses must have already issued a warning to the perpetrator, and the perpetrator needs to have declared verbally, in front of the witnesses, that he understands the prohibition and then verbally affirm his intention to commit the act anyway. These requirements, needless to say, relinquish the verdict of capital punishment to the realm of the theoretical. None of these requirements, it is critical to remember, appears in the Bible; they were constructed by a Rabbinic body concerned with the social and ethical ramifications of widespread capital punishment. This is yet another reminder that the word of God is not "the final word." The Rabbis' rulings utterly changed the way we understand the biblical text.

The covenant experience truly emerges when the people of Israel turn the written word into an open-ended creative word. The covenant, which is predicated on human responsibility, is strengthened when the Jewish people feel adequate to expand the implications of the spiritual guidance that began at Sinai. Revelation at Sinai then becomes a *derekh*—a pointing, a direction—and not the final consummation of the word of God. Cognitive dignity and intellectual adequacy transform the individual from a passive recipient into an active shaper of the future direction of Torah.

Stage Three: The Unfolding of History

While the Torah may not have been "in heaven" during the Rabbinic period, history certainly was. The Talmudic scholars and religious leaders who showed such agility in their textual interpretations made no attempt to alter the course of their own destiny. As Jews had always done, they waited patiently for the Messiah to bring an end to their exile.

The emergence of Zionism in nineteenth-century Europe marked a profound shift in the evolution of covenantal consciousness. The early Zionists realized that if they wanted to change their fate, they were going to have to take history into their own hands and learn the skills of building a new civilization. That was the great achievement of the State of Israel. In contrast to the ultra-Orthodox, who see the state in opposition to God's sovereignty, I believe that Zionism extended the covenantal tradition of empowerment by rejecting passivity as the hallmark of religious life.

This, then, is the third stage of the covenant: we are responsible not only for maintaining our own moral conscience and for taking on the role of interpreting God's law for our time and place, but we are also responsible for stepping outside of ourselves, and outside of the borders of our own reality, to take an active role in shaping our destiny. Some people disagree with this idea; they feel that history changes when—and only when—the divine will operates itself in the affairs of the universe. The ultra-Orthodox, for example, believe that human beings cannot take responsibility for history because history was, is, and always will be in the hands of God. I call this the Exodus paradigm of history. It is a way of looking at the world that positions us as passive and penitent, waiting for an interventionist God to rescue us from our realities.

The Exodus model of history does not credit human beings with the potential for empowerment or with the faculty to initiate change. In the Exodus model, people cannot have a role in history. In the covenantal model, people *must* have a role in history; it is part of our obligation to God. We are called to take responsibility for the direction of history and not wait for a supernatural God to rescue us. In this sense, the covenant is the opposite of waiting for divine grace.

This stage of the covenant began with the Zionist enterprise of the nineteenth century, but it did not end there. We are still in the embryonic stage of shaping a nation. Some six decades after the founding of the state, we are still finding our way regarding our attitude toward the Palestinians and how we treat "the other." The great achievement of Zionism was not the founding of the modern state per se, but an introduction into our consciousness of self-determination, an ongoing and ever-evolving quest. Taking responsibility for the unfolding of our history today means examining how we balance justice with compassion, security with human dignity, power with vulnerability.

———————

In the beginning, God says, "Let us make man in our image," and God creates man *betzelem Elohim*. But soon enough God learns that it is not possible to make humanity fully in God's image because God cannot make humanity moral. So the story of Genesis is, in a sense, a story about failure: God's failure to create a moral human being. Yet, at the same time, it is the story of God's realization that human beings possess the unique ability to play an active role in self-governance and, consequently, in the governance of the universe.

The covenant means history is not a chronicle of divine manipulation as described in the Exodus story; we cannot blame God for events in history, because God is fundamentally not engaged in history. God's covenantal consciousness has transformed history from a divine drama into a story of human achievement. Rather than hold God responsible for the world we live in, a covenantal perception of history understands that divine self-limitation has presented us with a world waiting to be shaped by human action.

———«()»———

10

MISHPACHTOLOGY
JUDAISM AS A FAMILY SYSTEM

Kaplan's Folkways:
The Significance of Jewish Practice

The Jewish people are a collective united by a prism of social, political, legal, and religious codes; members of the Jewish people may see themselves as sharing certain cultural habits or as bound to a common set of legal obligations. Yet, beginning with the book of Genesis, the Jewish people are conceived first and foremost as a family. Amidst our omnipresent political, religious, and cultural debates, it is often forgotten that the familial framework is our most essential foundation of peoplehood.

This idea is of great interest to Mordecai Kaplan, the great twentieth-century Jewish thinker and founder of the Reconstructionist movement. Kaplan's work is rarely studied today; it is considered, certainly in Orthodox circles, too far outside the pale, if not heretical. It is worth pointing out that although I am very far from Reconstructionism as a religious movement, I am very moved by Kaplan's thought.

For Kaplan, the concept of mitzvah is significant because it obligates you to participate as part of the community, not because of divine command. In Kaplan's conception, we observe mitzvot not because we are bound to the Divine, but because we are bound to our fellow Jews. Because we share common communal structures for living, we experience a powerful and deep sense of accountability to one another. It is in this sense that the connection among the Jewish people can be seen primarily as familial. This is what I call the Jewish people's sanctum, and what Kaplan refers to as "the folkways." In *Dynamic Judaism*, a book of his essential writings, Kaplan explains, "Folkways are the social practices by which a people externalizes the reality of its collective being. The more alive the collective being, the more it abounds in affirmative folkways."[1] He continues:

> It is of vital importance to have a significant term besides mitzvoth for those customs which have been referred to as "commandments pertaining to the relations between man and God." A term is needed that would indicate a different approach from that with which we come to positive law or jurisprudence. The term "folkways" meets that requirement…. If we were henceforth to designate all "commandments pertaining to the relations between man and God" as *minhagim* or "folkways," we would accomplish a twofold purpose. First, we would convey the thought that they should not be dealt with in a legalistic spirit, a spirit that often gives rise to quibbling and pettifogging. They should be dealt with as the very stuff of Jewish life, which should be experienced with spontaneity and joy, and which can be modified as circumstances require.[2]

By emphasizing a view of Judaism that foregrounds "the very stuff of Jewish life," Kaplan asserts his belief that it is the bond that exists among the Jewish people and their everyday patterns of living that define the religious experience. It is important to understand that Kaplan uses the term "folkways" as a counterpoint to viewing religious observance in a way that foregrounds its legal-authoritarian aspects. Kaplan was interested in how daily habit and ritual create opportunities for human beings to access their higher consciousness. His work is driven by an impulse to understand how the Jewish people created a way of life with the potential to redeem them from selfishness, narcissism, and cruelty and open them to a world of holiness.

In *The Meaning of God in Modern Jewish Religion*, Kaplan encapsulates his view of Judaism as a dynamic and organic system that can—and must—be understood within the context of how the community actually lives. In his introduction to the book, Kaplan writes:

> The very attempt to abstract Jewish religion from all the other aspects of Jewish life shows a woeful misunderstanding of the vital and organic relationship between religion and the other elements of a civilization. *The civilization of the Jewish people, with its long history and idealized future, has hitherto been the matrix of the ideas and practices by means of which the Jew expressed his relationship to God.*[3] [emphasis added]

In this passage, Kaplan clearly asserts his rejection of Judaism as a top-down legalistic structure centered on God's directives to the Jewish people and posits instead a conception of Judaism created by the community itself. Kaplan bases his understanding not on what God commands the Jewish people, but on how the Jewish people express their relationship to God.

Kaplan's writing on the meaning and purpose of Shabbat, the weekly day of rest that is the cornerstone of Jewish life, illustrates this idea:

> [The Sabbath's] significance must be judged by what it came to mean to the Jewish people. It became for them preeminently the occasion not only for rest from their labors, but for seeking satisfaction in that knowledge that their God helped them to live to achieve the purpose of life.[4]

What Kaplan is saying here (and he has been widely criticized for it) is that Judaism is not only about the voice heard at Sinai; it is also a living, changing organism, created in large part by the Jewish people themselves. This thinking extends beyond Shabbat to all the Jewish holy days; Kaplan is less interested in God's decrees than in what these observances came to mean to the Jewish people.

This idea is antithetical to many theologians, who are resistant to conceptions of Judaism as a human construct. People want to believe that they're living the word of God. Yet it is crucial to remember that we have never lived purely by the word of God. We have lived according to how the community *interpreted* that word. We live by divine word, but it is a divine word that has been transmuted and developed through human intellectual or spiritual aspirations.

In Kaplan's understanding, it's not that the Jewish people exist in order to serve God and to obey the commandments; the commandments exist to help the Jewish people access their own agency and sense of possibility for their moral future. Ritual and law for Kaplan are important only insofar as they propel us to become full human beings and reach our powers of ethical personality. The critical issue for Kaplan is how the commandments percolate into the lifestream of the Jewish people.

Tradition as Family Ritual: Maimonides and Halevi on the God of Being and the God of History

Over the years, Kaplan's conception of Judaism has become increasingly resonant for me. In my years as a congregational rabbi in Montreal, and in the decades I have spent since teaching in Jerusalem, it has become clear to me that the majority of Jews are driven in their religious observance by their associations with home and family. Whatever it may say in our sacred texts, in their actual lives people are motivated more by memories and emotions than they are by intellectual reasoning. We don't necessarily remember what it says in the Talmud about a particular commandment; we remember the way it was observed in our parents' home and in the community in which we were raised.

Building on Kaplan, I have come to believe that Jewish tradition is, in its most significant sense, a set of family rituals. The literal translation of the Yiddish term *mishpacha*, which has recently entered into the American vernacular, is "family." Yet *mishpacha* connotes more than just family; it refers to the feeling of being part of a web of human experience much larger than yourself—a web that extends from the past to the present to the future. *Mishpacha* places you in a relational context; it means you are connected by a thread of mutual responsibility stretching across time. *Mishpacha* is my mother reminding me of my *zayde*'s (grandfather's) moral stature; *mishpacha* means that sometimes I feel more obligated to uphold the legacy of my grandfather than I do to God. That is not an affront to the divine sensibility; God gave us the structure of family and community as the vehicles through which we might live out a life of spiritual authenticity. *Mishpacha* can be seen as a theological framework that, paradoxically, emphasizes the importance of lived tradition over theological principles. This is what I call mishpachtology.

The Bible begins with the story of a *mishpacha*. When we refer to God in our daily prayers as the God of Abraham, Isaac, and Jacob, we are saying that our concept of God is based on a spiritual inheritance. It's not a linguistic accident that we refer to Abraham, Isaac, and Jacob as our fathers and to Sarah, Rebecca, and Leah as our mothers; in doing so, we're saying we believe in this God because it's a family tradition. The book of Exodus introduces the concept of "nation"; but before we are a nation, we are a family. The covenant at Sinai is preceded by the lives and spiritual practice of Abraham and Sarah, Isaac and Rebecca, Jacob, Rachel, and Leah.

Mishpacha is an idea of critical importance for Judah Halevi, the medieval Spanish rabbi, philosopher, and poet. Throughout his writings, particularly in the *Kuzari*, Halevi foregrounds the importance of *mishpacha* in Judaism and articulates his own theology of mishpachtology. Halevi sees Judaism as a religion mediated by the Jewish people in their lived history. What is important to him is the feeling of being part of the family—the recognition that the story of the Jewish people is inseparable from our individual narratives, in the same sense that we experience our families' stories as our own.

Halevi's conception of Judaism as a family system grows out of his understanding of the Jewish God as a God who acts in history—and as such, is actively involved in the running of the universe and in the course of our everyday lives. For Halevi, it is through the history of Israel that we come to know the truth about God, because the God of Israel is involved in the lives of the people. The notion that God could be absent from history and from intimate involvement in our lives would, for Halevi, amount to a disqualification of God's divinity. The defining idea of Halevi's thought is the Jewish people's need to know that God is with them—to have the assurance a child has of a parent.

In a famous argument depicted in Halevi's *Kuzari* between a rabbi and a king, the rabbi attempts to prove God's existence by emphasizing God's role both in the lives of his ancestors and in the unfolding of Jewish history. In attempting to prove to the gentile king the existence of the Jewish God, the rabbi not only presents the patriarchs' personal experience of God's presence as authentication of the divine reality, but he also asserts that their experience serves as an ongoing spiritual legacy:

> Moses began addressing Pharaoh in the same way too, when he told him, "The God of the Hebrews has sent me to you," meaning, the God of Abraham, Isaac and Jacob, since their story was well-known among the nations as well as [the fact] that a divine order accompanied them, took interest in them, and performed wonders for them. He did not tell him, "the Lord of heaven and earth," or "my Creator and your Creator sent me." And God also began His address to the multitude

of the Children of Israel in the same way [by saying], "I am [the] God, whom you worship, who brought you out of the land of Egypt...." He did not say, "I am the Creator of the world and your Creator." Accordingly, I began [to speak to] you this way, O commander of the Khazars, when you asked me about my faith. I answered you in terms of what is compelling for me and for the community of the Children of Israel for whom that [which I have described] is well established on the basis of direct observation and subsequently, through uninterrupted tradition, which is as valid as direct observation.[5]

Halevi grasped that individuals are motivated not by abstract principles but by the sense that God is guiding their lives. It is the dynamic rhythm of God's involvement in history and the animating cadence of communal practice that informs Halevi's theology. For Maimonides, by contrast, Judaism is a religion based on God—on an affirmation of the reality of the divinity in its true form. As a rationalist philosopher, Maimonides based his theology on having the correct conception of God as the single source of existence. In the *Mishneh Torah*, his definitive halakhic work, Maimonides articulates his conception of the Jewish God in the first line of the first chapter, *Yesodei ha-Torah*, "The Basic Principles of the Torah":

The basic principle of all basic principles and the pillar of all sciences is to realize that there is a First Being who brought every existing thing into being. All existing things, whether celestial, terrestrial, or belonging to an intermediate class, exist only through His true existence.

Devoted to absolutist conceptions of faith and truth, Maimonides is unable to recognize the forces that actually drive human behavior; he doesn't really understand the Jewish people. His *Guide of the Perplexed* is the preeminent work of Jewish philosophy, yet it doesn't provide much guidance on how we might actually live. Halevi is concerned with human behavior; he is concerned that the human being feel loved and cared for and watched over by God.

"I Will Be What I Will Be": Toward an Understanding of the Jewish God

Maimonides and Halevi's differing conceptions of the Jewish God are based on their two different readings of the famous biblical verse in which God speaks to Moses at the burning bush and reveals Godself as *eheyeh asher eheyeh*, typically translated as "I will be what I will be" (Exodus 3:14). As I have written elsewhere, how a philosopher interprets this enigmatic phrase determines his understanding of Judaism. Maimonides translates *ehyeh asher ehyeh* as "I am that I am." In translating this statement in the way that he does, Maimonides asserts God's very Being as proof of the Divine. For Maimonides, *ehyeh asher ehyeh* means "I am the Being whose existence is not contingent on anything." Nature and being per se, and not the traditions of a particular community or history, create certainty about divine existence.

Halevi translates the phrase as "I will be present for you in the future as I have been present in the past." His reading reflects his view of God's role in history as proof of the Divine. For Halevi, the history of Israel makes the divine reality accessible to human beings. The triumphant story of the Exodus from Egypt and the spectacular miracles performed in the desert demonstrate the reality of the living God. As he writes in the *Kuzari*, Halevi understands *ehyeh asher ehyeh* to mean "I am the One who is present, who will be present with you when you seek Me. So, let them not seek any greater proof [of My true reality] than My being found together with them."[6]

Maimonides and Halevi provide us with two very different conceptions of the Jewish religion: one is an intellectual affirmation of the Divinity; the other stresses the importance of being an active, integral member of the Jewish family. For Maimonides, the very essence of being is proof of the Divine. For Halevi, it is God's hand in the unfolding of our individual and collective narratives that is evidence of God's existence.

Mishpachtology as a Corrective to Authoritarianism

In the Second Temple period, the *Beit ha-Mikdash*, the Holy Temple in Jerusalem, was the center of Jewish observance and ritual. Its seasonal pilgrimage festivals and sacrificial rites provided the structure for family and communal life. With the destruction of the Temple, the Jewish people lost not only the locus of their spiritual life but also the central organizing principle for their civic life. Halakha as we know it was developed by the leaders of the Sanhedrin in the wake of the Temple's destruction in 200 CE as a Rabbinic response to the urgent question of how to maintain a viable familial and communal framework in the wake of this loss. In this sense, halakha is a brilliant civic achievement: it provided the Jewish people with a workable structure for strengthening familial ties and for maintaining a vibrant communal life at the very moment those institutions seemed most vulnerable.

In the aftermath of the Temple's destruction, the Jewish people lost their primary medium for experiencing and relating to God. The elaborate set of rituals and observances that compose the body of halakha provided the Jewish people with a new one. The great achievement of halakha is that it also provided the Jewish people with a restored locus for their communal life. In this sense, halakha gave the Jewish people back their sense of being a *mishpacha*. In describing the development and purpose of halakha in the *Mishneh Torah*, Maimonides writes:

> The Great Sanhedrin of Jerusalem is the root of the Oral Law. The members thereof are the pillars of instruction; out of them go forth statutes and judgments to all Israel. Scripture bids us repose confidence in them, as it is said: "According to the law which they shall teach you" (Deuteronomy 17:11).

This is a positive command. Whoever believes in Moses our Teacher and his Law is bound to follow their guidance in the practice of religion and to lean upon them."[7]

In this passage, we see that Maimonides ascribes great importance to the Rabbinic body's obligation to interpret and determine halakhic practice for the community—and the obligation of the community, in turn, to observe its rulings. What Maimonides is emphasizing here is the human role in the shaping of halakhic observance. Maimonides is instructing us that halakha is not a voice heard from on high but a product of Rabbinic responsiveness created in conjunction with the community.

That is why for me Judaism is not an intellectual leap of faith, but a solidarity with the unfolding history of a living people. Halakha is merely the guideline that the Jewish people follow for how to live. When Soloveitchik was asked, "How do you know that there's a God?" his answer was, "My father told me."[8] To me this is not a glib retort but a serious philosophical response.

Those who have made a life's study of Jewish texts know the tremendous weight that the Torah gives to the concept of *minhag*. Typically translated as "custom," *minhag* more accurately refers to the deeply experiential aspect of religious observance that is transmitted across generations and across time and place. Growing up in my parents' home in Brooklyn, I had an ongoing debate with my father every year on Sukkot, the festival of huts. The Talmud states that on the last day of the festival, known as Shemini Atzeret, we sit in the sukkah but do not recite a blessing, as we do on the other days of the holiday. My father celebrated Shemini Atzeret but refused to sit in the sukkah on that day—with or without reciting a blessing—because that was not the custom among the community in Jerusalem where he was raised. My use of the Talmudic discussion had no effect on him. For my father, sitting in the sukkah and celebrating Shemini Atzeret were incompatible, irrespective of what the Talmud prescribes. The Judaism he carried with him was the Judaism of his mother and father and of the community where he grew up. It was the living practice of the Jerusalem community that was engraved in my father's memory and that trumped all formal halakhic considerations. Later in my life, in the course of my own rabbinic work, I quickly learned that what mattered most to my congregants was not what was written in our most sacred texts, but the ways their fellow Jews practiced. Communal life is not built upon the fullest intellectual tradition of mitzvah and halakha. Communities are built the way families are built: through the ongoing repetition of memory, narrative, and ritual.

The elaborate cleaning rituals associated with the holiday of Passover, for example, have become a hallmark of Jewish life. The halakhic obligations that involve the removal of *chametz*, leavened bread, occupies many Jewish households in the weeks leading up to Passover. The actual halakhic obligation to remove any trace of leavened food from one's home is actually quite basic, yet for centuries, the custom of Jewish households has been to see Passover as an opportunity for a thorough spring cleaning—spiritually as well as literally.

Every year at Passover I used to explain to my congregation that there is no halakhic obligation to wash the drapes or rewash laundry to fulfill the mitzvah of removing *chametz* from one's home. But my words had little meaning for the members of my community, who, like so many Jews, experienced the rigors of Passover cleaning as a spiritual catharsis: as a way to symbolically yet intimately connect them to the experience of slavery. The fact that the halakha doesn't demand weeks of cleaning as preparation for Passover is irrelevant. For many Jews, the catharsis of Passover cleaning—though "merely" a custom—is as vital to their experience as the celebration of the Seder night itself.

I bring these stories because they illustrate my understanding of Judaism as a system of folkways, in the phrasing of Kaplan: they demonstrate the great power of *minhag* to claim us, the power of family and custom to inform our religious observance.

Today, Orthodox Judaism has taken on an increasingly absolutist bent. Literalist forces within the community have promoted a religious agenda that promotes halakhic authority as the primary value. We must remember that Judaism, in its most essential form, is not an authoritarian system, but a pattern for how to live life within a familial framework. What the codes of Jewish law say about how to observe the Sabbath is ultimately of less importance than how the Sabbath was observed at my mother's table. It is the particular rhythms of family life that give meaning and context to Jewish ritual. How a family lives together, eats together, mourns and celebrates together is what creates the spiritual dynamicism that is the essence of Judaism.

11

CUSTOM AND INNOVATION

STEPPING BEYOND THE PARAMETERS OF THE PAST

It is out of my understanding of the value of *minhag* that I share a strong affinity with people who ascribe great importance to tradition. But there is a critical point at which I tend to diverge from other traditionalists. Tradition, in my view, should be encouraged to flourish, but it must not become idolized. The value of preserving the lived practices of the past must never eclipse the needs of the living community it is meant to nurture and serve.

Certainly, tradition is a powerful animating force in the Jewish religion. Custom provides the cartography for how we live out the halakhic imperative. Yet we cannot allow the weight of custom to obscure our need to reinterpret halakha for our own time and place. It is precisely the importance we place on communal practice for a vibrant sense of collective identity that demands that we pay attention to the shifting needs and sensibilities of the community itself.

As a young man, I often felt the weight of my family's anchorage in tradition more explicitly than I felt God. That anchorage inspired and impacted my religious identity permanently and profoundly. But that doesn't mean that I am obligated to observe halakha exactly as my father or grandfather did. Our ancestors may serve as our moral beacons, and their customs may be deeply etched on the canvas of our souls, yet we can—and must—simultaneously acknowledge that we are not living in the same world that they did.

Accepting the value of lived tradition does not mean ignoring our contemporary realities. We cannot permit the sense of obligation we feel to our ancestors to intimidate us. We cannot allow ourselves to become overwhelmed by guilt simply because we feel the need to step beyond the parameters of the past. We are, in many senses, obligated to the tradition of custom as it has been carried out throughout the generations, but we are equally obligated to examine how we observe the mitzvot in the context of our contemporary existence. Rabbinic attempts to ignore or disparage this reality will only diminish the strength and vitality of our communities. Without a sense of spiritually guided halakhic elasticity, our communities will break.

The notion of halakha as an objective and absolute reality is itself a human construct. As we have already discussed, Jews have never lived according to the literal meaning of the Torah; halakha has always been the product of human ingenuity and interpretation. Acknowledging the human contribution to the development of Judaism need not take away from the importance the tradition places on revelation. On the contrary, I would argue that it is in the very human adoption and adaptation of Jewish law and ritual that the true meaning of covenantal revelation is brought to light.

"Truth from Whatever Source": Maimonides and the Development of Moral Intuition

The past does not determine my understanding of what constitutes moral decency. I approach this issue from the perspective of my present reality, with all it entails. As a student of Judaism, I am interested in how the tradition can be understood in a new way so that it becomes an arena in which we give expression to our most fundamental values.

Many people in the halakhic community disagree with this approach; they maintain that any critique of the tradition is inherently baseless because the underlying assumptions driving that critique—equality, personal expression—are alien to the Jewish tradition.

A serious discussion about reinvigorating the tradition to reflect our values must begin with an examination of the sources that have shaped our moral intuition. What informs our understanding of what it means to live a life of dignity? From where do we draw our understanding of what a human being should strive for, morally? We must ask ourselves whether our conception of morality is derived exclusively from the Jewish canon or whether we allow ourselves to consider moral values that do not arise from the tradition itself.

I maintain that our moral life is not—and must not be—dictated exclusively by traditional halakha. Our conception of human dignity is derived not only from our deep and rich tradition, but from our involvement and participation in everyday modern life and culture. When we speak of moral intuition, we are speaking about a basic sense that is intrinsic to human beings but that is also informed by our experiences and education. Our moral intuition is at once innate and learned. It is God's unique gift to human beings, but it is shaped by all facets of our existence—by our parents, communities, and the larger world we live in.

In putting forth this argument, I am inspired by Maimonides, the greatest of all Jewish thinkers and halakhasists. A paradigm of intellectual honesty, Maimonides is prepared to accept the legitimacy of demonstrative truth, regardless of its source. The key question for Maimonides in examining the veracity of new ideas is not their origins but whether they are rational and well argued, whether they make sense on an empirical level. Maimonides's prime consideration is not pedigree, but an illuminated sense of understanding. In his introduction to the work known as *The Eight Chapters*, his commentary on the Mishnaic text "Ethics of Our Fathers," Maimonides writes:

> Know … that the ideas presented in these chapters and in
> the following commentary are not of my own invention;
> neither did I think out the explanations contained therein,
> but I have gleaned them from the words of the wise occur-
> ring in midrashim, in the Talmud, and in other of their
> works, as well as from the words of philosophers, ancient
> and recent, and also from the works of various authors,
> as one should accept the truth from whatever source it
> proceeds.[1]

By acknowledging that "truth from whatever source" has played a
role in the formulation of his ideas, Maimonides presents an inclusive
view of the development of knowledge. He boldly cites not only
Jewish scholars as the sources of his wisdom and understanding,
but secular thinkers and philosophers as well. Given that he worked
as a physician and philosopher in eleventh-century Morocco and
Egypt, those outside influences, particularly from Islamic thinkers,
were no doubt significant, although acquainted with the Jewish
people's suspicion of foreign spheres of influence, he was reluctant
to name them.

Maimonides's notion that our tradition can make room
for outside sources of knowledge shows that we need not blind
ourselves to the development of new ideas in an effort to preserve
the value of tradition. The Torah was intended, by design, to be
interpreted in every generation, in every time and place. Rather
than assume that shifting social and cultural norms will destroy the
tradition, we might acknowledge their potential to illuminate those
aspects of our inheritance that have served as forces of injustice
within our communities. I maintain that these external criteria not
only have a vital role to play in shaping the religious conversation,
but they also have the possibility to serve as a corrective to the
tradition itself.

(It is important to note that the reverse is also true. The Jewish
tradition in many ways acts as a corrective to modern life. The

Sabbath, for example, demands that we take the time to disconnect from the mode of "doing" and reorient to a deeper level of spiritual contemplation, the mode of "being." In this way, the Jewish tradition provides us with a spiritual refuge, an antidote to the daily toll extracted by the continuous demands of contemporary existence. Tradition and the modern world exist in a kind of dialectic.)

An honest confrontation with the tradition must begin with the acknowledgment that we are, in some very important way, shaped by the world we live in. We are social beings, affected by our environment. It would be disingenuous of me to claim, for example, that my philosophical conceptions of human decency and kindness are derived exclusively from codes of Jewish law; I learned these basic values as a youth watching the way the people in my neighborhood behaved. I learned about fairness and cooperation playing ball in Lincoln Terrace Park. I learned from my parents and brothers what it means to be a mensch.

In discussing the ways that we are shaped by the world we live in, it is important to note that we are living in a world of heightened consciousness: consciousness as to the basic rights of individuals to live as emancipated, dignified members of society, unimpeded by laws that discriminate or diminish them. Today, we live in a world that prizes the individual's ability to delineate between right and wrong based on his or her subjective moral sense. In the Western world, we've reached a point where our collective consciousness is almost totally shaped by these simple intuitions.

The rise of fundamentalism that we are witnessing today, across religious lines, is a response by people who cannot handle the shift represented by modern consciousness. Fundamentalist expression is the province of those who feel threatened by the intrusion of moral values into their preestablished worldview. The extreme move to the right that we see in so many spheres of life today is a direct result of the fear that's arisen in response to the new values that have surfaced.

"The Altar of Loyalty":
Heschel and the Need for
Contemporary Religious Relevance

As the rabbinic leader responsible for bringing traditional Judaism into the modern world, Joseph B. Soloveitchik deserves great credit for bringing the Western canons of theology and philosophy to bear on the Jewish imagination. Yet Soloveitchik and other leaders stopped short of bringing halakha into the realm of critical discourse. They could not bring themselves theologically, and perhaps also emotionally, to acknowledge that the tradition itself might bear serious moral flaws that it is our job to correct.

It is obvious that halakha does not carry the same weight in the modern world that it did generations ago, when the position of Jews within society at large was more circumscribed. In the past, it was self-evident that a person's life would be shaped by halakha. In the twenty-first century, religious observance is a matter of choice. In a free marketplace of identity, we can choose from a multitude of lifestyles that foreground our most deeply held values. We have the privilege of constructing our lives in a way that reflects our sensibilities. So today, the simple question that we must ask ourselves is whether Judaism is a credible system through which we might shape our lives.

It has become commonplace among the Jewish establishment to decry the apathetic attitude of younger generations toward the tradition. Yet from my perspective, I see a deep impulse in younger Jews to look to Judaism as an organizing framework for how to live a spiritual, meaningful life. We must acknowledge that for so many young Jews, raised in a culture that celebrates individual expression and subjective experience, the fact that many of the precepts underlying the tradition can be read as prejudiced or discriminatory destroys the very possibility of seeing Judaism as a viable structure. In many communities, it is the unbearable weight of the *minhag* imperative that precludes the potential for seeing Judaism as what William James would call "a live option."

We must allow for the fact that the current generation, exposed to a world of universalist ethics, cannot abide by statements in the Mishnah that if a non-Jew is dying on Shabbat we are not obligated to save him, or the Talmudic assertion that women are "light-headed," or Rav Elazar's statement that he'd rather burn the Torah than give it to women. We live today in a world that cannot countenance such assertions. If we do not allow ourselves to critique and, when possible, discover alternative interpretations of these statements, we risk a wholesale disaccreditation of Judaism's relevance and its viability within the modern world. The issues I present above are the tip of the iceberg; the deeper issue is Judaism's very ability to survive as a moral system in the contemporary scene.

In his philosophical work *God in Search of Man*, Abraham Joshua Heschel, one of the most important twentieth-century Jewish thinkers, writes about the religious quest to experience Jewish practice as relevant and meaningful:

> A serious difficulty is the problem of the meaning of Jewish observance. The modern Jew cannot accept the way of static obedience as a short cut to the mystery of the divine will. His religious situation is not conducive to an attitude of intellectual or spiritual surrender. He is not ready to sacrifice his liberty on the altar of loyalty to the spirit of his ancestors. He will only respond to a demonstration that there is meaning to be found in what is expected of him. His primary difficulty is not his inability to comprehend *the divine origin* of the law; his essential difficulty is in his inability to sense the *presence of divine meaning* in the fulfillment of the law.[2]

Heschel claims that tradition does not ask us to place our moral integrity on what he calls "the altar of loyalty." He claims that tradition asks us to take on the challenge of living a life of integrity; it asks us to find a way to live that balances our most deeply held values with our spiritual inheritance. I refuse to admit that a one-dimensional approach is the only path toward piety. I choose to remain loyal to my tradition, but not at any cost. The attempt on the part of the ultra-Orthodox to hermetically seal themselves off from the influences of contemporary culture as a way to perpetuate Jewish custom is not, in my analysis, what the tradition demands.

A Universe of Discourse: Experientialism as a Starting Point for Dialogue

Mordecai Kaplan's concept of "the folkways" posits that the meaning of Jewish law and ritual lies in how it was used by the Jewish people to create avenues for exploring their human potential. If we accept the premise of "the folkways," that the purpose of ritual is to create opportunities for us to access our higher consciousness, then we must ask ourselves, does the Jewish tradition open up those opportunities? Or does the status quo require us to compartmentalize our religious experience as divorced from our values?

Like Kaplan, I see Judaism as an experiential encounter. While the experiential aspect of observance connects us to the practice of past generations, I would like to suggest that a reexamination of those customs must also be based on the deeply experiential aspect of religious observance. When it comes to reinterpreting the tradition for our own time and place, we are not only permitted but also obligated to examine our experience of law and ritual as we live them. I maintain that our subjective piety is capable of guiding the way that we perceive and interpret the tradition.

The Talmud offers us a brilliantly nuanced portrait of a dynamic Jewish people who evolved through history, who had different perceptions and different values at different times. Our tradition teaches that there are seventy faces to the Torah; of course we share a multitude of views. But these differing views must be the starting point for dialogue. Heated discussion is our birthright; halakha has developed over time as a result of these very conversations. It is critical for us to understand that although halakha is infinitely complex, it's also intended to be flexible. What concerns me is rabbinic legislation that codifies a single interpretation as authoritative law.

If it is to survive, Jewish tradition must begin to accommodate a respectful dialogue of alternative opinions. And it is within our communities that this discourse will take shape. Relying on our subjective piety to guide the religious conversation does not mean anything goes. A community cannot survive if each of its members determines his or her own code of ethics. An individual's subjective experience is not the final word; it's the starting point for dialogue. When we make public our personal intuitions, they become part of an ongoing conversation. We live in a universe of discourse, where our deepest subjective impulses must be aired and exposed to critique. Just as a healthy family life must allow space for its members to give voice to their deepest thoughts and feelings, a healthy communal life must make room for the exchange of a multitude of views. Discourse rooted in a sense of familial bonds is the animating force that will give birth to a revitalization of the halakha.

Kaplan is interested in how the commandments percolate into the lifestream of the Jewish people; it is the communal structure for Kaplan that imbues ritual with meaning. I would take his concept one step further in positing that community is the source not just for meaning but also for change. That is why I see my theology as a grassroots approach. Change will not come from the rabbinic establishment; it will come when our communities experience the need for change as an organic and legitimate impulse. It is the very importance we ascribe to communal practice that demands that we examine all its facets with full clarity and conscience.

Power of the People:
Community as Antidote to Existentialism

Meaningful communal change will come when—and only when—communities become mobilized to give expression to their deepest spiritual impulses. Change will come when individuals raise their voices as a collective and command the communal structure as a locus for dialogue and innovation. We must seek to reinvigorate our communities based on our collective intuition; if not, we risk rendering ritual into meaningless exercise and our communal structures into soulless facades.

The ability of our communities to serve as places for spiritual expression and centers for moral vibrancy depends on the presence and participation of conscious, committed members. Our communities cannot serve as centers for moral and ethical living unless they have people actively and consciously involved in actualizing that ideal. Unless there are people who seek another form of spiritual expression and pursue it with passion, we'll stay stuck in a system that is a petrified replica of our true spiritual inheritance.

I maintain that there is a critical mass within the halakhic community that seeks to uncover the moral imperative at the core of tradition. Yet for many halakhically observant Jews who take seriously universalist ethical principles, breaking with the tradition is an emotionally daunting task. It often seems easier to abandon the tradition entirely or to passively follow suit, ignoring one's moral code, than to advocate for change. The specter of existential loneliness prevents many of us from listening to the still-small inner voice and confronting the tradition with legitimate critique.

Tradition has the power to claim us without argument; its very practice creates its authority. That is why the act of challenging it is so overwhelming. We cannot overestimate the psychological challenge of questioning the Jewish concept of *beit saba*, literally "the house of my grandfather." The power of longstanding tradition lies in its quality of self-evidence. We can easily argue that if the traditional interpretations of Judaism were not authentic, then they would not have persisted for so long. We can reason that the very proof of the correctness of the way in which the tradition has been interpreted is its longevity. So we must acknowledge that when we call into question certain aspects of the tradition, we are, in a certain sense, calling into question what are perceived as self-evident truths.

That is why challenging the tradition requires justification, while affirming the tradition requires only status quo.

Religion is fundamentally a form of group expression. The great Hasidic rabbis know there is great comfort in being part of thousands of followers singing and dancing. Without other people who share our passions and values, we feel lonely; religious group expression provides meaning and context to our lives. Without a viable communal structure, patterns for living can seem random or arbitrary. That is why the building of new communities in line with our values is of such critical importance. In order to bring about halakhic change, we must allow ourselves first to give voice to our claims and second to align ourselves with others who are motivated by a shared impulse. Being part of a spiritually vibrant community animated by ethical principles can serve to combat the existential loneliness that comes with challenging the tradition. I love the tradition, but I do not bow unconditionally to its authority. The time has come in the evolution of our collective human consciousness to acknowledge the need for historical reevaluation.

12

MY DAUGHTER IS NOT MY MOTHER

RETHINKING THE ROLE OF WOMEN IN TRADITIONAL JUDAISM

At Shira Hadasha, the congregation founded by my daughter Tova Hartman in Jerusalem, women participate fully in communal prayer. Shira Hadasha is a halakhically observant community that has worked to find room within the halakha for women to give expression to their religious yearnings. Women lead prayer services, maintain leadership positions in the community, give *drashot* (homilies) from the bimah, and read aloud from the Torah.

Shira Hadasha is but one among growing examples of Orthodox communities that have decided they cannot discredit the need for women to give full expression to their religious impulses any more than they can disregard the halakhic framework. When I attend Shira Hadasha and hear the voices of women raised in prayer, I don't feel that my relationship with God, or my sense of male identity, is diminished. On the contrary, I feel that women's voices raised in prayer, alongside those of men, draws the entire community closer to their experience of God and to the experience of their authentic selves. I maintain that it is through the full participation of women in communal religious life that the halakha finds its truest and most authentic expression.

I approach the issue of women's role in Judaism based on my understanding of what constitutes a decent human existence. My basic moral sense tells me that women should not be discriminated against by halakha, nor should they be prohibited from participating fully in public and religious life. My position on women's role in Judaism is based not on traditional justifications but on this basic moral intuition. Today, we no longer view personal and intellectual expression as the sole domain of men. Given that we have an awareness of the equality imperative, which I consider a forward step in the spiritual evolution of humanity, how can we interpret halakha in a way that ignores this new consciousness? Women of past generations may not have felt diminished by the circumscribed role that Jewish law and practice prescribed for them, but for increasing numbers of religiously observant women, that is no longer the reality.

That is not to say that communities that maintain the traditional division between the public sphere as the domain of man and the private sphere as the domain of woman do not experience authentic communion with God. Our obligation to interpret the halakha in a way that does not compromise our male or female identity does not give us license to denigrate those communities that wish to maintain the traditional approach. I do not wish to present women's increased role in religious communal life as a monolithic imperative, any more than I want to be coerced by those who seek to maintain the status quo. My aim is not to proselytize to those communities that feel their spiritual needs are being addressed in maintaining traditional gender roles, only to allow for diversity based on differing religious sensibilities.

Nor can we permit ourselves to take a condescending attitude toward the customs of the generations that preceded us. I do not believe that my mother was necessarily compromised by the fact that she was not permitted to read aloud from the Torah. On the contrary, I have the utmost respect for my mother's integrity, intellectual curiosity, and spiritual sense of wholeness. Yet, at the same time, I cannot allow my respect for her to prevent me from fully acknowledging the moral values I've learned from the world that I live in. I am not out to liberate my mother, but neither am I willing to oppress my daughter based on a perverse ideology that says that is the only way my mother's memory can be honored and her legacy upheld.

I use the terms "mother" and "daughter" not only as a metaphor for the past and present but also to highlight the fact that the question of women's role in Judaism is not just an individual or a communal issue, but a family issue. As I wrote in chapter 10 articulating my theology of mishpachtology, beginning with the book of Genesis and through to the present day, the Jewish people exist most fundamentally as an extended family unit. When we speak of women's role in Judaism, we are speaking about the dignity and full humanity of our wives, mothers, sisters, daughters, granddaughters, and ourselves. Approaching moral flaws within the tradition as a family issue brings to light the sense of immediacy that must accompany this conversation. Conversations about morality can quickly become abstract. When it is a question of whether the voices of the people closest to us will be able to find expression within our own communities, the discussion takes on a more personal and urgent dimension.

In the Tent:
Soloveitchik on the Essentialist Nature of Women

Over the years, halakhic apologists have tried to claim that the way in which Jewish law and custom have evolved vis-à-vis the role of women is the Torah's definitive and absolute intent. My teacher Joseph B. Soloveitchik, the Rosh Yeshiva of Yeshiva University, subscribed to the belief that women have an essentialist nature, rightly reflected in the halakha. Soloveitchik's conception of women's nature is based in part on his interpretation of the biblical passage in Genesis where the angels come to visit Abraham and, not encountering Sarah, ask him, *Ayeh ishtechca*, "Where is your wife?" Abraham's response—*Hinei va-ohel*, "She is in the tent"

(Genesis 18:9)—has been used to claim that the very essence of a woman, and the very thing on which her dignity depends, is her estrangement from the social-political arena. Her role, and her essential purity, can only flourish and take shape within the confines of the private sphere. The name for this concept, as it has developed throughout the Jewish tradition, is *Kol kevoda bat Melech penima*, literally, "The glory of the King's daughter is inward."

My critique of Soloveitchik in this case is that he refuses to acknowledge that his reading of the text reflects a particular understanding of gender roles. Instead, he cloaks his ideology with an authoritative fig leaf by claiming that his view is not his view per se, but simply the view of the Torah. Where he should more modestly (and accurately) claim that he is sharing one possible understanding of how the Bible can be read, he insists that he is presenting the Torah's definitive prescription for how all women, without exception, should be. This biblical passage has historically been used to claim not only that women have a particular nature, distinct from men, but also that it is explicitly prescribed by the Torah.

This precept finds myriad expressions in traditional halakhic life. Even with the dawn of modernity and the increasing awareness of the importance of girls' and women's education, the focal point of their (limited) emancipation remained confined to the private sphere. It is a historic fact that those who led the way for Jewish education for women maintained that it was necessary only insofar as it helped them to navigate the intricate laws of kashrut, Shabbat, and family purity. Education for Jewish women was not considered a value in and of itself as it is for Jewish men, but rather was considered necessary for instrumental purposes. The importance that Judaism places on intellectual rigor as a vehicle through which to attain knowledge of and closeness to the Divine excluded half of the community, as though the spirit of intellectual passion were irrelevant to them.

It's not a huge philosophical leap to see that an essentialist view of women is rooted in a fundamentally essentialist view of human beings. That is why a diminishment of women will always be accompanied by a diminishment of men. As feminist theorists have convincingly argued, the notion that women's self-negation can facilitate greater self-fulfillment for men is, in both psychological and sociological terms, a fallacy.[1] When we limit our conceptions of what a human being is, we lose not only the rich and multilayered contribution that women's full participation in communal life can bring, but we also lose the spiritual vitality that animates an entire community as it struggles to foreground its most basic moral values. When we circumscribe our notions of who we are and who we can become, as individuals and as communities, we are all diminished— men and women alike. That is why the question of women's role in Judaism cannot be seen merely as a "women's issue" but as an issue that confronts us all.[2]

The Dignity of the Congregation: The Need for Historical Reevaluation

I believe that the Talmud's understanding of women, as it has been translated into legal formulations, reflects a particular social and historical context. Normative halakha follows an atavistic claim: namely, that women are not entirely human in the same sense that men are. The Talmudic passage concerning the concept of *kavod ha-tzibur*, literally "the dignity of the congregation," is an example of how this fundamental misunderstanding became distilled into halakhic practice. The concept is first presented in the tractate *Megillah*, where the Rabbis of the Gemara discuss the eligibility to read aloud from the Torah:

> The Rabbis taught in the *baraita*, all Jews count toward the seven prescribed readers, even a minor and even a woman. But, the Sages said, a woman should not be called up to the Torah before the congregation for the dignity of the congregation.[3]

We see from this passage that there is no fundamental legal prohibition preventing women from having *aliyot*; the text clearly states that *all* Jews are eligible to read from the Torah—"even a minor and even a woman." (Seven prescribed readers refers to the seven sections of the given week's Torah portion.) This passage is supported by an early tannaitic source that states, "Everyone is called up to the seven readings of the Torah."[4]

Given that these Talmudic texts clearly prescribe a full participatory role for women, how do we understand the evolution of halakha to prohibit this very thing? The reason provided by the Sages is the so-called "dignity of the congregation." In the Rabbinic formulation of this concept, calling women to read aloud from the Torah might be taken as a sign that the women in the community are better educated or more intellectually competent than the men of the community. A footnote to this passage claims that if a woman were to be called up to the Torah, it would give the impression that men do not have the primary obligation of reading from the Torah or that they are incapable of doing so, which in turn reflects negatively on the congregational level of religious knowledge.

The Rabbinic body is unable to read women's participation in religious communal life in any way other than as a potential insult to men. In this sense, *kavod ha-tzibur* is a brilliant legalistic tool: it claims the power to predict the community's psychological response to a particular practice and, in so doing, forecloses its very possibility. I understand the Sages' concern for the emotional well-being of those who would feel threatened by female participation in ritual life. Human beings are built with the mortal flaws of envy, jealousy, small-mindedness, selfishness, and narcissism; I can appreciate the Rabbinic acknowledgment of the human condition. But what, we must ask, about the emotional well-being of the women that compose one-half of our communities? In the Sages' conception, human beings are inherently weak, prone to ignorance and the prejudice that accompanies it. The Sages offer us a portrait of humanity that must somehow be shielded from its perceived psychological failings. The Sages' development of the concept of *kavod ha-tzibur* is premised on a fundamentally pessimistic view of the human spirit.

The Sages' self-professed concern for the congregation's "dignity" betrays not only a fundamental misunderstanding of the meaning of the word but also a basic misconception of the human condition. True dignity is an internal state of being; it does not require external safeguards to "protect" it. Dignity is the inner sense that we are living in accordance with our values. It is the spiritual honor that comes from engaging with the world with moral and intellectual honesty.

It is clear to me that *kavod ha-tzibur* is not a halakhic construct, but a sociological one. It is absurd in our day and age to imagine that a woman delivering a lecture or teaching a class could be seen as humiliating the community. Few people today would claim that their *kavod*, their inherent human sacredness, is violated when they see a woman in a leadership role. We have to understand that there is nothing mystical or magical about the so-called dignity of the congregation; it is simply a legalistic tool designed by the Rabbis as a way to protect the egos of ignorant men. Today we must admit that maintaining a halakhic custom premised on such grounds is morally corrupt. We can no longer subscribe to a system of observance that bases its decision to prohibit women's full participation in communal religious life on a view of humanity so limited and belittling.

I would argue that that the deeper moral strain in our tradition requires us to confront the petty preoccupation with other people's behavior represented by the concept of *kavod ha-tzibur*. The role of the covenant is to give human beings, through ritual observances, the opportunities to overcome these very tendencies; halakha must be a vehicle through which we live out the struggle to overcome our self-limiting voices, not as a vehicle through which we might justify them.

Women and Minyan:
Historical Conceptions of Community

The concept of minyan, a prayer quorum, is one of the foundational structures of Jewish life and practice. The tradition teaches that a critical mass is required to recite "things of holiness," *davar shebikdushah*. The *Kedushah* prayer, for example, is not permitted to be said by a *yachid*, an individual, but only by a *tzibur*, a group. Sanctifying God's name requires a distinct bodily corpus. Minyan, as it has been handed down by the halakha, consists of ten Jewish adult males; traditional interpretations have historically excluded women. So our discussion must begin with the most basic question: can women compose a *tzibur*? This is a critical point, because if women can compose a *tzibur*, then they can participate in the mitzvah of minyan.

The halakhic language has maintained that women, by their very definition, cannot constitute a *tzibur*. The reason that is given is that women have the quality of *yechidim*, an essentially individualist nature, that prevents them from being able to participate in the communal experience. Based on this halakhic reasoning, they cannot compose a collective that merits uttering the sacred words of the *Kedushah* service. A woman, unequivocally, cannot participate in a minyan—even to say *Kaddish* for a parent.

The halakhic precept that informs this logic is *Meah nashim k'trei gavrei*, "A hundred women cannot create a community." That is to say, even when women do compose a group in the most literal sense, they do not constitute a group in the halakhic sense. This position claims that women retain an essential, ineffable singleness within themselves, even when gathered in large numbers. In this halakhic interpretation, women are somehow biologically inured to the psychological and spiritual dimensions of collective group experience.

Modern apologists like Moshe Meiselman, a leading halakhic authority and a nephew and student of Joseph B. Soloveitchik, have advanced this idea, giving it credence in modern halakhic observance. In *Jewish Woman in Jewish Law*, Meiselman posits that women's individual uniqueness cannot be integrated within a collective organism.[5] Meiselman couches his philosophy in sophisticated language, but his thought, as with that of other contemporary apologists, is fundamentally flawed, because it is premised on a limited conception of human personality and potential.

Men and women are equally deserving of the opportunity to explore both the individualist and the communal aspects of the human experience. Women, no less than men, benefit from the spiritual strength and social stability that collective experience can offer. We must give voice to our conscience and admit that *din tzibur*, the law of creating a group, as a formal halakhic category, does not make sense in our contemporary lives.

A rabbi in Jerusalem once came to me with a dilemma: on a recent morning his minyan service was attended by nine men and one woman; could the *Kaddish* blessing be recited? On one hand, he reasoned, there shouldn't be any real question: the recitation of *davar shebikdushah* requires a *tzibur*, which only ten men can create. Yet, at the same time, he held out the possibility that the people who had come to pray and study together that morning composed an authentic and viable community.

I asked him, "Were there ten people there?" and he responded, "There were nine men and one woman."

"But were there ten people?" I asked him again.

In approaching the fundamental question of whether or not women can constitute a *tzibur*, I maintain that it depends on the sensibility of each individual community. If Shira Hadasha and other congregations like it are able to reach a consensus that women can be legitimate members of a *tzibur*, then that, to me, is the fullest and most honest expression of minyan. The concept of minyan is based on God's command that God be sanctified *in the midst* of the Children of Israel; I read "in the midst" as conveying a divine imperative for the entire community of Israel to be involved in the mitzvah.

Peace in the Home:
Kook and Uziel on the Jewish Family Ideal

Even before the discussion about gender equality began populating the debates of the later decades of the twentieth century, there were voices among the Jewish religious leadership that advocated a fully participatory role for women in the sphere of public life. Ben-Zion Meir Hai Uziel, a prominent leader in pre-state Palestine and the chief Sephardi rabbi of Jaffa, was an early and vocal supporter of women's suffrage. Though the question seems hopelessly outdated today, Uziel's writing is instructive for the emphasis it places on the value of family relationships as the prism through which to understand Judaism.

As the issue of women's suffrage divided 1920s pre-state Palestine, Uziel came up against Abraham Isaac Kook, the Ashkenazi chief rabbi. A radical thinker regarding Zionism, Kook was nevertheless extremely conservative regarding the role of women in Jewish communal life. In his responsa to the issue of women's suffrage, "On the Election of Women," Kook writes:

> Roles of authority, judgment, and testimony are not for her [woman], as all her glory is within. Striving to prevent the mixing of the sexes in public gatherings is a theme that runs through the entire Torah. Thus, any innovation in public government that leads to a routine mixing … is certainly against the law.[6]

He continues:

> The spirit of the Bible is understood even now by the weightiest part of the world to require modesty and to avoid the social depravity that might result from human weakness with respect to the sexual inclination. The special feeling of respect toward women in the Bible is based and centered on domestic life and the improvement of inner life and of all the delicate human works branching out therefrom.[7]

For Kook, perhaps the most important leader of the Religious Zionist movement, the modesty imperative has a nationalistic component: it is for the sake of the nascent country's very viability that the sacredness of woman must be guarded. According to Kook, the defilement that would result from women's engagement in public and religious life has consequences not only for the individual and the community but also for Israel's ability to survive as a sovereign political entity. He continues in "On the Election of Women":

> Both the internal and external enemies of Israel make much use nowadays of the libel that young Israel has lost its link to the holy book and therefore has no right to the biblical land. Our duty is to stand guard and demonstrate to the whole world that the soul of Israel is alive in its true character and that the biblical land is deserved by the biblical people, for with all its soul it lives in the spirit of the holy land and this holy book....
>
> Hence it is our holy duty to ensure that the initial steps toward a political-social character of our own be clearly marked by the sign of biblical integrity and purity with which our life has been imbued from time immemorial. This will be obvious only if we avoid the European innovation—alien to the biblical spirit and to the national tradition deriving from it—of woman's entanglement in the tumultuous and multitudinous activities of elections and public life.[8]

Kook subscribes to a delusionary view that romanticizes the Jewish people and ascribes to them an essential purity that other nations lack. Like Soloveitchik, Kook sees the discussion of women's position in political communal life as stemming from a worldview that is utterly foreign to the biblical spirit. For Kook, the very notion of women's suffrage is premised on the non-Jewish world's presumed disregard for family unity. In Kook's understanding, the gentile world had to embrace equal voting rights to "compensate" for non-Jewish women's low stature within the home. Jewish women, in contrast, don't require such compensation; they receive full validation of their humanity within the family structure.

The reason Kook offers for his rejection of women's suffrage is *shalom bayit*, "peace in the home." Kook claims a woman's increased participation in political life will bring her into conflict with her husband and lead to friction in the family. For Kook, the notion that differing points of view can be mediated within a household is inconceivable, never mind that it is a couple's very ability to handle competing views with compassion and respect that is the hallmark of functional families. The *shalom bayit* that Kook is advocating is based not on the respectful resolution of a married couple's differences, but on the premise that there should be no differences in the first place.

What Kook offers up as the ultimate in family unity is merely a phantasm of unity. A happy family life does not demand that all of its members agree with each other. I would argue that it is in a family's very disagreements—and its very ability to overcome those disagreements—that the framework for harmonious family life is built.

Uziel takes a position that is very different from Kook's. As the contemporary scholar Michael Walzer has noted, Uziel, in keeping with the Sephardi tradition, expressed greater openness toward modern ideas and values than his Ashkenazi counterpart. Uziel maintains that it is immoral and unethical that a group of citizens would be obligated to obey the laws of their country but not be permitted to be part of the electorate. For Uziel, all citizens have the right to help determine the character of their government and elect the officials who would determine their fate. In his responsa "Women's Rights in Elections to Public Institutions," Uziel writes:

> It is inconceivable that women be denied this personal right. For in these elections we raise up leaders over us and empower our representatives to speak in our name, to organize the matters of our *yishuv* [the Jewish community in pre-state Palestine], and to levy taxes on our property. Women, whether directly or indirectly, accept the authority of these

representatives and obey their public and national directives and laws. How, then, can one simultaneously "pull the
rope from both ends": lay upon them the duty to obey those
elected by the people, yet deny them the right to vote in
elections?[9]

In this passage, Uziel makes a soundly reasoned argument in favor
of women's suffrage. Yet he is not content to let the discussion end
there. Anticipating a range of reactionary responses, Uziel goes on
to outline his rejoinders to the three primary claims of the anti-
suffrage camp: namely, that women are of weak character, that
women's right to vote will lead to licentiousness, and that it will
destroy *shalom bayit*, "peace in the home." Uziel refutes each of
these claims, beginning with the claim on women's character. His
responsa continues:

> It is argued that women should be excluded from the vot-
> ing public because "their character is weak" [*datan kalot*, BT
> *Shabbat* 33b] and they do not know how to choose who is
> worthy of leading the people, we reply: Well, then, let us
> also exclude from the electorate those men who are "of weak
> character" (and such are never lacking). However, reality
> confronts us clearly with the fact that both in the past and
> in our times, women are equal to men in knowledge and
> wisdom; they deal in commerce and trade and conduct all
> personal matters in the best possible manner.[10]

Regarding the claim of licentiousness, Uziel responds with
utter incredulousness, which is worth presenting in its original
formulation: "What licentiousness can there be in each person
going to the poll and entering a voting slip? If we start considering
such activities as licentious, no creature would be able to survive!"
In response to the claim the women's suffrage will destroy *shalom
bayit*, Uziel writes:

Or perhaps it should be prohibited for the sake of preserving domestic peace?... If so, we must also deny the right of voting to adult sons and daughters still living in their father's home. For in all cases where our Rabbis concerned themselves with ensuring tranquility, they gave equal treatment to the wife and to adult sons living at home (see BT *Bava Metzia* 12a).... The truth is that differences of opinion will surface in some form or other, for no one can suppress completely his opinions and attitudes. But familial love grounded in the shared enterprise [of the members] is strong enough to withstand such differences of opinion.[11]

Uziel makes two important arguments in this passage: first, that if it is domestic tranquility that is the goal, then grown children still living under their fathers' roofs must also be disqualified from voting, in keeping with the Talmudic precedent of according similar legal status to wives as to adult sons living with their parents. But it is Uziel's second argument that is most relevant to our contemporary dilemma. Here, Uziel reminds us that "differences of opinion will surface in some form or other" within a household irrespective of whether women are given the right to vote. Uziel reminds us that disagreements are an unavoidable part of family life; they certainly can't be kept at bay by barring women from the electorate. Rather than focusing on the question of whether women's suffrage will destroy family unity, as Kook claims, Uziel urges the community to focus on building a cohesive and collaborative family life that can weather its members' inevitable disagreements.

By bringing the reality and value of family life into the public religious discourse, Uziel offers a view of the Jewish tradition that places primary importance on lived family practice instead of on theoretical notions of "holiness" and "modesty." Uziel's theology can thus be seen as a sort of proto-mishpachtology theology, one that acknowledges that it is discourse and communication—not subjugation and disqualification—that lay the foundation for a peaceful home. While women were ultimately granted the right to vote in pre-state Palestine, Kook's essentialist conception of women and their place in society certainly took hold on a cultural level in many religious communities. That is why it is crucial for us to revisit the writings of Uziel, who correctly identifies familial love, and not political disengagement, as the true defining characteristic of a Jewish family life.

We cannot pretend that our daughters' needs are the same as our mothers' needs. My daughter studied psychological theory at Harvard and has led an intellectually and spiritually vibrant life; she cannot be expected to accept an authoritarian perspective regarding how she should live, speak, and dress. I cannot compare my daughter's religious authenticity to my mother's because my daughter is not my mother: I don't place them in the same perspective. There's always a move by tradition to spiritually intimidate us. I do not claim superior morality or intelligence; I claim only that my world is different than theirs. It's not a competition about whose religious path is more authentic; it's a question of how we give expression to our own spiritual needs and sense of religious identity. I refuse to be browbeaten by the holy men of the past. I respect their spiritual greatness and power, but I cannot permit myself to be intimidated or silenced by them. I utterly reject the notion that delving deep into our tradition's texts to try and understand them in a different way is in any sense combative or heretical; I maintain that the values we cherish as educated, moral beings, exposed to a modern world of ethical ideals, mirror the values of moral awareness and responsibility that lie at the heart of the covenantal relationship. And I maintain that the quest to unearth them is what the tradition demands.

13

HILLEL'S DECISION
SUBJECTIVE PIETY AS A RELIGIOUS VALUE

Morality and Traditional Authority

What is the relationship between allegiance to a tradition and an individual's personal moral autonomy? How does moral criticism work within a religious framework? In the medieval world, the major religious challenge was whether the authority of the Torah would be able to withstand the emergence of science and other new sources of knowledge. In the modern world, the major religious challenge is to what degree the halakha allows for the expression of a person's deepest moral conscience.

Abraham's moral confrontation with God at Sodom is the central paradigm for my philosophy of Judaism. The legitimacy of Abraham's claims—and God's fundamental acceptance of these claims—clearly illustrates for me the precept that our relationship with God must empower us to take responsibility for and trust our innermost convictions. The most important lesson we learn from our forefather Abraham is the legitimacy of personal moral intuition.

Yet taking seriously this intuition can, at times, bring us into direct conflict with the halakha. Often, we find ourselves faced with two conflicting impulses: the impulse, on the one hand, rooted in our ethical conscience, to innovate; and the impulse, on the other hand, rooted in our need to be part of a viable community, to maintain the rhythm of tradition as it has been practiced throughout the generations.

What do we do when we find ourselves presented with these simultaneously legitimate and contradictory impulses? Over the years, I have found myself struggling with the question of whether Judaism provides a way to express a person's moral convictions or whether it deems those very convictions illegitimate. It has never been my aim to undermine the semblance of halakhic authority; my goal is to see whether there is room *within* the halakhic structure to reconcile my personal moral instincts with the imperatives of the tradition.

I maintain that there are two perspectives from which to approach this question: from the perspective of my obligation as an individual, and from the perspective of my obligation as a member of the Jewish collective invested in the continuity of this way of life. As an individual, my job is to trust my inner moral voice; as a member of the community, my task is to see whether there is room in the canon to arrive at an alternative interpretation. As an individual, my instinct is to categorically reject halakhic rulings that are predicated on a view of humanity that foregrounds their mortal limitations instead of their moral potential. Yet, as a member of the Jewish collective and as someone deeply committed to the Jewish people's continuity, I have felt obligated to delve deep into our texts—to study, to probe, and to struggle—in the effort to demonstrate that the tradition *does* make room for the moral outrage we experience. And the way it makes room is by using methods of interpretation to neutralize morally problematic texts. My purpose in this chapter is to show that there are voices in the Talmud that allow for an expression of our moral convictions while also maintaining an adherence to halakhic structure.

"What He Saw":
Hillel's Moral Confrontation with the Law of *Shmita*

What are the religious currents in the tradition that enable me to feel that we can change things? What frees me from the paralysis of the authority of the written word? What gives me the impetus—from a religious perspective—to claim that although we are bound by the spirit of tradition, we are not necessarily bound by its halakhic formulations?

In my younger years, I was moved by a more radical spirit: I would simply deem a morally problematic aspect of the tradition wrong, and because I deemed it wrong, I deemed it unobligatory. When I was younger I believed that that which morally violates my conscience does not bind me. I would say that loud and clear. There was a time when I wasn't prepared to engage in exegetical gymnastics. I simply felt some things are wrong, pro forma; the Torah was given in a certain historical context, when there was an acceptance of a set of moralities to which we no longer subscribe. Therefore, laws that were applicable at one time are not necessarily applicable now.

I spent many years agonizing over the cost of this kind of stance. Over time, I came to realize that the problem with this approach is that it undermines the authority of tradition and, as a result, the religious communal structure. While unexamined adherence to established practice leads to moral stagnancy, rampant individualism has the potential to lead to moral anarchy. So today my aim is to maintain allegiance to our heritage by employing the Talmud's method of halakhic interpretation. My aim is to reinvigorate the tannaitic tradition of solving a moral issue not by aggressively announcing one's moral indignation, but through the framework of creative halakhic reasoning. In my eightieth decade, I am more interested in looking to see how the tradition provides me with the opportunity to give expression to my deepest religious feelings. There is a long-standing and deeply rooted Rabbinic precedent of employing exegesis as a method of moral confrontation. Examining this Rabbinic precedent is significant both for its independent historical veracity and for what it can teach us about how to approach the moral-religious dilemmas of our day. What moves me to challenge the accepted status quo is my firm belief that there are voices in the Jewish canon that nurture a morally guided approach to innovating halakha. There is a strain in our most sacred texts that supports and encourages responsive dialogue within the halakhic framework. My aim in this chapter is to illustrate that there is a historical precedent that acknowledges and makes space for the full range of human emotional, moral, and intellectual response. To me it is clear that innovation is tradition's very life force.

There are countless examples throughout the Rabbinic texts of religious leaders taking assertive stands against what they perceived to be morally or socially problematic halakhic injunctions. One of the most inspiring examples of this approach is the Mishnaic and Talmudic sage Hillel, one of the preeminent figures in all Jewish history. In several episodes recorded in the Talmud, Hillel shows himself to be a religious personality of great sensitivity and courage. In the spiritual legacy of Abraham, Hillel permits himself to trust his moral judgment—and to act on it.

As the leader of Jerusalem's Jewish community under Roman rule, Hillel was faced with a pressing moral dilemma. In the Second Temple's waning years, the Jewish community was beset with socioeconomic problems that resulted from *shmita*, the sabbatical year that is observed on the seventh year of the seven-year cycle prescribed by the Torah. While the laws of *shmita* are primarily agricultural, a second aspect concerns debts and loans. When the *shmita* year ends, personal debts are considered nullified and forgiven. Bountiful harvests are promised in Leviticus to those who observe *shmita* with the utmost seriousness.

> Every seventh year you shall practice remission of debts. This shall be the nature of the remissions; every creditor shall remit the due that he claims from his fellow; he shall

not dun his fellow or kinsman, for the remission proclaimed is of the Lord. You may dun the foreigner; but you must remit whatever is due from your kinsman.

(DEUTERONOMY 15:1–3)

This is the biblical source for the sabbatical year's cancellation of debts within the Jewish community. (This text actually presents us with another moral dilemma: the distinction the Talmud makes between Jew and non-Jew.) The text continues:

There shall be no needy among you—since the Lord your God will bless you in the land that the Lord your God is giving you as a hereditary portion—if only you heed the Lord your God and take care to keep all this Instruction that I enjoin upon you this day. For the Lord your God will bless you as He has promised you; you will extend loans to many nations, but require none yourself; you will dominate many nations, but they will not dominate you.

If, however, there is a needy person among you, one of your kinsmen in any of your settlements in the land that the Lord your God is giving you, do not harden your heart and shut your hand against your needy kinsman. Rather, you must open your hand and lend him sufficient for what he needs. Beware lest you harbor the base thought, "The seventh year, the year of remission, is approaching," so that you are mean to your needy kinsman and give him nothing. He will cry out to the Lord against you, and you will incur guilt. Give to him readily and have no regrets when you do so, for in return the Lord your God will bless you in all your efforts and in all your undertakings. For there will never cease to be needy ones in your land, which is why I command you: open your hand to the poor and needy kinsman in your land.

(DEUTERONOMY 15:4–11)

This passage illustrates the biblical awareness that the baser human instincts of selfishness and greed had the potential to hinder people's willingness to observe the *shmita* precept of debt forgiveness. Of course, it's only human nature that people would be reluctant to extend a loan with full knowledge that the arrival of *shmita* will erase the debtor's obligation to repay it. The Bible comes to warn against these "base thoughts," encouraging the Jewish people to reach out to those in need, regardless of whether the loan is likely to be repaid. Yet despite the biblical admonishment, the reality was a dramatic reduction in the number of loans in the lead-up to *shmita*, rendering the more vulnerable members of the community that much weaker and facing a crisis.

The *shmita* law, in its biblical origins, was intended to lessen dependency among the disenfranchised sectors of society. The purpose of the sabbatical remission of debts was to minimize the sense of perpetual helplessness that comes from living a life burdened by debt. The law of *shmita* is animated by a spiritual impulse to create a society of emancipated individuals unencumbered by the psychological tax of perpetual indigency. *Shmita* is driven by a biblical vision of economic equality and personal freedom.

Yet the reality of Jewish practice did not reflect the spirit of the law. In the year preceding *shmita*, potential lenders refused to heed the biblical warning and closed their doors to the needy, leaving them unable to procure the credit they needed to survive. Hillel, as the leader of the community, was confronted with the question of what to do with a law that, although intended to provide aid to the desperate, was in actuality preventing them from getting the very help they needed. Faced with the facts on the ground, Hillel was able to admit that *shmita*—the biblical strategy meant to implement a bold conception of equality and freedom—was instead subjugating the very people it was meant to protect.

Hillel faced a serious moral quandary. On the one hand, it was his duty as a political-religious leader and as the eminent halakhic mind of his generation to ensure that *shmita* was properly observed.

Yet his admonishments to the people went unheeded and brought them no closer to opening their coffers. Rather than allow the poor to starve and their families to be dismantled, Hillel was able to look at the socioeconomic predicament of his community and conclude that the law was not working:

> This is one of the regulations made by Hillel the Elder. For he saw that people were unwilling to lend money to one another and disregarded the precept laid down in the Torah: "Beware lest you harbor the base thought ..." (Deuteronomy 15:9). He therefore decided to institute the *prozbol*.... The text of the *prozbol* is as follows: I hand over to you, so and so, the judges of such and such a place, my bonds so that I may be able to recover any money owing to me from so and so, at any time I shall desire. The *prozbol* was to be signed by the judges or witnesses.[1]

Hillel acted spontaneously based on what he saw; he did not wait for reality to conform to lofty ideals, nor did he anticipate divine or Rabbinic permission. He saw a problem and he had the courage to respond. Instead of relying on halakhic precedent, Hillel relied on his own moral conviction. He employed a system of creative reasoning—couched in halakhic language—to significantly circumscribe the biblical *shmita* law and arrive at an alternative outcome. Hillel decided to institute a so-called *prozbol* (the term is Hebrew, of Greek origin), a technical mechanism with the ability to invert the meaning of the text with the express purpose of claiming never to have done so.

The *prozbol* had the legal power to transfer the status of individual private loans to the public domain, where the law of remission does not apply. The *prozbol* ensured that a legal document would accompany the loans stating explicitly that they were to be transferred to the courts at the end of the sabbatical year. The institution of *prozbol* was conceived by Hillel to restore faith among lenders: assured that their credit would be repaid, the wealthy were more likely to advance aid to those who urgently needed it. In its balance of pragmatism and compassion, Hillel's legal loophole is an inspired and groundbreaking example of religious leadership taking a bold moral stand in the service of the communal good. With this single stroke, Hillel responded to what had until then been a dire social problem with a wide-ranging effect on the entire community. In developing and implementing the tool of *prozbol*, Hillel addressed the predicament of the disadvantaged, whose hunger prohibits them the luxury of perseverating on halakhic intricacies.

"What They Saw": Two Models of Religious Response to a Community in Crisis

In describing Hillel's assessment of his community's predicament, the Talmud uses language that emphasizes Hillel's viewpoint: "He saw that people were unwilling to lend money to one another and disregarded the precept laid down in the Torah." The key words for me in this passage are "he saw," because they highlight not only the fact of Hillel's subjective perception but also the fact that this personal perspective compels him to action. It is crucial to understand that it was only allowing himself to see the human suffering of his community that enabled Hillel to address its predicament.

The Mishnaic example of Hillel stands in contrast to the biblical example of Pinhas, who was similarly faced with a widespread social problem. The text uses the language of *vayar*, "and he saw," to describe Pinhas's assessment of what was happening in his community—the same language used in the Mishnaic text about Hillel.

In the book of Numbers, the Bible describes the deteriorating moral behavior of the people of Israel, who have given in to rampant promiscuity and idol worship. This was not behavior that was hidden furtively behind closed doors, but a flagrant and very public rejection of their covenant with God, with the express purpose of further demoralizing the community. The situation is brought to a

head when a man of Israel brings a Midianite woman to the public
gathering place, in plain sight of Moses and the entire community,
with the intention of displaying his immoral impulses in flagrante.
Pinhas, witnessing the spectacle and the shamed weeping of the
Children of Israel, decides he cannot stand by and be silent:

> When Pinhas, son of Eleazar, son of Aaron the priest, saw
> this, he left the assembly and, taking a spear in his hand, he
> followed the Israelite into the chamber and stabbed both of
> them, the Israelite and the woman, through the belly.
>
> (NUMBERS 25:7–8)

Pinhas, impelled by the immorality in his midst, takes dramatic
and violent action in killing the two public fornicators. One would
assume that he was driven by the singular impulse of outraged
indignation. Yet the tradition clearly teaches that Pinhas did not act
in a rush of moral passion, but with careful consideration of halakhic
precedent. In commenting on the phrase "and Pinhas saw," Rashi,
the famed medieval commentator, writes, "He saw the situation and
remembered a halakha, taught to him by Moses." In other words,
Pinhas was not relying on the weight of his own moral intuition in
taking this dramatic and violent act—he was basing it on what he
had learned from his teacher. The Talmud further examines Pinhas's
basis for taking the action that he did:

> Scripture states further, "Pinhas the son of Eleazar saw ..."
> (Numbers 25:7). What did Pinhas see? Rav said: "He saw
> the incident involving Zimri and Cozbi and he recalled the
> ruling in this matter. Pinhas said to Moses: 'Brother of my
> father's father, did you not teach me upon your descent from
> Mount Sinai: Regarding one who cohabits with a Cuthean
> woman—zealots may kill him?' Moses replied to him: 'Let
> the one who reads the letter be the agent to carry out its
> instructions.'"[2]

We learn from this passage that although on the plain face of the biblical text, Pinhas's act seems rash, he was acting within the halakhic tradition. Unlike Hillel, Pinhas does not permit himself to make decisions based solely on his own intuition; he feels himself beholden to the weight of halakhic precedent. In seeing the moral chaos that had overtaken the community, Pinhas was reminded of the law he learned from Moses that permits one to murder a man who publicly fornicates with a non-Jewish woman. As such, it is the teachings of Moses—not Pinhas's independent authority—that inform his decision to act.

The figures of Hillel and Pinhas provide us with two different models of what it means to see and what it means to respond. In examining these texts side by side, we are presented with two examples of how to confront a social problem: one seeks halakhic legitimacy; the other acts simply because he sees the hunger of the poor. Hillel and Pinhas present us with different ways of understanding the meaning of *vayar*: Hillel acted spontaneously, based on what he saw, whereas Pinhas's action was mediated by the halakhic tradition. Hillel did not look for precedent; he saw the law was wrong and he acted, whereas Pinhas sublimated his moral impulse to the tradition.

These two positions are analogous to the two perspectives I previously delineated: my perspective as an individual, and my perspective as a member of the Jewish collective. The task of an individual is to trust his or her inner moral voice; the task of a Jew committed to his or her tradition is to see whether there is room in the canon to arrive at an alternative interpretation. In a certain sense, then, Hillel's position reminds us of our moral duty as individuals, while Pinhas embodies the duty of the rabbinic establishment to seek out the halakhic precedents that will enable us to religiously address our most serious moral concerns.

The Halakhization of Hillel:
A Comparison of Divergent Talmudic Approaches

The passage in which Hillel institutes his loophole is an early Mishnaic text, and it is reflective of the tannaitic approach. In early Rabbinic Judaism, when the Sages saw a moral problem, they acted. Yet as the tradition developed, bold halakhic moves such as Hillel's became rarer, as Mishnaic interpretive agility gave way to an increasingly legalistic and authoritarian Rabbinic culture. Halakha ceased to be understood as an organic and dynamic system for living with the built-in ability to respond to the needs of a given community at a given time and, instead, came to be seen as an inviolable framework of societal control.

Hillel's conception of *prozbol* was in keeping with the responsive and adaptive attitude of the Mishnaic Rabbinic body. Yet the later voices of the amoraic period, which populate the debates of the Gemara, are dumbfounded by Hillel's interpretive stance. Later generations, living at a time by which halakha had become crystallized, were incredulous at Hillel's audacity. For this Rabbinic body, Hillel's act is unfathomable; they cannot imagine how Hillel could have enacted a ruling that, in essence, overturned a biblical command. The Talmud asks the following question: "But is it possible that where according to the Torah the seventh year releases Hillel should ordain that it should not release?"[3]

How is it possible that the Torah states that the loan should be cancelled and Hillel goes against the Torah's prescription? In the Talmudic text, the question reads *Me ich kee medee*, "How is it possible?" What gave Hillel the authority to undermine a biblical law? The passage continues:

> Abaye said he was dealing with the sabbatical year in our time. And he went on the principle laid down by the Rabbi. As has been taught, Rabbi says: it is written, "Now is the matter of the release, every creditor shall release" (Deuteronomy 15:2). Text indicates here two kinds of release, one the release of land, and the other the release of money. When the release of land is in operation, the release of money is to be operative. And when the release of land is not operative, the release of money is not to be operative.

> The Rabbis, however, ordained that it should be operative in order to keep alive the memory of the sabbatical year. And when Hillel saw that people refrained from lending money to one another, he decided to institute the *prozbol*.[4]

When the Rabbinic sage Abaye says Hillel "was dealing with the sabbatical year in our time," he is emphasizing the historical point that Hillel was charged with instituting the laws of *shmita* in the postbiblical period. The Rabbinic aim in this passage is to erase the impact of Hillel's bold stance by undermining Hillel's obligation to observe *shmita* in the first place. According to this Talmudic reasoning, what is referred to as the sabbatical year "in our time"— that is, the Rabbinic period—is not the true sabbatical year; it is only a faint shadow of the sabbatical year as it once was observed.

If the sabbatical of the land is not in effect, the Rabbis argue, the remission of loans is not in effect. And if the remission of loans is not in effect, then Hillel did nothing questionable in overturning it. If the sabbatical year that Hillel faced was merely a proxy in its *remembrance*, then ultimately, the Rabbis reason, Hillel was not obligated in its observance. It is not, the Rabbis assert, an act of courage on Hillel's part to enact the *prozbol*; he was able to institute it only because the law of *shmita* did not apply to him.

It is clear that the Rabbis of this discussion are unsettled not only by Hillel's particular moral conviction but also by his independent moral authority. The amoraic body cannot understand Hillel's actions because they cannot understand his mindset; what they fail to grasp is that for Hillel, the question of the poor's accessibility to credit is not a question of halakhic authority, but an issue of moral and social responsibility. The *Amoraim* cannot permit themselves to say that Hillel defied the Torah, so they say that its precepts did not bind him. Rather than try to understand the sense of human concern and communal well-being that motivated Hillel in his halakhic ruling, they distort its very gravity and meaning. Because this later generation could not fathom Hillel's decision, they halakhasize it, affirming Hillel's legitimacy and his place in the halakhic system. In asserting that the sabbatical year that Hillel faced was not a true sabbatical year, the *Amoraim* claim that for Hillel, the law of *shmita* is not a *de-oraita*—a law commanded explicitly by the Torah—but a *de-rabanan*—a law of lesser legal authority instituted by the Rabbinic establishment. Thus, in overturning the law, they determine that Hillel did not violate a *de-oraita* law, which, for the Rabbinic body, is the ultimate heresy. In the Mishnaic text, Hillel stands independent of the halakhic tradition; it is the later discussion in the Talmud that attempts to plug him into that tradition and claims that he acted within its confines. The *Amoraim* could not absorb the fact of Hillel making a decision based on people's lived reality, so they had to reinvent the reality to suit their aims.

The Talmud's Internal Struggle: Halakhic Authority versus Moral Autonomy

It is important to ask ourselves, what are the two worldviews that emerge from examining the differing approaches of the Mishnah and the Gemara to the social dilemma presented by the observance of *shmita*? In the Mishnah, when the Rabbis see a moral or social problem, their goal is to address it. The Mishnaic approach is emblematic of Rabbinic sensitivity and responsiveness; it demonstrates an essential openness and adaptability. The Mishnaic worldview, as exemplified by Hillel, makes space for the human condition and takes seriously the need to address its most pressing concerns.

The framework of the Gemara does not always maintain that same spirit of alertness and empathy. For the *Amoraim*, living in a time of geographic dispersion among competing cultures (most notably Roman and Persian), the primary concern was maintaining the supremacy of the Torah and, thus, the continuity of the tradition. As we have seen, the amoraic generation would go to great exegetical lengths to protect the inviolability of the Torah's authority and to prove the loyalty of its adherents. Although the rabbis of the Gemara most certainly revered Hillel, they were, at the same time, uncomfortable with the blatant assertion of his moral autonomy. The Rabbis of the Gemara were estranged from their own moral impulses and, in a significant sense, from the real-life pressures faced by their communities. The ultimate value for them was the veracity of the Torah; they maintained that every human act requires halakhic legitimization. Rather than trusting their moral impulses and employing halakha as a tool of social and communal well-being, they chose to invert the system and use halakha as a justification of the status quo. In the amoraic worldview, individual moral autonomy—even for a revered Rabbinic leader such as Hillel—must be subordinate to the halakhic system; thus, moral authority becomes replaced by halakhic authority.

I bring this story about Hillel because I am not content to allow some of our most important Rabbinic voices to be written out of our history. I want to show that there are other voices in the tradition than the ones we're accustomed to hearing: there is the voice of Hillel, who offered a new method for confronting the moral dilemma of his time. Those voices were there. I want the Jewish people as a collective to be reminded that there were voices in our tradition that sought to respond to the needs of their followers and did not shy away from making bold decisions when the community's interest required it. Those voices existed and are preserved within the bedrock of our religious canon. Hillel did not look for any legitimization beyond his community's actual, lived experience. Hillel's example shows that moral and social awareness have a place in Jewish consciousness and legislation and that these are the values that must inform the decisions of our religious leadership.

Exegesis as Denial:
The Rebellious Son and Rabbinic Failure

The *shmita* law is one of many biblical prescriptions that present us with a moral challenge. I would like to introduce another morally confounding biblical injunction: the command to institute capital punishment to a minor gone astray. The injunction to kill the *ben sorer u-moreh* is among the most disturbing of our biblical commands. It is shocking that, on the face of it, the Bible approaches the (not atypical) problem of teenage rebellion with death. In the plain meaning of the text, this biblical law appears to be utterly lacking in mercy and strikes the reader as a distinct exception to a system of Jewish law that purports to foreground justice and compassion:

> If a man has a wayward and defiant son, who does not heed his father or mother and does not obey them even after they discipline him, his father and mother shall take hold of him and bring him out to the elders of his town at the public place of his community. They shall say to the elders of the town, "This son of ours is disloyal and defiant [*ben sorer u-moreh*]; he does not heed us. He is a glutton and a drunkard." Thereupon the men of his town shall stone him to death. Thus you will sweep out evil from your midst: all Israel will hear and be afraid.
>
> (DEUTERONOMY 21:18–21)

The Rabbis of the tannaitic period, discussing this passage in the Mishnah, are confronted with the basic immorality of the biblical text. From their discussion, we catch a revealing glimpse of the Rabbinic mind struggling to comprehend and negotiate with the biblical mind. It is clear that the Rabbis of the Mishnaic discussion instinctively feel that they cannot countenance the observance of this biblical decree. Yet the direct and clear-eyed approach of Hillel stands in stark contrast to that of the Rabbis of the Gemara. Hillel did not rely on exegetical interpretations or on halakhic antecedent to arrive at his decision. Hillel was able to *see* the moral flaw in the biblical injunction and respond. Yet the Rabbis in this discussion are unable to see; they are unable to admit that the biblical text might be flawed, that it might violate our conscience, that it might demand a critical response.

Instead, they create an intricate list of potential disqualifications, from the health and physical appearance of the defendant's parents to the precise circumstance of his alleged actions, to ensure that the law cannot be implemented:

> If one of them, his father or his mother, had a hand or fingers cut off, or is lame, dumb, blind, or deaf, he does not become a stubborn and rebellious son. Because it is written, "His father and mother shall take hold of him." This excludes those with hands or fingers cut off. "And bring him out," excluding lame parents. "And they shall say,'" excluding the dumb. "This is our son," excluding the blind. "He will not obey our voice," excluding the deaf.[5]

We see in this passage that the Rabbis are reading the text in such a way that brings the discussion into the realm of the absurd, reasoning that a physical impairment would prevent a parent from being able to fulfill the protocol of dealing with a rebellious son according to the letter of the law. If a person doesn't have fingers, the Rabbis reason, how can he "take hold" of his rebellious son? In devising this strange form of logic, the Rabbis are taking their interpretive prerogative to an extreme. Surely, no person reading the Bible would come to the conclusion that this description is meant to be read literally. But the text goes further in its bizarre reasoning:

> After all, his father is his father, and his mother is his mother, but he means not physically like his father. It has been taught likewise. Reb Judah said if his mother is not like his father in voice, appearance, and stature, he does not become the rebellious son. What is the reason for these requirements? It is as Scripture states: "He does not obey our voice." This teaches that the boy's parents must have similar voices. And from the fact that we require their voices to be similar, it follows that their appearance and height also must be similar.[6]

The Rabbinic body in this passage is actually suggesting that the parents must literally have the *same voice* in order for the law to apply. The Gemara logicizes that unless the purported rebellious son's parents have identical voices, they will be unable to fulfill the biblical command to speak as a unified entity. In case this were not an unlikely enough scenario, the Gemara goes on to stipulate that they must also have the same physical appearance and the same physical stature. Who would ever imagine that that is what the Bible means? Surely we don't think the Rabbis' strangely literal reading is reflective of the true meaning of the biblical text. Even the most casual reader would be unconvinced by the Rabbis' logic; so who are the Rabbis satisfying with their strange interpretations?

In discussing the biblical text concerning the *ben sorer u-moreh*, the Rabbis of the Talmud are clearly aware of the text's basic immorality. Yet rather than name their moral problem explicitly, they busy themselves constructing strange exegetical claims, interpretations so wild they undermine the very integrity of the biblical text.

After expending copious mental energy analyzing the biblical command and translating it into legalistic terms, the Talmudic discussion takes another strange turn when it states: "There never has been a stubborn and rebellious son and never will be. Why then was the law written? That you may study it and receive a reward."[7] In other words, the Rabbis posit that in discussing and analyzing the law, they are fulfilling its very intent. The law was never meant to be implemented, the Rabbis thus explain; it exists only to be contemplated. The Rabbis are drawing here on the Rabbinic tradition of *drosh ve-kabel sakhar*, "learn and you shall receive a reward." Yet in using this idea in this way, I claim *drosh ve-kabel sakhar* is an admittance of failure on the Rabbis' part—the failure to adequately respond to the moral problem in front of them.

But just as it seems that the Rabbis have exhausted the subject of the rebellious son, the text suddenly offers a poignant and perplexing coda by introducing the voice of Rav Jonathan, who says of the rebellious son, "I saw him and sat on his grave."[8] After many twists and turns, the Rabbinic discussion takes on an almost surrealist dimension. Rav Jonathan essentially says: *I want you to know that I was on the grave of the rebellious son. You think you solved the problem, but you didn't.* The voice of Rav Jonathan exposes the inherent limitations of employing interpretive strategies to confront moral dilemmas. No amount of interpretation can alter the original biblical precept. That requires explicit, vocal critique.

By including this countervoice, the Talmud is allowing a form of self-criticism to surface. Rav Jonathan rejects the approach of using interpretive gymnastics to solve moral issues and asserts instead the necessity of addressing them head-on. In including this voice, the Rabbis, in a certain sense, admit their failure; perhaps they wish they could be bolder and act with the full weight of their moral convictions.

The Rabbis' exegetical approach, with its wild interpretive claims, shows how far they were willing to go to protect the inviolability of the biblical verse. The passage on *ben sorer u-moreh* presents a serious moral issue: it is advocating the death of a child simply for eating and drinking too much. Rather than name the immoral claims of the text, the Rabbis instead go to great exegetical lengths to prove that the text never meant what it says. Without realizing it, the Rabbis thus undermine the very biblical tradition they claim to uphold.

The Rabbis are willing to utterly distort the meaning of the text in the paradoxical effort to protect their belief that the Bible is morally absolute; they go to great lengths to protect their claim that the Bible does not violate their moral sense. We understand from their discussion that the Rabbinic body is invested in maintaining the illusion that the Bible does not mean what it says, that it does not ask us to violate our moral conscience. In trying to maintain this illusion, the Rabbis inadvertently render the biblical text absurd. They create an illusion of continuity in a vain effort to protect the tradition from moral critique.

It is my claim that the exegetical model fails, in the sense that it does not offer a coherent or compelling alternative reading. The inclusion of the voice of Rav Jonathan—"I sat on his grave"—shows that the Rabbis' copious exegesis in the end achieved nothing and convinced no one.

The problem with attempting to use internal mechanisms within the tradition to resolve moral quandaries is that the moral problematic is never named, much less explicitly critiqued. By hiding moral anxiety with exegetical maneuvers, moral conscience per se is never encouraged or cultivated. The Rabbinic body's attempt to safeguard the tradition ultimately has the effect of undermining it, because its very interpretations diminish the need to directly confront the biblical text. Engaging authentically with our most sacred book means acknowledging when it arouses our sense of injustice or compassion—and admitting that some of its injunctions may be flawed. The Talmudic discussion about the rebellious son demonstrates the misguided attempt on the part of the Rabbis to hide behind bizarre exegetics. Where they failed was in their refusal to confront the words of the Bible directly, to grapple with the text's *actual* meaning. The voice of Rav Jonathan comes to remind us that at the end of the day, we are still faced with the inherent immorality of the text. The lesson I learn from the Talmudic discussion about the rebellious son is that ultimately, the tradition can't save itself from itself.

14

HALAKHA AS RELATIONSHIP

TOWARD A GOD-CENTERED CONSCIOUSNESS

Biblical versus Rabbinic Conceptions of the God Relationship and the Three Stages of Jewish Practice

How does God enter into a Jew's religious consciousness? In the biblical period, God was made known through the ten plagues, the splitting of the sea, the revelation at Sinai. The drama of history, in other words, was the framework in which the presence of an active and caring God was made manifest. The Jewish people's awareness of the Divine was mediated by the miraculous, beyond the laws of nature, beyond the ken of human comprehension.

Yet the miraculous becomes patently absent as Jewish history moves beyond the biblical and into the Rabbinic period. The God of miracles, the God of History, seems to be deafeningly silent during this era, when the body of Jewish legality known collectively as halakha emerged. With the destruction of the First Temple and the Babylonian Exile (c. 586 BCE), Jews faced the trauma of attempting to understand the role of God—a God who appears to have abandoned them to the whims of other rulers, servitude, forced wandering, and slaughter—in the life of God's elected nation.

This struggle is reflected powerfully and poignantly in the following Talmudic passage:

> Rabbi Joshua ben Levi said: Why were they called the Men of the "Great" Assembly? Because they restored the crown of the divine attributes to its ancient completeness [i.e., brought about a renewal of God's "greatness"]. Moses came and said: "The great, mighty, and awesome God." Jeremiah [who prophesied during the destruction of the First Temple] followed and said: "Strangers are frolicking in His sanctuary! Where are the displays of His 'awesomeness'?" Therefore he omitted "awesome" [i.e., he removed it from his prayer]. Daniel [who lived during the Babylonian Exile that followed the First Temple's destruction] followed and said: "Strangers are enslaving His children! Where are the displays of His 'might'?" And so he did not say "mighty" in his prayer. [The Men of the Great Assembly] followed and said: "On the contrary! This is His magnificent strength, for He restrains His will, showing forbearance to the wicked. And these are the displays of His 'awesomeness': because, were it not for the awe [i.e., of the nations] of the Holy One, blessed be He, how could one solitary, singular nation survive among the nations of the world?"[1]

Moses, who is the authority for the correct notion of divine power as well as for the normative behavior of the community, had described God in prayer as "great, mighty, and awesome" (Deuteronomy 10:17). In the biblical context, "mighty and awesome" refers to God's victorious power in history, which enables a prophet to defeat a Pharaoh, but Jeremiah and Daniel's experience of history did not correspond with the portrait of God's power depicted by Moses. This is how the Talmud explains why in their prayers we find God addressed only as "great and mighty" (Jeremiah 32:18) and "great and awesome" (Daniel 9:4). When they were unable to see God's might or awesomeness, they did not want to "ascribe false things to Him" (BT *Yoma* 69b; PT *Berakhot* 7:3).

The men of the Great Assembly, on the other hand, demonstrated *their* greatness by finding a way to restore the full Mosaic formula when they offered prayer at the renewal of the Sinai covenant. They were able to recognize the might and awesomeness of God in God's ability to show restraint and not wrathfully strike down the oppressors of Israel.

The Talmud further confirms this picture of an uninvolved, non-miraculous God when it asks, "Who is as silent as you, God?"[2] It is this silence that presented the Rabbinic body with a serious and profound dilemma: how to cultivate consciousness of the Divine when the God of the Jewish people, the God of the Bible, is absent from their lived reality.

I would suggest that it is God's very silence that gave rise t o the Rabbinic body's articulation and codification of Jewish law. Halakha surfaced within Rabbinic Judaism out of a desire to forge a new type of relationship with this new type of God, as the Rabbinic leadership struggled with the question of how to develop a new understanding of Judaism that would somehow compensate for the absence of the omnipresent and omnipotent God of the Bible. Having inherited the legacy of Rabbinic Judaism, we forget that the development of halakha in fact represented a dramatic shift in how a Jew accesses God-consciousness.

Halakha as a Relational Matrix
for Connecting to God

A relationship with God mediated by the miraculous is by nature unstable and unpredictable, dependent upon God's inscrutable will for how history should unfold. Halakha, by contrast, creates a continuous frame of reference for a relationship with the Divine. It is in the very minutia of halakha, observed day to day, week to week, month to month, year to year, that signifies the Jew's ongoing quest for that relationship. In this sense, halakha is the relational matrix that connects us to God.

In developing my conception of halakha, I turn, once again, to the metaphor of family life: revelation corresponds to the time when a couple first meets and falls in love. Yet, after a couple marries, they suddenly find themselves in the prosaic business of building a home and raising children. What happens to the early rush of passion and excitement? In a functional marriage, that passion and excitement get translated into the daily acts of running a household together: taking out the garbage, paying the bills, changing the baby's diapers. Certainly, no one is without their complaints in maintaining the routines that keep the structure of family life intact. Yet, there is the implicit understanding that these routine tasks are somehow imbued with larger purpose, that it is life's details that create the nexus of connection. From this perspective, every mundane chore serves in its own way to strengthen and intensify the family bond.

As any schoolchild knows, God's profound biblical miracles seemed to have a less than lasting impact on the Jewish people's collective imagination. From the vantage of our contemporary world—in which the question of God's existence continues to polarize our political, religious, and cultural conversations—this seems strange. The obviousness of God's existence as depicted in the Bible would seem to answer all questions and squelch any dissent. If *we* were able to experience the presence of God with such palpable immediacy, we think, it would no doubt become imprinted upon our consciousness in such a way that would forever transform us. Yet no sooner have the Children of Israel been freed from slavery in Egypt than they complain about being thirsty in the desert; no sooner do they receive the Torah—the very word of God—amidst thunder and lightning than they turn to the idolatry of the golden calf.

Revelation does not solve anything for the Jewish people. As I have written elsewhere, the Bible is, in many ways, a story of failure: the failure of God to create an absolutely moral human being, and the failure of revelation to create absolute faith. The Bible teaches us, in some sense, that no matter how great the historical revelatory moment, revelation does not change the human personality. So what does change the human personality? Paradoxically, it is not the dramatic tidal wave of miracles of biblical Judaism, but the cyclical rhythms of halakhic observance that have the power to effect change on the human character and help us access consciousness of the Divine. Revelation, in the end, does not have a transformative effect; it is a cataclysmic moment that then has to be translated and integrated into the details of daily life.

In terms of understanding the shift from the biblical mindset to the Rabbinic mindset, it is important to recall the three essential levels of Jewish practice: mitzvah, halakha, and *talmud Torah* (Torah study). Mitzvah, though typically translated as "commandment," would be more accurately described as the initial mode in which the individual is brought into consciousness of the divine will. It is the hearing of oneself in the presence of God. At the same time, the notion of mitzvah imbues a sense of duty; it is the hearing of the call, the first frame of reference for human responsibility.

In this sense, mitzvah is analogous to revelation, in that it is the catalyst, the initial spark of human awareness that we are accountable to God and are called upon to act.

The notion of mitzvah is the starting point for any discussion of Jewish theology—the way it unfolds historically, in the concrete reality of community, constitutes the detailed life system we know as halakha. It is the Rabbinic mind that renders mitzvah into halakha, translating the presence of God not through history, but through daily acts of living. The third stage of Jewish practice, Torah study, is a further outgrowth and elaboration of the Rabbinic mindset; because the Rabbis understood that dramatic events do not fundamentally alter the human personality, they placed tremendous emphasis on the study of the Torah and the halakha.

Understanding the development of these three stages of practice demonstrates the profound shift that occurred in the Rabbinic period: from drama to sobriety, from poetry to prose.

The Middle Path:
Maimonides and the Purpose of Halakha

In my conception of halakha I am inspired, as I so often am, by Maimonides. In the first chapter of the section of the *Mishneh Torah* regarding the laws of moral disposition and ethical conduct, he writes:

> The right way is the mean in each group of dispositions common to humanity: namely, the disposition that is equally distant from the two extremes in its class not being nearer to the one than to the other. Hence our ancient Sages exhorted us that a person should also evaluate his dispositions and so adjust them so that they shall be at the mean between extremes.[3]

Maimonides then goes on to elaborate on what a life of balance and moderation in all things should look like:

> Thus a man shall not be collared, easily moved to anger, nor be like the dead without feeling, but should aim for the happy medium. Be angry only for grave cause that rightly caused indignation so that the like shall not be done again. Only desire that which the body absolutely needs and cannot do without, as it is said, "The righteous eats to satisfy himself" (Proverbs 13:25).... He will not be tight-fisted, nor yet a spendthrift, but will bestow charity according to his means and give a suitable loan to whoever needs it. He will be neither frivolous and given to gesturing nor mournful and melancholy but will rejoice all his days tranquilly and cheerfully. And so will he comport himself with regard to all his other dispositions. That is the way of the wise. Whoever observes in his dispositions the mean is termed wise.... We are bidden to walk in the middle paths that are the right and proper, as it is said, "And you shall walk in His ways" (Deuteronomy 28:9).[4]

Of course, Maimonides is well known for the emphasis he places on the golden mean, an idea that originated with Aristotle. But it is

Maimonides who attributes the way of "the middle path" to God: "We are bidden to walk in the middle paths that are the right and proper, as it is said, 'And you shall walk in His ways'" (Deuteronomy 28:9). Maimonides begins with a worldview developed by Aristotle and integrates it to become a cornerstone of Jewish theology. Given that the golden mean is the way of God, Maimonides then expands upon what is meant by the command to "walk in His ways":

> The explanation of the text just quoted, the Sages taught: Even as God is called gracious, so shall you be gracious. Even as He is called merciful, so shall you be merciful. Even as He is called holy, so shall you be holy. Thus too the prophets described the Almighty by all the various attributes, long-suffering and abounding in kindness, righteous and upright ... to teach us that these qualities are good and right and that a human being should cultivate them and thus imitate God as far as he can.[5]

How then, asks Maimonides, do people train themselves in these dispositions so that they become ingrained?

> Let him practice again and again the actions prompted by those dispositions that are the mean between extremes. And repeat them continually so they become easy and are no longer irksome to him. And so the corresponding dispositions will become a fixed part of his character.[6]

The text continues:

> A man should aim to maintain physical health and vigor in order that his soul shall be upright in a condition to know God. For it is impossible for one to understand sciences and meditate upon them when he is hungry or sick, or when any of his limbs is aching.... Whoever throughout his life

follows this course will continually be serving God, even while engaged in business and even during cohabitation, because his purpose in all that he does will be to satisfy his need so as to have a sound body with which to serve God. Even when he sleeps and seeks repose to calm his mind and rest his body, so as not to fall sick and be incapacitated from serving God, his sleep is service of the Almighty.[7]

In this passage, Maimonides suggests that our every mundane act—from eating to exercise to sex—can be viewed in a religious framework if our overarching goal is to follow God in all God's ways, if they are an instrument to living a spiritual life. In the relational matrix, every act has meaning. I am partial to noting that Maimonides, the greatest halakhic thinker of all time, understood its limits. Halakhic practice is not an end unto itself, but rather the vehicle through which human beings engage with the awareness and yearning for God. It is, in his view, the very psychological and moral discipline provided by halakha that enables us to enter into the realm of God-consciousness. Put more simply, the entire purpose of halakha is to take one beyond halakha.

Halakha as Idolatry

A question I sometimes find myself asking is how to distance myself from those who have turned halakha into a form of idolatry, who ascribe to it such ultimate importance that they have no time for the broader issues toward which it is intended to point us. We see this in countless examples of modern Jewish life: When we say the *Shema* in synagogue on Friday night, are we focused on expressing our awareness of and relationship to God? Or are we more preoccupied with technical questions, like whether it was read before or after *tzet ha-kokhavim* (the emergence of the night's first stars)—the former rendering its recitation, from a formally halakhic perspective, null and void? Are our religious lives defined by debating the various levels of kashrut certification, or are we thinking about what the God who created us wants from us as morally accountable human beings? Inheritors of Rabbinic Judaism, we must remember the imperative of making God-consciousness the centerpiece of how we meet the intricacies of halakha.

I believe that Judaism has no future if the halakhic system does not survive. We need halakha—but the question is, what kind of halakha? When we are deadened to its true purpose, the details of halakha, no matter how meticulously observed, do not create a relational mode and fail to lead us to the further stages of spiritual life. Halakha does not necessarily lead us to moral behavior. As we are well aware, a halakhically observant person is not always an ethical person. Personal morality and *menschlichkeit* (being a mensch) are beyond halakha's purview. What halakha can do is keep us in relationship with a world in which God is present. And when that takes place, it creates an opening for the larger purpose of halakha to infuse our thinking.

———•———

15

AMONG ABRAHAM'S CHILDREN

THE CONFRONTATION OF THE PARTICULAR WITH THE UNIVERSAL

As the pioneer of monotheism, and as the progenitor of a nation—a status promised to him in his covenant with God—we often speak of Abraham as the forefather of the Jewish people. But Abraham is, of course, the father not only of Isaac but also of Ishmael. The midrash, moreover, makes the intriguing claim that he is the "father of many nations" (Genesis 17:5). In examining the character of Abraham, we are thus in some sense also called to examine the relationship between the Jew and the non-Jew, between those we consider *mishpacha* and those outside the family structure. Is Judaism a religion that celebrates our shared humanity, or is it a private arena in which the nonmember has no place?

Many apologetics have been offered to explain the notion of exclusivity that is built into the Jewish people's conception of itself; what I am interested in exploring is whether there is a strain in the Jewish tradition that incorporates the universal themes of free will and human dignity that are equally present in our spiritual inheritance.

As a young man, I wasn't interested in this question. Ensconced in the all-encompassing universe of the yeshiva, I had little interest in how Judaism relates to the outside world, because within the yeshiva's four walls, there is no outside world. In my later years, I came to see that how we understand our relationship to the non-Jew is a serious philosophical issue vital to the integrity of our religious lives.

Over time, I came to realize that, paradoxically, it is the very notion of "chosenness" that places us in relationship with the outside world. Being Jewish means being cast into a polemical dialogue with the cosmic order of the universe. It means being called to examine how Jewish consciousness relates to Christianity and Islam, with people whose foundations of faith differ from ours. (Certainly, there is no question that Judaism is premised on the notion of a special, intimate relationship with God. Yet today we forget that historically there was a deep question about who was meant to be the carrier of this intimacy. In the ancient world, many early Christians observed the biblical laws that have over the centuries come to be seen as exclusively Jewish observances, most notably the Sabbath.)

How does the inherent tension between intimacy—that is, the intimate relationship between God and the Jewish people—and universality—that is, the commonalities of the human experience—find expression in the Jewish religion? Do we share the same story, or must we see our stories as separate? If, as I have elucidated in earlier chapters, our understanding of ourselves and of our relationship to God grows out of our most sacred narratives, then how we answer that question depends, in large part, on how we read the biblical accounts of the Sabbath and the Exodus.

The Paradox of Shabbat

In the book of Exodus, God expands on the commandment to observe the Sabbath day and keep it holy:

> And the Lord said to Moses: Speak to the Israelite people and say: Nevertheless you must keep my Sabbaths, for this is a sign between Me and you throughout the ages, that you may know that I the Lord have consecrated you. You shall keep

the Sabbath, for it is holy for you. He who profanes it shall be put to death: whoever does work on it, that person shall be cut off from among his kin. Six days work may be done, but on the seventh day there shall be a Sabbath of complete rest, holy to the Lord; whoever does work on the Sabbath day shall be put to death. The Israelite people shall keep the Sabbath, observing the Sabbath throughout the ages as a covenant for all time: it shall be a sign for all time between Me and the people of Israel. For in six days the Lord made heaven and earth, and on the seventh day He ceased from work and was refreshed.

(EXODUS 31:12–17)

In describing the Sabbath as "a sign between Me and you," the biblical text highlights the intimate aspect of the Sabbath, presenting it as a symbol of the unique bond between God and the Jewish people. The midrash on this passage extends this idea further by pointedly adding that the Sabbath is "between Me and the Children of Israel but not with between Me and the nations of the world."[1]

Why do the Rabbis feel called upon to paint the Sabbath in such exclusivist terms? We must remember that the leaders of the Rabbinic period lived in a polemical environment, in which the question of who is the true mediator of God and history was a central theme of both Jewish-Christian and Jewish-Muslim relations. Thus, the Rabbis feel they must assert their claim as "the true Israel," as the carriers of the intimate relationship between God and God's chosen people.

I can appreciate the historical context that gave rise to this Rabbinic assertion, but in their need to claim the exclusive God relationship, the Rabbis premise the very meaning of election on a *rejection* of the world. I do not believe that the primary value of the Sabbath lies in its exclusivity, nor do I think the biblical passage need be read in that vein, for this passage also presents an echo of the Creation story, the source for the original day of rest, and the paradigmatic universal narrative:

> The heaven and the earth were finished, and all their array. On the seventh day God finished the work that He had been doing and He rested on the seventh day from all the work that He had done. And God blessed the seventh day and declared it holy, because on it God rested from all the work of creation that He had done.
>
> (Genesis 2:1–3)

In its first mention in Genesis, the Sabbath is described in the broadest cosmic terms—as a day of rest for God after creating heaven and earth. Here, in the passage that introduces to the world the concept of the Sabbath, there is no hint of the particular. Thus, we come to see that the Sabbath contains two distinct elements: it reflects at once the special relationship between God and the Jewish people on the one hand, and the far-reaching spiritual principles of work and rest, productivity and rejuvenation, on the other.

This is the paradox of the Sabbath. The book of Genesis presents the day of rest as the culmination of Creation and as a day for God— and by extension, it implies, for all human beings; it would seem to have no relationship to the specificity of God's relationship with Israel. Yet in the book of Exodus, the Sabbath is presented as both a remembrance of Creation ("For in six days the Lord made heaven and earth, and on the seventh day He ceased from work and was refreshed") and as a symbol of the special relationship between God and the Jewish people ("The Israelite people shall keep the Sabbath, observing the Sabbath throughout the ages as a covenant for all time: it shall be a sign for all time between Me and the people of Israel"). The Sabbath separates the Jewish people from the rest of the world, as an expression of their uniqueness, at the same time that it draws them closer to notions of Creation and eternity.

Therefore, I suggest that the Sabbath, the cornerstone of Jewish life, exemplifies the way the Jewish religion absorbed the universal into the particular. In observing the Sabbath according to the dictates of Jewish tradition, we experience a brief glimpse into the cosmic order of the universe, the cycles of creativity and rest that are endemic to all life. The Sabbath offers us the weekly opportunity to celebrate not only our Jewish identity but also our human identity. Yet it is *through* the intimate covenantal relationship that we are able to access the universal aspects of our consciousness.

In my reading of the Sabbath as a prism that filters the universal into the particular, I am inspired by the nineteenth-century German-Jewish thinker Samson Raphael Hirsch, who reads the first of the biblical formulations for the Sabbath commandment—"Remember the Sabbath day" (Exodus 20:8)—as evocative of its universal principles, while he reads the second part—"Observe the Sabbath day" (Deuteronomy 5:12)—as reflective of the way those principles were woven into Jewish spirituality.

This theme is also played out in a more literal sense, at the end of the book of Isaiah. In describing the approbation promised to the son of a non-Jew, perhaps the son of a foreign worker, who has come to identify with the Jewish people, this passage illuminates yet another way in which the Sabbath serves as an example of the universalistic spirit underlying the Jewish people's distinct practices:

> Let not the son of the foreigner say, who has attached him-self to the Lord, "The Lord will keep me apart from His people"; and let not the eunuch say, "I am a withered tree." For thus said the Lord: "As for the eunuchs who keep My Sabbaths, who have chosen what I desire and hold fast to My covenant—I will give them, in My house and within My walls, a monument and a name better than sons and daughters. I will give them an everlasting name which shall not perish.
>
> (ISAIAH 56:3–5)

Isaiah takes an inclusive stance toward this person—"Let not the foreigner say he has been excluded." And how does Isaiah propose that he be included? Through his observance of the Sabbath. Thus, the Sabbath is put forth as the defining rite of Jewish identification and identity even as it serves as the portal through which "the other" may become part of the Jewish community.

The Exodus Story:
Theocentric versus Humanistic Conceptions

Just as the Sabbath can be seen as a kind of spiritual prism for the universal and particular, how we read the Exodus narrative also sheds light on the tension between inclusivity and exclusivity in the Jewish tradition. How does the story of a slave-people liberated from Egypt inform our conceptions of ourselves and the other? Put another way, how do we reconcile the distinct notion of Jewish chosenness depicted in the Exodus story with its larger themes of human freedom and personal liberty?

The book of Leviticus, in discussing the freeing of slaves in the jubilee year, references the Exodus story and, in so doing, helps illuminate our understanding of it:

> If he has not been redeemed in any of those ways, these years, then he and his children with him shall go free in the jubilee year. For it is to Me that the Israelites are servants; they are My servants, whom I freed from the land of Egypt. I am the Lord your God.
>
> (LEVITICUS 25:54–55)

Here, the biblical text clearly instructs that Jewish slaves be freed in the jubilee year. But the reason cited by the text is not some sweeping universalistic notion of human freedom, but because Jews are already beholden to the God who took them out of Egypt. God "purchased" the Jewish people by liberating them; no human being can possess them, because they are the exclusive possession of God. This is a theocentric view of God's relationship with the Jewish people, one in which the will toward self-determination is utterly negated. That is one way of understanding a Jew's sense of freedom; it is a freedom borne of complete dependence on the God relationship.

Of course, that is not the beginning, middle, and end of the Exodus story, which inspires us anew every year at Passover. In an alternate reading of the Exodus narrative, the focus is not on how God's liberation made the Jewish people God's property, but on how God's liberation of a slave-people instructs us that human beings are not objects to be manipulated and exploited. In this reading, the Exodus story is a clarion call for the inherent dignity of all human beings, a reminder that our collective humanity precludes ownership or enslavement.

We can read the Exodus from a humanistic perspective, as a narrative of empowerment, or from a theocentric perspective, as a narrative of submission. If we read Exodus from a humanistic perspective, we must conclude that slavery is prohibited for any human being, whereas if we read the narrative from a theocentric perspective, then slavery for non-Jews is not precluded because only the Jewish people were emancipated by God. Is the Exodus the story of God's abhorrence of exploitation, or is it the story of how God acquired the Jewish people and made them God's own? Both are possible readings. The Exodus story, I claim, is at once a chapter in the unfolding drama of God's covenantal relationship with Israel and a celebration of the universal yearning for freedom.

The Sabbath and the Value of Human Life

How do we reconcile the notion of the intrinsic dignity of human life with the idea that the Jewish people are, by virtue of their relationship with God, somehow unique? How do we understand the value of basic human existence if we believe that the Jewish people in some sense "belong" to God? Again, the answer is to be found in a discussion of the Sabbath, as it appears in the Talmud. The Gemara depicts Rabbi Samuel, Rabbi Akiba, and Rabbi Elazar ben Azariah debating the origin for the law that a person may violate the Sabbath in order to save a human life:

Rabbi Ishmael, Rabbi Akiba, and Rabbi Elazar ben Azariah were once on a journey with Lavee Sadar, and Rabbi Ishmael son of Rabbi Elazar ben Azariah following them. Then this question was asked of them. Whence do we know in the case of danger to human life the laws of the Sabbath are suspended? Rabbi Ishmael answered and said: If a thief be found breaking in, now if in this case of this one it is doubtful whether he came to take money or life, and although the shedding of blood pollutes the land so that the *Shekhinah* departs from Israel, yet it is lawful to save oneself at the cost of his life, how much more then may one suspend the laws of the Sabbath to save a human life.[2]

In an attempt to trace back the reasoning that permits a person to break the laws of the Sabbath in order to save a life, Rabbi Ishmael draws on the legal precedent of self-defense. If a thief were breaking into your home, you are permitted to kill him—whether or not you know his intention is to kill. Even though murder is, obviously, a grievous sin, it is allowed to save a life; so too, Rabbi Ishmael reasons, even though the violation of the Sabbath is a sin, it is necessary in life-or-death emergencies.

A lengthy discussion proceeds from there, with each Talmudic figure putting forth various legal-religious inferences to justify the law of *pikuach nefesh* (saving a life). Among other halakhic precedents the Rabbis bring to bear on the discussion, Rabbi Elazar puts forth the example of *brit milah*, male ritual circumcision performed eight days after a boy's birth; if the eighth day happens to fall on the Sabbath, the regular laws of the Sabbath are suspended, and the circumcision is performed. Rabbi Elazar's logic proceeds thus: "If circumcision, which attaches to only one of the 248 members of the human body, suspends the Sabbath, how much more shall the saving of the whole body suspend the Sabbath."[3] Another opinion worth noting is that of Rav Simon ben Menashe, who suggests that it is permissible to violate one Sabbath if it will enable a person to keep many Sabbaths in the future.[4] In this argument, which applies the value of expediency to halakhic reasoning, saving a life on the Sabbath is legitimized only by the fact that the individual saved from death will presumably then be able to observe many more mitzvot.

After a protracted analysis of numerous halakhic precedents, the Talmudic discussion is abruptly upended by an independent voice, that of Samuel:

> Rab Judah in the name of Rav Samuel said: "If I had been there, I should have told them something better than what they said: 'He shall live by them [Leviticus 18:5], not die by them.'" Raba said the position of all of them could be refuted, except that of Samuel, which cannot be refuted.[5]

Rather than draw an analogy from a previous law, Rav Samuel posits the intrinsic value of human life as the only necessary legitimization for suspending the laws of the Sabbath. In Samuel's conception, life is of a priori value: "He shall live by them, not die by them." Samuel's position does not ask Rabbinic permission nor seek halakhic justification. One need not extrapolate from halakhic precedents or principles to arrive at the simple understanding that no value can supersede that of human life.

The discussion ends with the word of Raba, who states authoritatively that only Samuel's argument stands on its own merits and cannot be discounted. Why is Samuel's position the one that "cannot be refuted"? Because Samuel refuses to rely on inference or analogy. Instead, he taps into his moral awareness to arrive at an independent judgment—and the Talmudic narrative gives its approval.

What I learn from Samuel's position is that neither the Sabbath—nor any religious law—can ever be permitted to contradict the unqualifiable worth of human existence. In Samuel's thought, I see a possible answer to the question of how to reconcile the Jewish people's particular relationship to God with the universal value of human life. The voice of Samuel suggests that as members of the Jewish people, we can belong to God without denying our humanness. The covenant does not mean we sacrifice our universalistic aspirations; it means we live out those aspirations through the specificity of Jewish practice. In "belonging" to God, we do not deny our human existence—we acknowledge and embrace it.

Notes

1. The Joy of Torah

1. BT *Rosh ha-Shanah* 28a.

2. BT *Avodah Zarah* 3a; BT *Kiddushin* 31a.

3. See Moses Maimonides, *Guide of the Perplexed* (Chicago: University of Chicago Press, 1974), 3:34.

4. For a selection of Rabbinic material on the joy of the law, see Solomon Schechter, *Aspects of Rabbinic Theology* (New York: Schocken Books, 1961), pp. 148–69.

5. See Maimonides, *Guide*, and Joseph B. Soloveitchik, *Halakhic Man*, trans. L. Kaplan (Philadelphia: Jewish Publication Society, 1983), pp. 75–94. For a mystic theocentric orientation, see Gershom Scholem, *On the Kabbalah and Its Symbolism* (New York: Schocken Books, 1965), chap. 2, and *Major Trends in Jewish Mysticism* (New York: Schocken Books, 1941), chap. 1.

6. See Ephraim E. Urbach, *The Sages: Their Concepts and Beliefs*, trans. Israel Abrahams (Jerusalem: Magnes Press, 1975), pp. 286–314; Schechter, *Aspects of Rabbinic Theology*, pp. 138–47.

7. Maimonides, *Guide* 2:6 and 3:53. See Arthur O. Lovejoy, *The Great Chain of Being* (New York: Harper & Row, 1960), chap. 3.

8. Maimonides, *Guide* 3:1213, 3:23.

9. See David Hartman, *Maimonides: Torah and Philosophic Quest* (Philadelphia: Jewish Publication Society, 1976), pp. 139–87.

10. *Pesikta de-Rab Kahana*, trans. W. C. Braude and I. J. Kapstein (Philadelphia: Jewish Publication Society, 1975), *piska* 12, pp. 248–49; see *Pesikta Rabbati*, *piska* 21.

11. See BT *Nedarim* 34a; Maimonides, *Mishneh Torah*, Laws of Torah Study 1:7.

12. We fully realize that the medieval language of overflow and self-sufficiency used to characterize Creation is philosophically incompatible with such notions as divine anger and rage, i.e., with the characterization of the God who causes the flood. Nevertheless, as a metaphorical or symbolic portrayal, we allow our "midrash" the license of extracting from anthropomorphic biblical descriptions the spirit of the philosophical ideas and the religious orientations under discussion. Relying on the literary strands in the Bible and in Rabbinic and Maimonidean thought (much of our description of the God of Sinai is colored by Rabbinic characterizations), we seek to illustrate how the interplay of God-centered Creation and human-centered revelation permeate a halakhic perception of the Bible.

13. Our analysis of Sinai is not, strictly speaking, direct exegesis of the Bible. Sinai, for our purposes, represents and embodies a spiritual outlook mediated by halakha. Although there is considerable evidence in the Bible confirming our hypothesis, various features of God's relationship to humans after Sinai do not easily fit our categories. For example, God's rage and apparent willingness to destroy the people are hardly compatible with our linking Sinai with halakha and the characterization of God as the patient, accepting teacher. It is, however, interesting and supportive of our approach to halakha to examine the following Rabbinic midrash:

> Why does God say: *"Now therefore let Me alone"*? Was Moses holding Him? To what can the thing be compared? To a king who was angry with his son, and when the son was brought into the chamber and about to be beaten, the king cried from the chamber: "Let me alone, that I might smite him." Now the instructor [of the son] happened to be standing without and he thought to himself: If both the king and the son are within the chamber, then why does he say: "Let

me alone"? It must be because the king is desirous that I should entreat him on his son's behalf and for this reason does he say: "Let me alone." Similarly, God said to Moses: "Now therefore let Me alone," and from this Moses inferred, "God is desirous that I should intercede with Him on Israel's behalf and hence is He saying: 'Now therefore let Me alone.'" Forthwith Moses began to plead for mercy on their behalf, as it says, *And Moses besought the Lord his God*.

> (MIDRASH RABBAH, EXODUS, TRANS. S. M. LEHRMAN
> [LONDON: SONCINO, 1939], KI TISSA, 42:9, P. 493)

Where the biblical text appears to portray an enraged God bent on destroying the people, who is mollified by Moses, the midrash, on the basis of subtle textual evidence, presents God as initiating the "cooling off" by prodding Moses to act the role of the defender of Israel. To the midrashic writer, God, the teacher of Torah, is ultimately accepting of human weakness and imperfection. See BT *Berakhot* 32a for a slightly different version of this midrash.

In Numbers 14, where God desires to destroy the people and Moses pleads, "I pray, let my Lord's forbearance be great, as You have declared" (v. 17), the midrash writers present the prophet as being intolerant and God as teaching the prophet to feel compassion for the wicked.

When Moses ascended on high, he found the Holy One, blessed be He, sitting and writing "Long-suffering." Said he to Him, "Sovereign of the universe! Long-suffering to the righteous?" He replied, "Even to the wicked." He urged, "Let the wicked perish!" "See now what thou desirest," was His answer. "When Israel sinned," He said to him, "didst thou not urge Me, [let Thy] long-suffering be for the righteous [only]?" "Sovereign of the universe!" said he, "but didst Thou not assure me, Even to the wicked!" Hence it is written, "And now, I beseech Thee, let the power of my Lord be great, according as Thou hast spoken ..." (Numbers 14:17).

> (BT SANHEDRIN 3A–B)

14. For other explanations, see *Mekhilta, Bachodesh*, 5; Schechter, *Aspects of Rabbinic Theology*, pp. 131–32; Moshe Greenberg, *Understanding Exodus* (New York: Behrman House, 1969), pp. 9–17.

15. Martin Buber, *Moses: The Revelation and the Covenant* (New York: Harper & Brothers, 1958), pp. 101–9. Buber's understanding of the nature of the covenant cannot be separated from his general belief that revelation is incompatible with institutionalized halakha. See *Moses*, p. 104, and Buber's letter to Rosenzweig in Franz Rosenzweig, *On Jewish Learning* (New York: Schocken Books, 1955), p. 111.

16. BT *Shabbat* 88b–89a.

17. *Sifre Shelach*, 112; BT *Bava Metzia* 31b; see Abraham Joshua Heschel, *Theology of Ancient Judaism* (New York: Soncino, 1962), p. 3; *Talmudic Encyclopedia*, vol. 7 (Hebrew), pp. 77–82; Maimonides, *Guide*, 1:33.

18. BT *Kiddushin* 21b.

19. See Soloveitchik, *Ish ha-Halakhah*, pp. 86–87, 142–43.

20. See BT *Kiddushin* 36a.

21. Evening Service, *The Daily Prayer Book*, trans. P. Birnbaum (New York: Hebrew Publishing Co., 1949), p. 192.

22. See Urbach, *The Sages*, p. 393, for the connection between *lishmah* (doing commandments for their own sake) and *simchah shel mitzvah* (the joy of commandments) and *ahavah* (love).

23. This psychological insight may shed light on the apparently opposite theological conceptions in Maimonides's *Guide*. Although a thoroughly theocentric perspective is required for understanding Creation, the revelation at Sinai is anthropocentric. The portrait of God the Teacher in *Guide* 3:32 should be contrasted with the description in 3:13.

24. See Maimonides, *Introduction to Helek*, Laws of Repentance 10, and Laws of *Lulav*.

25. See the description of Adam the Second in Joseph B. Soloveitchik's "The Lonely Man of Faith," *Tradition* (Summer 1965).

26. See Maimonides, *Guide* 3:27.

27. See Hartman, *Maimonides*, pp. 70–78.

28. See Maimonides, *Mishneh Torah*, Laws of the Foundations of the Torah, and the comment of *Kesef Mishneh*. Although many attacked

Maimonides for grounding love of God in philosophical knowledge, Soloveitchik feels comfortable in applying the Maimonidean pathos to engagement in the study of legal sections of the halakha. See Joseph B. Soloveitchik, *In Aloneness, In Togetherness* [Hebrew], ed. P. H. Peli (Jerusalem: Orot, 1976), p. 233.

29. See Soloveitchik, *Ish ha-Halakhah*, pp. 118–31.

30. BT *Menachot* 29b. See contrasting interpretations of this midrash in Menahem Elon, *Jewish Law: History, Sources, Principles* (Jerusalem: Magnes Press, 1973), pp. 319–20; and in Gershom Scholem, "Revelation and Tradition as Religious Categories in Judaism," in *The Messianic Idea in Judaism* (New York: Schocken Books, 1971), pp. 282–303.

31. See Urbach, *The Sages*, pp. 298–302.

32. "Scripture, Mishnah, Halakhoth, Talmud, Toseftoth, Haggadoth, and even what a faithful disciple would in the future say in the presence of his master, were all communicated to Moses on Sinai"; *Midrash Rabbah, Leviticus*, trans. H. Freedman and M. Simon (London: Soncino, 1939), chap. 2 (*Ahare Moth*), p. 277. Such statements are not merely polemical in the light of the Christian challenge, nor solely intended to support the legitimacy of Rabbinic authority, but also express the experience of the student of Torah who is devoted to serving God out of love.

33. BT *Gittin* 60b; JT *Peah* 2:4.

34. "If you have heard Torah from the mouth of a scholar, let it be in your estimation as if your ears had heard it from Mount Sinai"; *Midrash Rabbah, Ecclesiastes*, trans. A. Cohen (London: Soncino, 1939), p. 34.

35. See Soloveitchik, *In Aloneness, In Togetherness*, pp. 109–12, 125–30, 235.

36. Maimonides, *Commentary to the Mishnah, Chulin* 7:6. For a contemporary application of this notion, see chapters 5 and 6 of this book.

37. The Talmud (BT *Megillah* 23b; BT *Berakhot* 26b) explores the personal and collective dimensions of prayer. The *rachamim* (need for compassion) motif is individualistic; the *kedushah* ("I shall be sanctified in the midst of the people of Israel"; Leviticus 22:32) and the *bimkom korbanot* (prayer in the place of the sacrificial cult) motifs reflect the collective dimension. See BT *Berakhot* 30a and the last *Tosafot* on 26a. See Ramban (Nachmanides), *Milchamot Hashem, Megillah* 5a, for an

interesting distinction regarding the role of community in halakha; Soloveitchik, "The Lonely Man of Faith," pp. 34–43.

38. The relationship between community and joy is explicitly formulated in the halakhic use of the categories *simchah* (joy) and *tzibur* (community). Halakhically speaking, the applicability of the concept of *tzibur* is a necessary condition for *simchah*. Whenever one finds a situation defined in terms of the category *simchah*, one finds the category of *tzibur*. When *tzibur* is absent, there can be no *simchah*. The possibility of joy emerges where the community meets, e.g., on Pesach, Shavuot, and Sukkot. Joy is fundamentally an experience nurtured by one's feeling organically related to a broader collectivity.

The relationship of joy and community is further revealed in the relationship of their opposites. Mourning involves deep feelings of isolation. The practice of mourning involves being cut off from one's social reality. Therefore, halakha considers the mitzvah of mourning *aseh de-yachid* (a positive commandment of the individual). When there is conflict between *avelut* (mourning) and *simchah* (joy), the mitzvah expressing collective consciousness takes precedence over and cancels the performance of a mitzvah symbolically expressing a person's isolation and loneliness. See BT *Mo'ed Katan* 14b and comment of Rashi.

39. See Maimonides, *Guide* 3:27–28, and compare with the philosopher's approach to the law as described in 3:51. See Hartman, *Maimonides*, chap. 5, pp. 187–214; BT *Kiddushin* 32b; Maimonides, *Mishneh Torah*, Laws of Torah Study, and compare with BT *Menachot* 99b, regarding different approaches to *talmud Torah*.

40. *Pesikta de-Rab Kahana*, piska 12, pp. 249–50.

41. Maimonides, *Mishneh Torah*, Laws of Moral Disposition and Ethical Conduct 3:3.

42. Maimonides, *Mishneh Torah*, Laws of the Foundations of the Torah 5:2.

43. For a fuller analysis of the relationship of the individual and the community in Rabbinic and Maimonidean thought, see Hartman, *Maimonides*, pp. 66–101.

2. The Body as Spiritual Teacher: Learning to Accept Interdependency

1. Morning Service, *The Daily Prayer Book*, trans. Birnbaum.

2. Maimonides, *Mishneh Torah*, Laws of Gifts to the Poor 10:7.

3. Ibid., 10:8.

4. Ibid., 10:4.

5. Ibid., 10:5.

6. Martin Buber, *I and Thou*, trans. R. G. Smith (New York: Scribner, 1958), p. 16.

3. Democratizing the Spiritual: The Risks and Rewards of Halakha

1. Benedict de Spinoza, *A Theologico-Political Treatise*, trans. R. H. M. Elwes (New York: Dover, 1951). See D. Hartman, *Maimonides*, chap. 3, "Reason and Traditional Authority," and n. 6 and n. 42.

2. Compare Judah Halevi, *Kuzari* 2:47–48 and 3:7, with Maimonides, *Guide of the Perplexed* 3:32, 3:54.

3. Ramban (Nachmanides), *Commentary on the Torah: Leviticus*, trans. Charles B. Chavel (New York: Shilo, 1974), pp. 283–84.

4. Ramban (Nachmanides), *Commentary on the Torah: Deuteronomy*, trans. Charles B. Chavel (New York: Shilo, 19), p. 88.

5. See Aaron Lichtenstein, "Does Jewish Tradition Recognize an Ethic Independent of Halakha?" in *Modern Jewish Ethics*, ed. Marvin Fox (Columbus: Ohio State University Press, 1975), pp. 62–88; and Hartman, *Maimonides*, pp. 86–98.

6. See Chaim Perelman, "Equity and the Rule of Justice," in *Justice* (New York: Random House, 1967), p. 29.

7. BT *Sanhedrin* 6b.

8. Ibid.

9. BT *Yoma* 69b.

10. *Midrash Rabbah, Genesis* 9:7. See Maimonides, *Guide* 3:10.

11. For an approach that neutralizes the significance of history for halakhic practice, see Yeshayahu Leibovitch, *Judaism, the Jewish People*

and the State of Israel (Hebrew) (Tel Aviv: Schocken Books, 1975), pp. 13–16; Nathan Rotenstreich, *Reflections on Contemporary Jewish Philosophy* (Hebrew) (Tel Aviv: Am Oved-Tarbut Vechinuch, 1978), pp. 84–103.

12. G. E. Mendenhall, "Covenant Forms in Israelite Tradition," in *The Biblical Archaeologist Reader*, ed. E. F. Campbell Jr. and D. N. Freedman (New York: Doubleday, 1970), pp. 33–34.

13. See Brevard S. Childs, *The Book of Exodus* (Philadelphia: Westminster Press, 1974), p. 401: "In the act of creating a people for himself [God], history and law are not antagonistic but different sides of the one act of divine self-manifestation."

14. See BT *Bava Batra* 12a–b; BT *Sanhedrin* 11a.

15. See BT *Yoma* 69b.

16. *Mekhilta, Bachodesh,* 5. See Maimonides, *Sefer ha-Mitzvot,* first commandment and comments of Nachmanides; Hartman, *Maimonides,* p. 221, n. 51.

17. See M. M. Kasher, *The Israel Passover Haggadah* (New York: American Biblical Encyclopedia Society, 1956), pp. 56–59, for numerous examples of how the theme of the Exodus from Egypt enters halakhic practice.

18. See *Mishnah Berakhot* 1:5.

19. See Brevard S. Childs, *Memory and Tradition in Israel* (London: CSM, 1962), pp. 50–65.

20. BT *Berakhot* 13a.

21. Maimonides's *Mishneh Torah* reflects the integration of legality and of relationship with (knowledge of) God. The first of the fourteen books of *Mishneh Torah*—*The Book of Knowledge*—deals primarily with themes that broaden one's understanding of God. *The Book of Knowledge* is followed by *The Book of Love.* This sequence indicates that Maimonides deals with the full legal scope of halakha only after establishing the centrality of knowledge and love of God. See Hartman, *Maimonides,* pp. 62–65.

22. *The Evening Service Daily Prayer Book,* trans. Birnbaum, p. 192.

23. BT *Avodah Zarah* 3a; BT *Kiddushin* 31a.

24. See chap. 1, "The Joy of Torah," for a description of how love for God influenced Rabbinic perception of intellectual creativity within Torah.

25. "Our Rabbis taught: Once the wicked government issued a decree for-
bidding the Jews to study and practice the Torah. Pappus ben Judah
came and found Rabbi Akiba publicly bringing gatherings together
and occupying himself with the Torah.... When Rabbi Akiba was
taken out for execution, it was the hour for the recital of the *Shema*,
and while they combed his flesh with iron combs, he was accepting
upon himself the kingship of heaven. His disciples said to him: 'Our
teacher, even to this point?' He said to them: 'All my days I have
been troubled by this verse, '[You shall love the Lord your God] with
all your soul," [which I interpret] even if He takes your soul! I said:
"When shall I have the opportunity of fulfilling this?" Now that I have
the opportunity, shall I not fulfill it?' He prolonged the word *echad*
[one] until he expired while saying it" (BT *Berakhot* 61a). See Urbach,
The Sages, pp. 268–70, 417, for his treatment of how Rabbi Akiba's
death establishes a new understanding of the relationship of suffering
and the observance of the commandments.

26. *Mishnah Yadaim* 3:5.

27. Maimonides, *Guide* 3:52.

28. *Midrash Rabbah, Genesis* 8:4–5.

29. See Urbach, *The Sages*, pp. 496–98; *Midrash Rabbah, Leviticus*, 36:6.
See the comments of Rabbenu Tam regarding the distinction between
the merit of the fathers and the covenant of the fathers; *Tosafot*, "And
Samuel said"; BT *Shabbat* 55a.

30. *Mishnah Avot* 3:18.

31. BT *Kiddushin* 36a.

32. See BT *Eruvin* 13b for an account of Rabbi Meir's and his students'
masterful competence in legal argumentation.

33. *Avot de-Rabbi Nathan* 12.

34. See Maimonides, *Mishneh Torah*, Laws of Repentance 6:10; Hartman,
Maimonides, chap. 4.

35. For a fuller analysis of this relationship, see chapter 5 of this book.

36. See Alfred North Whitehead, *Religion in the Making* (New York: Meridian
Books, 1960); Kierkegaard's portrayal of Abraham at the *Akedah* (bind-
ing of Isaac), in *Fear and Trembling* (Cambridge: Cambridge University
Press, 2006), is a classic formulation of this approach.

37. BT *Berakhot* 32a; see Maimonides, *Iggeret Hashemad*.

38. See Soloveitchik, "The Lonely Man of Faith," p. 40: "The democratization of the God-man confrontation was made possible by the centrality of the normative element in prophecy." See Maimonides, *Guide* 3:34.

39. See Abraham Joshua Heschel, *God in Search of Man* (New York: Farrar, Straus & Cudahy, 1955), pp. 320–48.

40. BT *Pesachim* 8a–b. Both Rashi and *Tosafot* were concerned with the exaggerated praise accorded such a person. Rashi argues that acting on the basis of self-interest is not incompatible with acting from a sense of duty. A person may act because of numerous reasons. According to *Tosafot*, whether a person later regrets an action when the anticipated interest is not realized is a criterion for deciding whether the act in question was motivated solely by self-interest. Someone is a "perfectly righteous person" only if he or she does not later regret an act when it fails to lead to the anticipated interest. See Meiri on BT *Rosh ha-Shanah* 4a.

41. BT *Rosh ha-Shanah* 28a–b.

42. Medieval commentators struggled with this text and added qualifications. See Ran and Meiri, and Meiri's introduction to BT *Berakhot*.

43. See Maimonides's introduction to *Helek* (chap. 10 of *Sanhedrin*). Leibovitch, in his approach to halakha, has difficulty explaining this process; see *Judaism, the Jewish People and the State of Israel*, pp. 311–14.

44. *Midrash Rabbah, Lamentations*, trans. A. Cohen (London: Soncino Press, 1939), pp. 2–3.

45. BT *Menachot* 99b.

46. *Mishnah Avot* 2:18.

47. *Sifre Deuteronomy, Ekev*, 41.

48. Maimonides, *Mishneh Torah*, Laws of Prayer 1:1–6.

49. BT *Berakhot* 28b.

50. See Hartman, *Maimonides*, pp. 66–79.

51. Soloveitchik, like Maimonides, gave expression to this profound tension. See Hartman, *Maimonides*, chap. 5.

52. See Soloveitchik, "The Lonely Man of Faith," p. 40.

53. *Mishnah Avot* 4:22.

54. Urbach, *The Sages*, p. 18: "Their eyes and their hearts were turned Heavenward, yet one type was not to be found among them—not even among those who occupied themselves with the 'Work of the Chariot' and the 'Work of Creation'—namely the mystic who seeks to liberate himself from his ego, and in doing so is preoccupied with himself alone. They saw their mission in work here in the world below."

55. See Gershom Scholem, "Toward an Understanding of the Messianic Idea in Judaism," in *The Messianic Idea in Judaism* (New York: Schocken Books, 1971), p. 1.

56. BT *Shabbat* 31a.

57. Ibid.

58. Ibid.

59. This chapter, as originally published, was written in collaboration with Elliot Yagod.

4. Embracing Covenantal History: Compassion, Responsibility, and the Spirituality of the Everyday

1. These remarks, which conclude James's essay "On a Certain Blindness in Human Beings," capture the intellectual orientation of this essay. Rather than claim to speak on behalf of "religious people" in general, I base my remarks on the memories and experiences of a people's history, knowing full well that our particular tradition does not exhaust the "vast field." That one's ideas must be relevant to people outside of one's tradition is not a necessary requisite of rationality. Religious philosophers think dangerously, even arrogantly, when they attempt to explain what is beyond their experience. This essay will approach the issue of secularism from the perspective of the national renewal of the Jewish people in the present century. The return of the Jewish people to national self-determination is, *inter alia*, Judaism's return to and confrontation with secularism.

2. See Robert Charles Zaehner, "On the Self-Exposure of Faith to the Modern-Secular World," in *Quest for Past and Future,* ed. Emil L. Fackenheim (Boston: Beacon Press, 1968), pp. 278–305.

3. Ibid.

4. Alasdair MacIntyre, *Secularization and Moral Change* (London: Oxford University Press, 1967), p. 68.

5. Ibid., pp. 61–65.

6. Soloveitchik, "The Lonely Man of Faith." For a discussion of *imitatio dei*, see *Midrash Rabbah, Leviticus*, 15:13; *Sifre, Deuteronomy, Ekev* 48 and *Sotah* 14a. For the use of Creation as a model for the political leader, see Maimonides, *Guide* 1:54.

7. Soloveitchik, "Lonely Man of Faith," pp. 14–15.

8. For the commandment of work during *chol* (the six weekdays), see *Mekhilta de-Rabbi Simeon ben Yohai, Yitro* 20:9, and *Avot de-Rabbi Nathan* 11.

9. *Midrash Rabbah, Genesis* 8:10.

10. See *Mekhilta, Shabbata*, 1.

11. *Midrash Rabbah, Genesis* 8:45.

12. See Soloveitchik, "The Lonely Man of Faith," pp. 38–43.

13. See chap. 1, "The Joy of Torah."

14. BT *Kiddushin* 36a.

15. *Midrash Rabbah, Exodus* 43:1.

16. See *Midrash Rabbah, Deuteronomy* 2:12: "The gates of prayer are sometimes open and sometimes closed, but the gates of repentance always remain open."

17. BT *Berakhot* 5a: "If a man sees that painful sufferings visit him, let him examine his conduct."

18. See Ephraim E. Urbach, "Redemption and Repentance in Talmudic Judaism," in *Types of Redemption*, ed. J. Z. Werblowsky and C. J. Bleeker (Leiden: E. J. Brill, 1970), pp. 190–206.

19. See Hartman, *Maimonides*, chap. 4; and David Hartman "Maimonides's Approach to Messianism and Its Contemporary Implications," *Da'at: Journal of Jewish Philosophy*, (Fall 1978).

20. See *Mekhilta, Yitro*, 7; and Nachmanides, *Commentary to the Torah*, Exodus 12:2, 20:8.

21. See BT *Pesachim* 117b; and JT *Rosh ha-Shanah* 1:3.

5. Creating a Shared Spiritual Language: The Urgency of Community and the Halakhic Roots of Pluralism

1. Joseph B. Soloveitchik, "Kol Dodi Dofek," in *Ish ha-Emunah* (Jerusalem: Mossad Harav Kook, 1968), pp. 65–106. Soloveitchik perceives *berit goral*, covenantal destiny, as creating the halakhic ground of collective responsibility. The law, which derives from *berit ye'ud*, covenantal purpose, requires that individual members of Israel sense their collective responsibility. Common historical fate has a normative significance in Soloveitchik's philosophy (see ibid., pp. 89–91).

   Soloveitchik is also careful to distinguish between theodicy and the human response to suffering. He does not pretend to offer a solution to the metaphysical problem of evil. His approach is practical; he is concerned with developing a halakhic response to events in history. His theology of history is a logic of response and not a logic of description. Action, not metaphysical truth, is his concern, and it is in this light that we must appreciate his theological approach to the State of Israel. See as well the opening remarks in "The Lonely Man of Faith," p. 9.

2. Soloveitchik, "Kol Dodi Dofek," pp. 103–7.

3. For approaches to the loss of tradition and its possible renewal, as reflected in the Israeli reality, see Natan Rotenstreich, *Tradition and Reality* (New York: Quadrangle Press, 1974); Eliezer Schweid, *Israel at the Crossroads* (Philadelphia: Jewish Publication Society, 1973).

4. Maimonides's introduction to *Guide of the Perplexed*, trans. Shlomo Pines (Chicago: University of Chicago Press, 1974), pp. 5–6.

5. See the suggestive remarks by Soloveitchik in "Sacred and Profane," *Gesher* (June 1966): 23–28. Throughout Soloveitchik's writings, one discerns how struggle, doubt, and failure can be utilized to deepen religious commitment. One senses, at times, a romaniticization of the darker side of human beings in the creation of new religious energy. See Soloveitchik, *Al ha-Teshuvah* (Jerusalem: World Zionist Organization, 1974), pp. 175–87.

6. Gershom Scholem, "Revelation and Tradition as Religious Categories in Judaism," in *The Messianic Idea in Judaism* (New York: Schocken Books, 1971); "Religious Authority and Mysticism," in *On the Kabbalah and Its Symbolism* (New York: Schocken Books, 1965). In the former

essay, Scholem sees the achievement of the biblical scholar as an example of "spontaneity in receptivity." He writes that "out of the religious tradition [these scholars] bring forth something entirely new, something that itself commands religious dignity: commentary.... Commentary thus became the characteristic expression of Jewish thinking about truth, which is another way of describing the rabbinic genius."

Scholem is sensitive to the profound dialectic that is expressed in commentary. "There is ... a striking contrast between the awe of the text, founded on the assumption that everything already exists in it, and the presumptuousness of imposing the truth upon ancient texts. The commentator, who is truly a biblical scholar, always combines both attitudes" (pp. 289–90).

Scholem believes that the mystic understanding of revelation illuminates the boldness reflected in Rabbinic commentary. Because mystics confirm and perpetuate authority, they are able to express unlimited freedom in their exegesis ("Religious Authority and Mysticism," pp. 12–13, 22).

For a discussion on the possibility of continuing in the tradition of commentary without the ancient belief in revelation, see Gershom Scholem, "Reflections on the Possibility of Jewish Mysticism in Our Time," *Ariel* 26 (1970): 49–50.

Julius Guttmann claims that commentary is not possible for a generation that has lost faith in a literal revelation. He therefore attempts to clarify essential principles in the tradition that can act as a framework for continuity within change. See Julius Guttman, "The Principles of Judaism," trans. David W. Silverman, *Conservative Judaism* 14, no. 1 (Fall 1959): 1–24.

7. For different approaches to the significance of sacrifices, see Halevi, *Kuzari* 2:26; Maimonides, *Guide* 2:32; and commentary of the Ramban (Nachmanides) on Leviticus 1:9.

On the contrast between mystic and rational sensibilities, see Scholem, *Major Trends*, pp. 28–37. Contrast the approach to Shabbat taken by Maimonides, *Guide* 2:31, with the mystic approach discussed by Scholem in "Tradition and New Creation in the Ritual of the Kabbalists," in *On the Kabbalah*, pp. 118–58.

8. The need to find ways to understand and apply the Torah to one's generation is a vital way of realizing the Rabbinic attitude toward *kabbalat ha-Torah*. "Let the Torah never be for you an antiquated decree, but rather like a decree freshly issued, no more than two or three days old.... But Ben Azzai said: 'Not even as old as a decree issued two or three days ago but as a decree issued this very day'" (*Peskita de-Rab Kahana, piska* 12, section 12). "When you study My words of Torah, they are not to seem antiquated to you, but as fresh as though the Torah were given this day" (*piska* 12, section 21). "Rabbi Judah spoke further in honor of the Torah, expounding the text: 'Attend [*hasket*] and hear, O Israel: this day thou art become a people unto the Lord thy God' [Deuteronomy 27:9]. Now was it on that day that the Torah was given to Israel? Was not that day the end of the forty years (of the wandering)? It is, however, to teach thee that the Torah is as beloved every day to those that study it as on the day when it was given from Mount Sinai" (BT *Berakhot* 63b). See also *Sifre* 23:6.

9. See B. M. Levin's *Otzar ha-Geonim*, 4, *Chagigah*, p. 60; Maimonides's introduction to *Guide*, pp. 18–20.

10. Soloveitchik is concerned with showing how the detailed objective prescriptions of halakha do not exhaust the full richness of the halakhic experience. He does this by showing the relationship between the inner realization (*kiyyum she-balev*) and the outward act (*ma'aseh*) of a mitzvah. In examining the writings of Soloveitchik, we note the lengthy treatment he gives to the mitzvot of prayer, repentance, joy, and mourning. Those mitzvot illuminate the relationship of internal experience and objective form in halakha. See "Lonely Man of Faith," pp. 34–43.

    For a discussion of the way autonomy and spontaneity may be expressed within halakha, see the chapter on mitzvot in Ephraim Urbach's *The Sages*, pp. 317–42. See also Heschel, *God in Search of Man*, pp. 281–348, for a modern attempt at integrating halakha and *aggadah*.

11. See David Hartman, "Torah Mi-Sinai BeDorenu," *Petachim* 33 (June 1975): 10–16; and Hartman, *Maimonides*, chap. 3.

12. *Midrash Tehillim* 12:4.

13. BT *Eruvin* 13b.

14. See Benjamin N. Cardozo, *The Growth of the Law* (New Haven: Yale University Press, 1963), pp. 64–70; H. L. A. Hart, *The Concept of*

Law (London: Oxford University Press, 1964), chap. 7; Perelman, *Justice*, pp. 91–110; Julius Stone, *Legal Systems and Lawyers' Reasoning* (London: Stevens and Sons, 1964), chap. 8.

15. Julius Stone, *Social Dimensions of Law and Justice* (London: Stevens and Sons, 1966), chap. 14; Chaim Perelman, *The Idea of Justice and the Problem of Argument* (New York: Humanities Press, 1963), pp. 98–134.

16. See the fundamental disagreement between Maimonides and Nachmanides regarding the relationship between authority based upon revelation and the content of revelation (Maimonides, *Sefer ha-Mitzvot*, first and second principles, and the comments of Nachmanides). See also Menahem Elon, *Mishpat Ivri* (Jerusalem: Magnes Press, 1975), pp. 223–32.

17. Maimonides, *Guide* 3:31.

18. Yeshayahu Leibovitch's exaggerated claim that if the mitzvot reflect any human value they are empty of religious significance is a modern application of the *Akedah* consciousness. To Leibovitch, anything that deviates from the model of the *Akedah* is self-worship, that is, idolatry. It is doubtful whether his understanding of Judaism can illuminate a tradition that recognized stages of growth in people's religious development and allowed for a variety of motives in the performance of mitzvot. Given the tradition's uncompromising attitude toward idolatry, this tolerance toward practice is not understandable within Leibovitch's categories. See his *Yahadut, Am Yehudi U'Medinat Yisrael* (Jerusalem: Schocken Press, 1975), p. 26.

19. Maimonides, *Guide* 3:31.

20. Maimonides, *Helek*, 136, 137.

21. On some of the possible differences between Aristotelian and Maimonidean ethics, see Eliezer Schweid, *Iyyunim biShmonah Perakim* (Jerusalem: Jewish Agency, 1969), p. 63. See also the comment of Leo Strauss, "Notes on the Book of Knowledge," in *Studies in Mysticism and Religion, presented to G. Scholem* (Jerusalem: Magnes Press, 1967), pp. 277–78.

22. Maimonides, *Mishneh Torah*, Laws of Moral Disposition and Ethical Conduct 1:3–4.

23. Ibid., 2:5–7.

6. Conquering Modern Idolatry: Building Communities of Meaning around Shared Aspirations

1. See Emil Fackenheim's profound treatment of what constitutes modern idolatry, in "Idolatry as a Modern Possibility," in *Encounters Between Judaism and Modern Philosophy* (New York: Basic Books, 1973).

2. BT *Megillah* 13a.

3. BT *Horayot* 8a.

4. Maimonides, *Mishneh Torah*, Laws of Idolatry 2:4. It is interesting to observe that Maimonides introduces the laws relating to idolatry with a long statement regarding both the historical origin of idolatry and how the philosophical way of Abraham leads to the halakhic way of Moses. Possibly, Maimonides wants us to understand that only within the context of the struggle against idolatry is man best able to appreciate the relationship between philosophy and law. For a further understanding of Maimonides's approach to idolatry, see *Guide* 1:36, 3:29, 3:30, 3:37, 3:41.

5. Although the Talmud speaks of the destruction of the evil instinct toward idolatry, Soloveitchik nevertheless describes how modern idolatry may manifest itself in unconditional allegiance to family or state. See BT *Yoma* 69b; BT *Sanhedrin* 63b–64a; and Soloveitchik, *Al ha-Teshuvah*, pp. 140–43.

6. Lon L. Fuller, *The Morality of Law* (New Haven: Yale University Press, 1964).

7. Fackenheim's remarks are germane to this question: "Whether or not idolatry could be possible if there were no God, or if He were not jealous, idolatry in any case achieves its full religious meaning only in the context of a covenant with a jealous God" (Emil Fackenheim, "Idolatry as a Modern Possibility," p. 176). See also Urbach, *The Sages*, pp. 21–23; Fuller, *The Morality of Law*, pp. 10–13.

8. Ephraim Urbach, "The Rabbinical Laws of Idolatry, Part II," *Israel Exploration Journal* 4 (1960): 238–45. See Saul Lieberman, "Rabbinic Polemics Against Idolatry," in *Hellenism in Jewish Palestine* (New York: Jewish Theological Seminary, 1950), pp. 115–27.

9. BT *Sotah* 4b.

10. Ibid., 5a.

11. BT *Shabbat* 105b.

12. Seminal for our discussion is the following remark: "Rav Huna and Rabbi Jeremiah said in the name of Rabbi Hiyya ben Abba: 'It is written, They have forsaken Me and have not kept My law (Jeremiah 16:11)—i.e., would that they had forsaken Me but kept My law, since by occupying themselves therewith, the light which it contains would have led them back to the right path.' Rav Huna said: 'Study Torah even if it be not for its own sake, since even if not for its own sake at first, it will eventually be for its own sake.' Rabbi Joshua ben Levi said: 'Every day a *bat kol* issues from Mount Horeb, declaring, "Woe to mankind for slighting Torah!"'" (*Midrash Rabbah, Lamentations*, Soncino ed., pp. 2–3). See *Pesikta de-Rab Kahana*, piska 15:5; JT *Hagigah* 1:7. This statement would be unintelligible if faith were the exclusive and primary focus of the tradition. Similarly, the discussion in BT *Rosh ha-Shanah* 28a about whether mitzvot require *kavanah* would also be unintelligible.

13. See *Sifre*, 48; *Mishnah Berakhot* 2:1; BT *Kiddushin* 30b, 31a, 40a; BT *Yevamot* 78b, 79a; Maimonides, *Mishneh Torah*, Laws of Repentance 2:10, Laws of Forbidden Relations 12:22–24.

14. MacIntyre's critique of modern Protestant theology does not fit a theology where halakha is central: "Injunctions to repent, to be responsible, even to be generous, do not actually tell us what to *do*. And about the content of the moral life Christians in fact have no more to say than anyone else. Christians behave like everyone else but use a different vocabulary in characterizing their behavior, and so conceal their lack of distinctiveness" (*Against the Self-Images of the Age* [London: Duckworth, 2007], p. 24).

    MacIntyre sees partial significance in the work of Bonhoffer because there was a social context that affected practice: "One gets from Bonhoffer's writings no clear picture of what type of action he would actually be recommending now, but one gets the clearest picture of what Bonhoffer means if one sees it in the context out of which he wrote. For in Nazi Germany, and in the Europe of the 1930s, the Christian role was at best one of suffering witness. The Nazi regress to gods of race made relevant a Christian regress to a witness of the catacombs and of the martyrs. There was available then a simple form in which to relive Christ's passion. Bonhoffer lived it.

And in all situations where nothing else remains for Christians, this remains. But what has this Christianity to say not of powerlessness, but of handling of power? Nothing; and hence the oddity of trying to reissue Bonhoffer's message in our world" (ibid., p. 19).

MacIntyre's critique of modern theological attempts at translation, i.e., at creating general intelligibility of religious language, is related to his strong claim that "urbanization and industrialization produced a new form of social life, in which religious utterance and activity were necessarily contextless gestures" (*The Religious Significance of Atheism* [New York: Columbia University Press, 1970], p. 43). His important critique, however, may not be applicable to Judaism, which defines the cultural life of a community. The living Jewish community in the State of Israel seeks cultural forms to give expression to its collective life. The attempt to see whether Judaism can be concretized within the political structure of the community provides a social context for the meaning of religious language. The important place that peoplehood, land, history, and law occupy in Jewish theology may provide the modern framework for the renewal of faith in God. See Ernst Simon, "The Way of the Law," in *Tradition and Contemporary Experience*, ed. Alfred Jospe (New York: Schocken Books, 1970), pp. 221–38; Gershom Scholem, "Some Reflections on Jewish Theology," *The Center Magazine* (1973).

15. See Maimonides, *Guide* 1:54, 2:36–40, 3:34, 3:41; and the introductory comments of S. Pines, lxxxvii–xcii, cxx–cxxiii; Leo Strauss, *Persecution and the Art of Writing* (Chicago: University of Chicago Press, 1988), pp. 7–21; Julius Guttman, *Philosophies of Judaism*, trans. David W. Silverman (New York: Anchor Books, 1966), pp. 203–5 and n. 125; and Julius Guttman, "Filosfia shel ha-Dat o Filosofia shel ha-Hok?" *Proceedings of the Israel Academy of Sciences and Humanities* 5, no. 9 (1975): 188–207.

16. See Maimonides, *Commentary to the Mishnah, Chulin* 7:6; *Mishneh Torah*, Laws of Idolatry 1:3, Laws of Moral Disposition and Ethical Conduct 1:7; *Guide* 1:63, 2:39. Notice the repeated emphasis in Maimonides that the patriarchs only teach.

17. See Maimonides, *Guide* 3:51, 3:54; and David Hartman, *Maimonides*, chap. 5.

18. Maimonides, *Mishneh Torah*, Laws of Idolatry 1:16–18.

19. Maimonides, *Guide* 3:32.

20. See Maimonides, *Mishneh Torah*, Laws of the Foundations of the Torah 4:13, and comments on the *Kesef Mishneh*, Laws of Torah Study 1:12. Maimonides never intended that a person must first be a master of Talmudic thought before engaging in philosophical reflection.

7. Learning to Hope: A Halakhic Approach to History and Redemption

1. See John Bright, *Covenant and Promise* (Philadelphia: Westminster Press, 1976), for an analysis of how memories affect biblical eschatology.

2. See William James, "The Will to Believe," in *Essays on Faith and Morals* (New York: Meridian, 1962), pp. 32–62.

3. Gershom Scholem, *The Messianic Idea in Judaism*, p. 10.

4. See ibid.; Gerson D. Cohen "Messianic Postures of Ashkenazim and Sephardim," in *The Leo Baeck Memorial Lecture* (New York: Leo Baeck Institute, 1967).

5. BT *Sanhedrin* 97b.

6. Ibid. For discussion on the views of Rabbi Eliezer and Rabbi Joshua, see Urbach, *The Sages,* pp. 668–73; and Ephraim E. Urbach, "Redemption and Repentance in Talmudic Judaism," in *Types of Redemption*, ed. Z. Werblowsky and J. Bleeker (Leiden: Brill, 1970), pp. 190–206.

7. BT *Sotah* 49b.

8. BT *Sanhedrin* 98a.

9. Maimonides, *Mishneh Torah*, Laws of Kings, chap. 11–12.

10. "The words of Isaiah: 'And the wolf shall dwell with the lamb, and the leopard shall lie down with the kid' (Isaiah 11:6) are to be understood figuratively, meaning that all Israel will live securely among the wicked of the heathens, who are likened to wolves and leopards (Jeremiah 5:6).... All similar expressions used in connection with the messianic age are metaphorical" (ibid.).

11. Cf. Maimonides, *Mishneh Torah*, Laws of Repentance 9:11; *Guide* 2:36, 3:11, 3:27.

12. Nachmanides, *Commentary on the Torah*.

13. Cf. also Nachmanides's commentary on Leviticus 26:16 and Deuteronomy 28:42.
14. Scholem, *The Messianic Idea in Judaism*, pp. 30–31.
15. Maimonides, *Mishneh Torah*, Laws of Repentance 7:5.
16. See Maimonides, *Guide* 2:47.
17. *Genesis Rabbah* 9:11.
18. Maimonides, *Commentary to the Mishnah*, Avot 2:6; cf. the commentary on *Peah* 1:1.
19. Maimonides, *Mishneh Torah*, Laws of Repentance 6:10; cf. Maimonides's treatment of the statement of the Sages, "Whoever comes to purify himself receives aid" (BT *Yoma* 38b; BT *Avodah Zarah* 55a; BT *Shabbat* 104a; BT *Menachot* 29b).
20. BT *Berakhot* 33b.
21. Maimonides, *The Eight Chapters*, ed. and trans. Joseph Gorfinkle (New York: AMS Press, 1966), p. 89.
22. *Genesis*, introduction, trans., and notes by E. A. Speiser, Anchor Bible, vol. 1 (Garden City, N.Y.: Doubleday, 1964), p. 28.
23. Maimonides, *Guide* 2:48.
24. Maimonides, *The Eight Chapters*, p. 90.
25. Maimonides, *Mishneh Torah*, Laws of Repentance 6:11.
26. Ibid., 6:8.
27. Maimonides, *Guide* 2:25.
28. Ibid.
29. Ibid., 2:27.
30. Ibid., 2:29.
31. See *Guide* 3:27, and Hartman, *Maimonides*, pp. 83–101.
32. Maimonides should not be interpreted as maintaining a Marxist type of historical determinism. Rare individuals may achieve the goals of a messianic era (intellectual love of God) even within an unredeemed world. It was for such individuals that he wrote *Guide of the Perplexed*.
33. Maimonides, *Mishneh Torah*, Laws of Repentance 9:7–8.

34. For a phenomenology of halakhic activism, see Soloveitchik, *Ish ha-Halakhah*; *In Aloneness, In Togetherness*, pp. 37–188; and "The Lonely Man of Faith," pp. 34–44.

35. BT *Berakhot* 5a. The following statement characterized Rabbinic spirituality: "The gates of prayer are sometimes open and sometimes closed, but the gates of repentance always remain open" (*Midrash Rabbah, Deuteronomy* 2:12).

36. Maimonides, *Mishneh Torah*, Laws of Public Fasts 1:1–3.

37. Cf. ibid., Laws of Repentance 3:14; chap. 4. It is not accidental that Maimonides seriously deals with his philosophy of history in chaps. 5–9 of the Laws of Repentance.

38. In *Guide* 2:29, Maimonides interprets the prophet Joel's expression "the great and terrible day of the Lord" as referring to the destruction of Sennacherib. He adds, "Every day in which a great victory or a great disaster comes to pass is called 'the great and terrible day of the Lord.'" In chapter 2 of the *Guide*, Maimonides aims at dispelling the belief that prophetic texts indicate a change in the order of nature in the messianic age. The permanence of the messianic period does not challenge Maimonides's naturalism as long as it does not imply a new natural order.

39. *Perek Helek*, introduction to BT *Sanhedrin* 11, in "Maimonides on the Jewish Creed," trans. J. Abelson, *Jewish Quarterly Review* (Oct. 1906): 43–44.

40. Shlomo Pines, "Histrabrut ha-Tekumah me-Hadash shel Medinah Yehudit lefi Yosef ibn Kaspi u-lefi Spinoza," *Riv'on Philosophe* 14 (1964): 301–9.

41. Pines rightly claims that Maimonides is silent about the transition from dispersion to messianism. However, it is consistent with Maimonides's approach to claim that were he alive after this transition, he would attempt to understand it without appealing to miracles. Messianism, as distinct from resurrection, is organically related to Maimonides's philosophy of Judaism. Resurrection is a miracle that Maimonides accepted simply because the tradition demanded this of him. He did not attempt to explain its significance. His extended treatment of the significance of messianism in his legal writings suggests that messianism (as distinct from resurrection) indeed is essen-

tially related to his philosophy of Judaism. See Maimonides, *Epistle to Yemen*, ed. A. S. Halkin (New York: PAAJR, 1952), p. 28.

42. BT *Sanhedrin* 97b.

43. See Soloveitchik, "The Lonely Man of Faith," pp. 28–30.

44. See chap. 1, "The Joy of Torah."

45. Compare Plato's arguments for the philosopher to return to the cave of the community, with Maimonides, *Guide* 2:37. See Hartman, *Maimonides*, p. 246, n. 7, 19; p. 261, n. 39.

46. This understanding of the implications of the giving of Torah may shed light on the Talmudic preference for action based on divine commandment over spontaneous behavior: "Greater is he who does an act that he is commanded to do than he who does an act that he is not commanded to do" (BT *Avodah Zarah* 3a; BT *Kiddushin* 31a). This approach should not be confused with the Kantian preference for duty. Being commanded reflects the added dimension of divine loving acceptance of limited human beings.

47. See Yehezkel Kaufmann, *The Religion of Israel,* trans. Moshe Greenberg (Chicago: University of Chicago Press, 1960), pp. 425–26; and M. Goshen-Gottstein, "Ezekiel and Ijob: Zur Problemgeschichte von Bundestheologie und Gott-Mensch-Verhaltnis," *Festschrift fur Joseph Zeigler,* vol. 2 (Wurzburg: Echten-Verlag, 1972), pp. 155–70.

48. See Soloveitchik, "The Lonely Man of Faith," pp. 11–16.

49. Ernst Cassirer, *The Myth of the State* (New Haven: Yale University Press, 1946), pp. 371–75.

8. Abraham's Argument: Empowerment, Defeat, and the Religious Personality

1. Joseph Epstein, ed., *Shiurei Harav—A Conspectus of the Public Lectures of Rabbi Joseph B. Soloveitchik* (Hamevaser, Israel: Yeshiva University, 1974), p. 45.

2. Ibid., p. 46.

9. A Covenant of Empowerment: Divine Withdrawal and Human Responsibility

1. BT *Bava Metzia* 59b.
2. *Makkot* 1:10.

10. Mishpachtology: Judaism as a Family System

1. Mordecai Kaplan, *Dynamic Judaism: The Essential Writings of Mordecai Kaplan*, ed. Emanuel S. Goldsmith and Mel Scult (New York: Fordham University Press, 1991), p. 431.
2. Ibid., p. 17.
3. Mordecai Kaplan, *The Meaning of God in Modern Jewish Religion* (Detroit: Wayne State University Press, 1994), p. 40.
4. Ibid.
5. Judah Halevi, *Kuzari* 1:25.
6. Ibid., 4:3. See David Hartman, *Israelis and the Jewish Tradition: An Ancient People Debating Its Future* (New Haven: Yale University Press, 2000), p. 37.
7. Maimonides, *Mishneh Torah*, *Book of Judges*, Laws of Rebels 1:1.
8. Personal reflection.

11. Custom and Innovation: Stepping Beyond the Parameters of the Past

1. Raymond Weiss with Charles Butterworth, *Ethical Writings of Maimonides* (New York: New York University Press, 1975), p. 10.
2. Abraham Joshua Heschel, *God in Search of Man*.

12. My Daughter Is Not My Mother: Rethinking the Role of Women in Traditional Judaism

1. See, e.g., Carol Gilligan and David A. J. Richards, *The Deepening Darkness: Patriarchy, Resistance, and Democracy's Future* (New York: Cambridge University Press, 2008), introduction.

2. See Tova Hartman, *Feminism Encounters Traditional Judaism: Resistance and Accommodation* (Waltham, Mass.: Brandeis University Press, 2007).

3. BT *Megillah* 7b.

4. BT *Megillah* 11a.

5. Moshe Meiselman, *Jewish Woman in Jewish Law* (New York: Ktav, 1978).

6. Abraham Isaac Kook, "On the Election of Women," in *Edah Journal*, trans. Tzvi Zohar, 1:2 (2001): 3.

7. Ibid.

8. Ibid.

9. Ben-Zion Meir Hai Uziel, "Women's Rights in Elections to Public Institutions," in *Edah Journal*, trans. Tzvi Zohar, 1:2 (2001): 8.

10. Ibid.

11. Ibid.

13. Hillel's Decision: Subjective Piety as a Religious Value

1. BT *Gittin* 36a.

2. BT *Sanhedrin* 82a.

3. BT *Gittin* 36a.

4. Ibid.

5. BT *Sanhedrin* 71a.

6. Ibid.

7. Ibid.

8. Ibid.

14. Halakha as Relationship: Toward a God-Centered Consciousness

1. BT *Yoma* 69b.

2. See David Hartman, *A Heart of Many Rooms: Celebrating the Many Voices within Judaism* (Woodstock, Vt.: Jewish Lights, 1999).

3. *Mishneh Torah*, Laws of Moral Disposition and Ethical Conduct 1:4.

4. Ibid., 1:4–5.

5. Ibid., 1:6.

6. Ibid., 1:7.

7. Ibid., 3:3.

15. Among Abraham's Children: The Confrontation of the Particular with the Universal

1. *Mekhilta, Shabbat*, ch. 1.

2. BT *Yoma* 85a.

3. BT *Yoma* 85b.

4. Ibid.

5. Ibid.

Bibliography

Birnbaum, Phillip, ed. and trans. *The Daily Prayer Book*. New York: Hebrew Publishing Co., 1949.

Bright, John. *Covenant and Promise*. Philadelphia: Westminster Press, 1976.

Buber, Martin. *I and Thou*. Translated by R. G. Smith. New York: Scribner, 1958.

———. *Moses: The Revelation and the Covenant*. New York: Harper & Brothers, 1958.

Cardozo, Benjamin N. *The Growth of the Law*. New Haven: Yale University Press, 1963.

Cassirer, Ernst. *The Myth of the State*. New Haven: Yale University Press, 1946.

Childs, Brevard S. *The Book of Exodus*. Philadelphia: Westminster Press, 1974.

Cohen, Gerson D. "Messianic Postures of Ashkenazim and Sephardim." In *The Leo Baeck Memorial Lecture*. New York: Leo Baeck Institute, 1967.

Elon, Menahem. *Jewish Law: History, Sources, Principles*. Jerusalem: Magnes Press, 1973.

———. *Mishpat Ivri*. Jerusalem: Magnes Press, 1975.

Fackenheim, Emil. "Idolatry as a Modern Possibility." In *Encounters between Judaism and Modern Philosophy*. New York: Basic Books, 1973.

———. "On the Self-Exposure of Faith to the Modern-Secular World." In *Quest for Past and Future*. Boston: Beacon Press, 1968.

Fuller, Lon L. *The Morality of Law*. New Haven: Yale University Press, 1964.

Genesis. Introduction, translation, and notes by E. A. Speiser. Anchor Bible, vol. 1. Garden City, N.Y.: Doubleday, 1964.

Gilligan, Carol, and David A. J. Richards. *The Deepening Darkness: Patriarchy, Resistance, and Democracy's Future.* New York: Cambridge University Press, 2008.

Goshen-Gottstein, M. "Ezekiel and Ijob: Zur Problemgeschichte von Bundestheologie und Gott-Mensch-Verhaltnis." In *Festchrift fur Joseph Zeigler.* Wurzburg: Echten-Verlag, 1972.

Greenberg, Moshe. *Understanding Exodus.* New York: Behrman House, 1969.

Halevi, Judah. *Kuzari: An Argument for the Faith of Israel.* New York: Schocken Books, 1987.

Hart, H. L. A. *The Concept of Law.* London: Oxford University Press, 1964.

Hartman, David. *The God Who Hates Lies: Confronting and Rethinking Jewish Tradition.* Woodstock, Vt.: Jewish Lights, 2011.

———. *A Heart of Many Rooms: Celebrating the Many Voices within Judaism.* Woodstock, Vt.: Jewish Lights, 1999.

———. *Israelis and the Jewish Tradition: An Ancient People Debating Its Future.* New Haven: Yale University Press, 2000.

———. *Maimonides: Torah and Philosophic Quest.* Philadelphia: Jewish Publication Society, 1976.

———. "Maimonides' Approach to Messianism and Its Contemporary Implications." *Da'at: Journal of Jewish Philosophy* (Fall 1978).

———. "Torah Mi-Sinai BeDorenu." *Petahim* 33 (June 1975).

Hartman, Tova. *Feminism Encounters Traditional Judaism: Resistance and Accommodation.* Waltham, Mass.: Brandeis University Press, 2007.

Heschel, Abraham Joshua. *God in Search of Man.* New York: Farrar, Strauss and Cudahy, 1955.

———. *Theology of Ancient Judaism.* New York: Soncino, 1962.

James, William. "The Will to Believe." In *Essays on Faith and Morals.* New York: Meridian, 1962.

Kaplan, Mordecai. *Dynamic Judaism: The Essential Writings of Mordecai M. Kaplan.* Edited by Emanuel S. Goldsmith and Mel Scult. New York: Fordham University Press, 1991.

Kasher, Menahem M. *The Israel-Passover Haggadah.* New York: American Biblical Encyclopedia Society, 1956.

Kaufmann, Yehezkel. *The Religion of Israel*. Translated and abridged by Moshe Greenberg. Chicago: University of Chicago Press, 1960.

Kierkegaard, Søren. *Fear and Trembling and Sickness unto Death*. Princeton: Princeton University Press, 1954.

Leibovitch, Yeshayahu. *Judaism, the Jewish People and the State of Israel* (Hebrew). Tel Aviv: Schocken Books, 1975.

———. *Yahadut, Am Yehudi U'Medinat Yisrael*. Jerusalem: Schocken Press, 1975.

Lichtenstein, Aaron. "Does Jewish Tradition Recognize an Ethic Independent of Halakha?" In *Modern Jewish Ethics*. Edited by Marvin Fox. Columbus: Ohio State University Press, 1975.

Lieberman, Saul. "Rabbinic Polemics Against Idolatry." In *Hellenism in Jewish Palestine*. New York: Jewish Theological Seminary, 1950.

Lovejoy, Arthur O. *The Great Chain of Being*. New York: Harper & Row, 1960.

MacIntyre, Alasdair. *Against the Self-Images of the Age: Essays on Ideology and Philosophy*. London: Duckworth, 2007.

———. *The Religious Significance of Atheism*. New York: Columbia University Press, 1970.

———. *Secularization and Moral Change*. London: Oxford University Press, 1967.

Maimonides, Moses. *The Eight Chapters*. Edited and translated by Joseph J. Gorfinkle. New York: AMS Press, 1966.

———. *Epistle to Yemen*. Introduction and notes by A. S. Halkin. New York: PAAJR, 1952.

———. *Guide of the Perplexed*. Translated by Shlomo Pines. Chicago: University of Chicago Press, 1974.

———. *Introduction to Helek*.

———. *Mishneh Torah*.

Meiselman, Moshe. *Jewish Woman in Jewish Law*. New York: Ktav, 1978.

Mendenhall, George E. "Covenant Forms in Israelite Tradition." In *The Biblical Archaeologist Reader*. Edited by Edward F. Campbell Jr. and David Noel Freedman. New York: Doubleday, 1970.

Midrash Rabbah, Ecclesiastes. Translated by A. Cohen. London: Soncino, 1939.

Midrash Rabbah, Exodus. Translated by S. M. Lehrman. London: Soncino, 1939.

Midrash Rabbah, Leviticus. Translated by H. Freedman and M. Simon. London: Soncino, 1939.

Nachman, Moses ben (Nachmanides). *Commentary on the Torah: Leviticus.* Translated and annotated by Charles B. Chavel. New York: Shilo Publishing House, 1974.

Perelman, Chaim. *The Idea of Justice and the Problem of Argument.* New York: Humanities Press, 1963.

————. *Justice.* New York: Random House, 1967.

Pesikta de-Rab Kahana. Translated by W. C. Braude and I. J. Kapstein. Philadelphia: Jewish Publication Society, 1975.

Pines, Shlomo. "Histrabrut ha-Tekumah me-Hadash shel Medinah Yehudit lefi Yosef ibn Kaspi u-lefi Spinoza." *Riv'on Philosophe.* 14 (1964).

Rosenzweig, Franz. *On Jewish Learning.* New York: Schocken Books, 1955.

Rotenstreich, Natan. *Reflections on Contemporary Jewish Philosophy.* (Hebrew). Tel Aviv: Am Oved-Tarbut Vechinuch, 1978.

————. *Tradition and Reality.* New York: Quadrangle Press, 1974.

Schechter, Solomon. *Aspects of Rabbinic Theology.* New York: Schocken Books, 1961.

Scholem, Gershom. *Major Trends in Jewish Mysticism.* New York: Schocken Books, 1941.

————. *On the Kabbalah and Its Symbolism.* New York: Schocken Books, 1965.

————. "Revelation and Tradition as Religious Categories in Judaism." In *The Messianic Idea in Judaism.* New York: Schocken Books, 1971.

————. "Some Reflections on Jewish Theology." *The Center Magazine* (1973).

Schweid, Eliezer. *Israel at the Crossroads.* Philadelphia: Jewish Publication Society, 1973.

————. *Iyyunim biShmonah Perakim.* Jerusalem: Jewish Agency, 1969.

Simon, Ernst. "The Way of the Law." In *Tradition and Contemporary Experience*. Edited by Alfred Jospe. New York: Schocken Books, 1970.

Soloveitchik, Joseph B. *Al ha-Teshuvah*. Jerusalem: World Zionist Organization, 1974.

————. *In Aloneness, In Togetherness* (Hebrew). Edited by P. H. Peli. Jerusalem: Orot, 1976.

————. *Halakhic Man*. Translated by L. Kaplan. Philadelphia: Jewish Publication Society, 1983.

————. "Kol Dodi Dofek." In *Ish ha-Emunah*. Jerusalem: Mossad Harav Kook, 1968.

————. "The Lonely Man of Faith." *Tradition* (Summer 1965).

Spinoza, Benedict de. *A Theologico-Political Treatise*. Translated by R. H. M. Elwes. New York: Dover, 1951.

Stone, Julius. *Legal Systems and Lawyers' Reasoning*. London: Stevens and Sons, 1964.

————. *Social Dimensions of Law and Justice*. London: Stevens and Sons, 1966.

Strauss, Leo. "Notes on the Book of Knowledge." In *Studies in Mysticism and Religion, presented to G. Scholem*. Jerusalem: Magnes Press, 1967.

Urbach, Ephraim E. "The Rabbinical Laws of Idolatry, part II." *Israel Exploration Journal* 4 (1960).

————. "Redemption and Repentance in Talmudic Judaism." In *Types of Redemption*. Edited by R. J. Zwi Werblowsky and C. Jouco Bleeker. Leiden: E. J. Brill, 1970.

————. *The Sages*. Jerusalem: Magnes Press, 1975.

————. *The Sages: Their Concepts and Beliefs*. Translated by Israel Abrahams. Jerusalem: Magnes Press, 1975.

Whitehead, Alfred North. *Religion in the Making*. New York: Meridian Books, 1960.

Index

Abraham: and the *Akedah*, 159–61, 164–67; and covenantal relationship with God, 169–70, 174, 178, 181, 227, 257; and Sodom and Gomorrah, 107, 159–61

Akedah (binding of Issac), 103–7, 159–61, 163–67, 171–75, 282n18

autonomy and human perfection, 26–29

charity, 33–36

circumcision, 264

commandments. *See* mitzvot (commandments)

community: as creator of Judaism, 187–90; diverseness in, 96–101; God dwelling in, 90; and halakha, 119–25, 195–98, 236–40; and halakhic change, 206–9; in Israel, 91–96, 279n1, 279n3, 279n5; joy of, 18–23, 272n38; and observance of Sabbath, 261–62; and prayer, 62–65; primacy of, 58–62; and shared aspirations, 107–10, 111, 114; and tradition, 199–200; and understandable values, 106–7; value and risks of, 66–70

compassion/unconditional love (*rachamim*) and judgment/justice (*din*), 55–58, 82–90, 275n29

congregation, dignity of, 215–17

covenantal consciousness, 174–75, 183–85

covenantal theology, 178, 181

Creation (of the world): divine speech of, 6–8; and eternity, 140–43; and Exodus from Egypt, 148; God of, 179–81; and human responsibility, 77–79, 278n6; and the Sabbath, 79–83, 259–60

custom (*minhag*), 196–98, 199–200, 204

dependency relationships: and the body, 29–31; and empathy, 34–37; and Jewish spirituality, 25–26; prevention of, 32–34; and Western thought, 26–29; and the whole person, 37–38

doctor-patient relationships, 25, 30–31, 34–38

education, 125–26, 214, 286n20

empathy, 34–37

Exodus from Egypt narrative, 147–49, 152–53, 262–63

memories and hope for redemption, 127–28, 146–47, 152–53

messianic era, 131–35, 142–43, 145–49, 286n10, 287n32, 288n38, 288n41

minyan (prayer quorum), 18, 217–19

mitzvot (commandments): and choosing life, 181; and community, 18, 187–90; and the divine will, 251; and halakha, 15; and idolatory, 119–21; and joy, 3–4, 14, 270n22; and love, 53–54, 274n24, 275n25; subjective, 97–101, 280n7, 281n8, 281n10; understanding of, 103–7, 282n18. *See also* custom (*minhag*); halakha (Jewish body of law)

morality: and the halakha, 227–30, 234–36; relational, 51–53, 55–56, 274n21; and the Talmud, 236–45; and tradition, 170–71, 200–203

mortal life and the Sabbath, 79–82, 278n8

Nachmanides (Nachman, Moses ben): on free will and punishment, 140; on the messianic era, 132–33, 143; on the Torah, 42–44

Noah, covenant with, 180–81

people of Israel. *See* Jewish people

Pinhas and an immoral situation, 234–36

prayers: of Abraham, 168–69; collective dimensions of, 18, 271n37; and halakha, 62–65; interpretations of, 136; quorum for, 18, 217–19; and repentance, 144

prophets, role of, 58, 75–76, 85–86

punishment: capital, 182–83, 240–45; interpretations of, 135–40

rebellious son, capital punishment of, 240–45

redemption: and compassion, judgment, and repentance, 86–87; and Exodus from Egypt, 147–49, 152–53; and repentance, 129–35, 147, 286n6; and the revelation at Sinai, 149–53; self-defeat as, 161–64

relationship between God and the people of Israel: and account of Sodom, 170–71; autonomy vs. interdependency, 27–29; as expressed by the Jewish people, 187–90; and the halakha, 15, 54–55, 247–51, 254, 255, 270n28; and human dependency, 36–37; and narratives, 157–61, 174–75, 178, 262–63; people as children of God, 56–57, 275n36; and prophets, 58; and the Sabbath, 260–61; and spirituality, 47–48; and the value of human life, 265–66. *See also* revelation at Sinai

relationships: dependency, 25–38; doctor-patient, 25, 30–31, 34–38; "I-It" vs. "I-Thou", 37–38

Bar/Bat Mitzvah

The Mitzvah Project Book
Making Mitzvah Part of Your Bar/Bat Mitzvah ... and Your Life
By Liz Suneby and Diane Heiman; Foreword by Rabbi Jeffrey K. Salkin; Preface by Rabbi Sharon Brous
The go-to source for Jewish young adults and their families looking to make the
world a better place through good deeds—big or small.
6 x 9, 224 pp, Quality PB Original, 978-1-58023-458-0 **$16.99** *For ages 11–13*

The JGirl's Guide: The Young Jewish Woman's Handbook for Coming of Age
By Penina Adelman, Ali Feldman and Shulamit Reinharz
6 x 9, 240 pp, Quality PB, 978-1-58023-215-9 **$14.99** *For ages 11 & up*

The JGirl's Teacher's and Parent's Guide 8½ x 11, 56 pp, PB, 978-1-58023-225-8 **$8.99**

The Bar/Bat Mitzvah Memory Book, 2nd Edition: An Album for Treasuring the
Spiritual Celebration *By Rabbi Jeffrey K. Salkin and Nina Salkin*
8 x 10, 48 pp, 2-color text, Deluxe HC, ribbon marker, 978-1-58023-263-0 **$19.99**

For Kids—Putting God on Your Guest List, 2nd Edition: How to Claim the
Spiritual Meaning of Your Bar or Bat Mitzvah *By Rabbi Jeffrey K. Salkin*
6 x 9, 144 pp, Quality PB, 978-1-58023-308-8 **$15.99** *For ages 11–13*

Putting God on the Guest List, 3rd Edition: How to Reclaim the Spiritual
Meaning of Your Child's Bar or Bat Mitzvah *By Rabbi Jeffrey K. Salkin*
6 x 9, 224 pp, Quality PB, 978-1-58023-222-7 **$16.99**; HC, 978-1-58023-260-9 **$24.99**

Putting God on the Guest List Teacher's Guide
8½ x 11, 48 pp, PB, 978-1-58023-226-5 **$8.99**

Tough Questions Jews Ask, 2nd Edition: A Young Adult's Guide to Building a Jewish Life
By Rabbi Edward Feinstein 6 x 9, 160 pp, Quality PB, 978-1-58023-454-2 **$16.99** *For ages 11 & up*

Tough Questions Jews Ask Teacher's Guide 8½ x 11, 72 pp, PB, 978-1-58023-187-9 **$8.95**

Bible Study/Midrash

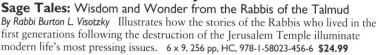

Sage Tales: Wisdom and Wonder from the Rabbis of the Talmud
By Rabbi Burton L. Visotzky Illustrates how the stories of the Rabbis who lived in the
first generations following the destruction of the Jerusalem Temple illuminate
modern life's most pressing issues. 6 x 9, 256 pp, HC, 978-1-58023-456-6 **$24.99**

The Modern Men's Torah Commentary: New Insights from Jewish Men on the
54 Weekly Torah Portions *Edited by Rabbi Jeffrey K. Salkin*
6 x 9, 368 pp, HC, 978-1-58023-395-8 **$24.99**

The Genesis of Leadership: What the Bible Teaches Us about Vision, Values and
Leading Change *By Rabbi Nathan Laufer; Foreword by Senator Joseph I. Lieberman*
6 x 9, 288 pp, Quality PB, 978-1-58023-352-1 **$18.99**

Hineini in Our Lives: Learning How to Respond to Others through 14 Biblical Texts and
Personal Stories *By Rabbi Norman J. Cohen, PhD* 6 x 9, 240 pp, Quality PB, 978-1-58023-274-6 **$16.99**

A Man's Responsibility: A Jewish Guide to Being a Son, a Partner in Marriage, a Father and a
Community Leader *By Rabbi Joseph B. Meszler* 6 x 9, 192 pp, Quality PB, 978-1-58023-435-1 **$16.99**

Moses and the Journey to Leadership: Timeless Lessons of Effective Management
from the Bible and Today's Leaders *By Rabbi Norman J. Cohen, PhD*
6 x 9, 240 pp, Quality PB, 978-1-58023-351-4 **$18.99**; HC, 978-1-58023-227-2 **$21.99**

Righteous Gentiles in the Hebrew Bible: Ancient Role Models for Sacred Relationships
By Rabbi Jeffrey K. Salkin; Foreword by Rabbi Harold M. Schulweis;
Preface by Phyllis Tickle 6 x 9, 192 pp, Quality PB, 978-1-58023-364-4 **$18.99**

The Wisdom of Judaism: An Introduction to the Values of the Talmud
By Rabbi Dov Peretz Elkins 6 x 9, 192 pp, Quality PB, 978-1-58023-327-9 **$16.99**

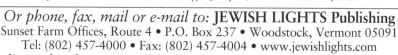

Or phone, fax, mail or e-mail to: **JEWISH LIGHTS Publishing**
Sunset Farm Offices, Route 4 • P.O. Box 237 • Woodstock, Vermont 05091
Tel: (802) 457-4000 • Fax: (802) 457-4004 • www.jewishlights.com
Credit card orders: (800) 962-4544 (8:30AM–5:30PM EST Monday–Friday)
Generous discounts on quantity orders. SATISFACTION GUARANTEED. Prices subject to change.

Congregation Resources

Empowered Judaism: What Independent Minyanim Can Teach Us about Building Vibrant Jewish Communities
By Rabbi Elie Kaunfer; Foreword by Prof. Jonathan D. Sarna
Examines the independent minyan movement and the lessons these grassroots communities can provide. 6 x 9, 224 pp, Quality PB, 978-1-58023-412-2 **$18.99**

Spiritual Boredom: Rediscovering the Wonder of Judaism *By Dr. Erica Brown*
Breaks through the surface of spiritual boredom to find the reservoir of meaning within. 6 x 9, 208 pp, HC, 978-1-58023-405-4 **$21.99**

Building a Successful Volunteer Culture
Finding Meaning in Service in the Jewish Community
By Rabbi Charles Simon; Foreword by Shelley Lindauer; Preface by Dr. Ron Wolfson
Shows you how to develop and maintain the volunteers who are essential to the vitality of your organization and community. 6 x 9, 192 pp, Quality PB, 978-1-58023-408-5 **$16.99**

The Case for Jewish Peoplehood: Can We Be One?
By Dr. Erica Brown and Dr. Misha Galperin; Foreword by Rabbi Joseph Telushkin
6 x 9, 224 pp, HC, 978-1-58023-401-6 **$21.99**

Inspired Jewish Leadership: Practical Approaches to Building Strong Communities
By Dr. Erica Brown 6 x 9, 256 pp, HC, 978-1-58023-361-3 **$27.99**

Jewish Pastoral Care, 2nd Edition: A Practical Handbook from Traditional & Contemporary Sources *Edited by Rabbi Dayle A. Friedman, MSW, MAJCS, BCC*
6 x 9, 528 pp, Quality PB, 978-1-58023-427-6 **$30.00**

Rethinking Synagogues: A New Vocabulary for Congregational Life
By Rabbi Lawrence A. Hoffman, PhD 6 x 9, 240 pp, Quality PB, 978-1-58023-248-7 **$19.99**

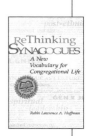

The Spirituality of Welcoming: How to Transform Your Congregation into a Sacred Community *By Dr. Ron Wolfson* 6 x 9, 224 pp, Quality PB, 978-1-58023-244-9 **$19.99**

Children's Books

Around the World in One Shabbat
Jewish People Celebrate the Sabbath Together
By Durga Yael Bernhard
Takes your child on a colorful adventure to share the many ways Jewish people celebrate Shabbat around the world.
11 x 8½, 32 pp, Full-color illus., HC, 978-1-58023-433-7 **$18.99** *For ages 3–6*

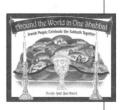

What You Will See Inside a Synagogue
By Rabbi Lawrence A. Hoffman, PhD, and Dr. Ron Wolfson; Full-color photos by Bill Aron
A colorful, fun-to-read introduction that explains the ways and whys of Jewish worship and religious life.
8½ x 10½, 32 pp, Full-color photos, Quality PB, 978-1-59473-256-0 **$8.99** *For ages 6 & up*
(A book from SkyLight Paths, Jewish Lights' sister imprint)

Because Nothing Looks Like God
By Lawrence Kushner and Karen Kushner Introduces children to the possibilities of spiritual life. 11 x 8½, 32 pp, Full-color illus., HC, 978-1-58023-092-6 **$17.99** *For ages 4 & up*

The Book of Miracles: A Young Person's Guide to Jewish Spiritual Awareness
Written and illus. by Lawrence Kushner
6 x 9, 96 pp, 2-color illus., HC, 978-1-879045-78-1 **$16.95** *For ages 9–13*

In God's Hands *By Lawrence Kushner and Gary Schmidt* 9 x 12, 32 pp, Full-color illus., HC, 978-1-58023-224-1 **$16.99** *For ages 5 & up*

In Our Image: God's First Creatures *By Nancy Sohn Swartz*
9 x 12, 32 pp, Full-color illus., HC, 978-1-879045-99-6 **$16.95** *For ages 4 & up*

The Kids' Fun Book of Jewish Time
By Emily Sper 9 x 7½, 24 pp, Full-color illus., HC, 978-1-58023-311-8 **$16.99** *For ages 3–6*

What Makes Someone a Jew? *By Lauren Seidman*
Reflects the changing face of American Judaism.
10 x 8½, 32 pp, Full-color photos, Quality PB, 978-1-58023-321-7 **$8.99** *For ages 3–6*

Ecology/Environment

A Wild Faith: Jewish Ways into Wilderness, Wilderness Ways into Judaism
By Rabbi Mike Comins; Foreword by Nigel Savage 6 x 9, 240 pp, Quality PB, 978-1-58023-316-3 **$16.99**

Ecology & the Jewish Spirit: Where Nature & the Sacred Meet
Edited by Ellen Bernstein 6 x 9, 288 pp, Quality PB, 978-1-58023-082-7 **$18.99**

Torah of the Earth: Exploring 4,000 Years of Ecology in Jewish Thought
Vol. 1: Biblical Israel & Rabbinic Judaism; Vol. 2: Zionism & Eco-Judaism
Edited by Rabbi Arthur Waskow Vol. 1: 6 x 9, 272 pp, Quality PB, 978-1-58023-086-5 **$19.95**
Vol. 2: 6 x 9, 336 pp, Quality PB, 978-1-58023-087-2 **$19.95**

The Way Into Judaism and the Environment *By Jeremy Benstein, PhD*
6 x 9, 288 pp, Quality PB, 978-1-58023-368-2 **$18.99**; HC, 978-1-58023-268-5 **$24.99**

Graphic Novels/History

The Adventures of Rabbi Harvey: A Graphic Novel of Jewish Wisdom and Wit in
the Wild West *By Steve Sheinkin* 6 x 9, 144 pp, Full-color illus., Quality PB, 978-1-58023-310-1 **$16.99**

Rabbi Harvey Rides Again: A Graphic Novel of Jewish Folktales Let Loose in the
Wild West *By Steve Sheinkin* 6 x 9, 144 pp, Full-color illus., Quality PB, 978-1-58023-347-7 **$16.99**

Rabbi Harvey vs. the Wisdom Kid: A Graphic Novel of Dueling
Jewish Folktales in the Wild West *By Steve Sheinkin*
Rabbi Harvey's first book-length adventure—and toughest challenge.
6 x 9, 144 pp, Full-color illus., Quality PB, 978-1-58023-422-1 **$16.99**

The Story of the Jews: A 4,000-Year Adventure—A Graphic History Book
By Stan Mack 6 x 9, 288 pp, Illus., Quality PB, 978-1-58023-155-8 **$16.99**

Grief/Healing

Facing Illness, Finding God: How Judaism Can Help You and
Caregivers Cope When Body or Spirit Fails *By Rabbi Joseph B. Meszler*
Will help you find spiritual strength for healing amid the fear, pain and chaos of
illness. 6 x 9, 208 pp, Quality PB, 978-1-58023-423-8 **$16.99**

Midrash & Medicine: Healing Body and Soul in the Jewish Interpretive
Tradition *Edited by Rabbi William Cutter, PhD; Foreword by Michele F. Prince, LCSW, MAJCS*
Explores how midrash can help you see beyond the physical aspects of healing to
tune in to your spiritual source.
6 x 9, 352 pp, Quality PB, 978-1-58023-484-9 **$21.99**; HC, 978-1-58023-428-3 **$29.99**

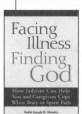

Healing from Despair: Choosing Wholeness in a Broken World
By Rabbi Elie Kaplan Spitz with Erica Shapiro Taylor; Foreword by Abraham J. Twerski, MD
5½ x 8½, 208 pp, Quality PB, 978-1-58023-436-8 **$16.99**

Healing and the Jewish Imagination: Spiritual and Practical Perspectives on
Judaism and Health *Edited by Rabbi William Cutter, PhD*
6 x 9, 240 pp, Quality PB, 978-1-58023-373-6 **$19.99**

Grief in Our Seasons: A Mourner's Kaddish Companion *By Rabbi Kerry M. Olitzky*
4¼ x 6¼, 448 pp, Quality PB, 978-1-879045-55-2 **$15.95**

Healing of Soul, Healing of Body: Spiritual Leaders Unfold the Strength & Solace
in Psalms *Edited by Rabbi Simkha Y. Weintraub, LCSW*
6 x 9, 128 pp, 2-color illus. text, Quality PB, 978-1-879045-31-6 **$16.99**

Mourning & Mitzvah, 2nd Edition: A Guided Journal for Walking the Mourner's
Path through Grief to Healing *By Rabbi Anne Brener, LCSW*
7½ x 9, 304 pp, Quality PB, 978-1-58023-113-8 **$19.99**

Tears of Sorrow, Seeds of Hope, 2nd Edition: A Jewish Spiritual Companion
for Infertility and Pregnancy Loss *By Rabbi Nina Beth Cardin*
6 x 9, 208 pp, Quality PB, 978-1-58023-233-3 **$18.99**

A Time to Mourn, a Time to Comfort, 2nd Edition: A Guide to Jewish
Bereavement *By Dr. Ron Wolfson; Foreword by Rabbi David J. Wolpe*
7 x 9, 384 pp, Quality PB, 978-1-58023-253-1 **$21.99**

When a Grandparent Dies: A Kid's Own Remembering Workbook for Dealing
with Shiva and the Year Beyond *By Nechama Liss-Levinson, PhD*
8 x 10, 48 pp, 2-color text, HC, 978-1-879045-44-6 **$15.95** *For ages 7–13*

Inspiration

God of Me: Imagining God throughout Your Lifetime
By Rabbi David Lyon Helps you cut through preconceived ideas of God and dogmas that stifle your creativity when thinking about your personal relationship with God. 6 x 9, 176 pp, Quality PB, 978-1-58023-452-8 **$16.99**

The God Upgrade: Finding Your 21st-Century Spirituality in Judaism's 5,000-Year-Old Tradition *By Rabbi Jamie Korngold; Foreword by Rabbi Harold M. Schulweis* A provocative look at how our changing God concepts have shaped every aspect of Judaism. 6 x 9, 176 pp, Quality PB, 978-1-58023-443-6 **$15.99**

The Seven Questions You're Asked in Heaven: Reviewing and Renewing Your Life on Earth *By Dr. Ron Wolfson* An intriguing and entertaining resource for living a life that matters. 6 x 9, 176 pp, Quality PB, 978-1-58023-407-8 **$16.99**

Happiness and the Human Spirit: The Spirituality of Becoming the Best You Can Be *By Rabbi Abraham J. Twerski, MD* Shows you that true happiness is attainable once you stop looking outside yourself for the source. 6 x 9, 176 pp, Quality PB, 978-1-58023-404-7 **$16.99**; HC, 978-1-58023-343-9 **$19.99**

A Formula for Proper Living: Practical Lessons from Life and Torah
By Rabbi Abraham J. Twerski, MD 6 x 9, 144 pp, HC, 978-1-58023-402-3 **$19.99**

The Bridge to Forgiveness: Stories and Prayers for Finding God and Restoring Wholeness *By Rabbi Karyn D. Kedar* 6 x 9, 176 pp, Quality PB, 978-1-58023-451-1 **$16.99**

The Empty Chair: Finding Hope and Joy—Timeless Wisdom from a Hasidic Master, Rebbe Nachman of Breslov *Adapted by Moshe Mykoff and the Breslov Research Institute* 4 x 6, 128 pp, Deluxe PB w/ flaps, 978-1-879045-67-5 **$9.99**

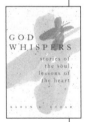

The Gentle Weapon: Prayers for Everyday and Not-So-Everyday Moments— Timeless Wisdom from the Teachings of the Hasidic Master, Rebbe Nachman of Breslov *Adapted by Moshe Mykoff and S. C. Mizrahi, together with the Breslov Research Institute* 4 x 6, 144 pp, Deluxe PB w/ flaps, 978-1-58023-022-3 **$9.99**

God Whispers: Stories of the Soul, Lessons of the Heart *By Rabbi Karyn D. Kedar* 6 x 9, 176 pp, Quality PB, 978-1-58023-088-9 **$15.95**

God's To-Do List: 103 Ways to Be an Angel and Do God's Work on Earth
By Dr. Ron Wolfson 6 x 9, 144 pp, Quality PB, 978-1-58023-301-9 **$16.99**

Jewish Stories from Heaven and Earth: Inspiring Tales to Nourish the Heart and Soul *Edited by Rabbi Dov Peretz Elkins* 6 x 9, 304 pp, Quality PB, 978-1-58023-363-7 **$16.99**

Life's Daily Blessings: Inspiring Reflections on Gratitude and Joy for Every Day, Based on Jewish Wisdom *By Rabbi Kerry M. Olitzky* 4½ x 6½, 368 pp, Quality PB, 978-1-58023-396-5 **$16.99**

Restful Reflections: Nighttime Inspiration to Calm the Soul, Based on Jewish Wisdom *By Rabbi Kerry M. Olitzky and Rabbi Lori Forman-Jacobi* 4½ x 6½, 448 pp, Quality PB, 978-1-58023-091-9 **$15.95**

Sacred Intentions: Morning Inspiration to Strengthen the Spirit, Based on Jewish Wisdom *By Rabbi Kerry M. Olitzky and Rabbi Lori Forman-Jacobi* 4½ x 6½, 448 pp, Quality PB, 978-1-58023-061-2 **$16.99**

Kabbalah/Mysticism

Jewish Mysticism and the Spiritual Life: Classical Texts, Contemporary Reflections *Edited by Dr. Lawrence Fine, Dr. Eitan Fishbane and Rabbi Or N. Rose* Inspirational and thought-provoking materials for contemplation, discussion and action. 6 x 9, 256 pp, HC, 978-1-58023-434-4 **$24.99**

Ehyeh: A Kabbalah for Tomorrow
By Rabbi Arthur Green, PhD 6 x 9, 224 pp, Quality PB, 978-1-58023-213-5 **$18.99**

The Gift of Kabbalah: Discovering the Secrets of Heaven, Renewing Your Life on Earth *By Tamar Frankiel, PhD* 6 x 9, 256 pp, Quality PB, 978-1-58023-141-1 **$16.95**

Seek My Face: A Jewish Mystical Theology *By Rabbi Arthur Green, PhD* 6 x 9, 304 pp, Quality PB, 978-1-58023-130-5 **$19.95**

Zohar: Annotated & Explained *Translation & Annotation by Dr. Daniel C. Matt; Foreword by Andrew Harvey* 5½ x 8½, 176 pp, Quality PB, 978-1-893361-51-5 **$15.99** *(A book from SkyLight Paths, Jewish Lights' sister imprint)*

See also *The Way Into Jewish Mystical Tradition* in The Way Into... Series.

Meditation

Jewish Meditation Practices for Everyday Life
Awakening Your Heart, Connecting with God
By Rabbi Jeff Roth
Offers a fresh take on meditation that draws on life experience and living life with greater clarity as opposed to the traditional method of rigorous study.
6 x 9, 224 pp, Quality PB, 978-1-58023-397-2 **$18.99**

The Handbook of Jewish Meditation Practices
A Guide for Enriching the Sabbath and Other Days of Your Life
By Rabbi David A. Cooper Easy-to-learn meditation techniques.
6 x 9, 208 pp, Quality PB, 978-1-58023-102-2 **$16.95**

Discovering Jewish Meditation, 2nd Edition
Instruction & Guidance for Learning an Ancient Spiritual Practice
By Nan Fink Gefen, PhD   6 x 9, 208 pp, Quality PB, 978-1-58023-462-7 **$16.99**

Meditation from the Heart of Judaism
Today's Teachers Share Their Practices, Techniques, and Faith
Edited by Avram Davis   6 x 9, 256 pp, Quality PB, 978-1-58023-049-0 **$16.95**

Ritual/Sacred Practices

The Jewish Dream Book: The Key to Opening the Inner Meaning of Your Dreams   *By Vanessa L. Ochs, PhD, with Elizabeth Ochs; Illus. by Kristina Swarner*
Instructions for how modern people can perform ancient Jewish dream practices and dream interpretations drawn from the Jewish wisdom tradition.
8 x 8, 128 pp, Full-color illus., Deluxe PB w/ flaps, 978-1-58023-132-9 **$16.95**

God in Your Body: Kabbalah, Mindfulness and Embodied Spiritual Practice
By Jay Michaelson
The first comprehensive treatment of the body in Jewish spiritual practice and an essential guide to the sacred.
6 x 9, 272 pp, Quality PB, 978-1-58023-304-0 **$18.99**

The Book of Jewish Sacred Practices: CLAL's Guide to Everyday & Holiday Rituals & Blessings *Edited by Rabbi Irwin Kula and Vanessa L. Ochs, PhD*
6 x 9, 368 pp, Quality PB, 978-1-58023-152-7 **$18.95**

Jewish Ritual: A Brief Introduction for Christians
By Rabbi Kerry M. Olitzky and Rabbi Daniel Judson
5½ x 8½, 144 pp, Quality PB, 978-1-58023-210-4 **$14.99**

The Rituals & Practices of a Jewish Life: A Handbook for Personal Spiritual Renewal *Edited by Rabbi Kerry M. Olitzky and Rabbi Daniel Judson*
6 x 9, 272 pp, Illus., Quality PB, 978-1-58023-169-5 **$18.95**

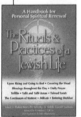

The Sacred Art of Lovingkindness: Preparing to Practice
By Rabbi Rami Shapiro 5½ x 8½, 176 pp, Quality PB, 978-1-59473-151-8 **$16.99**
(A book from SkyLight Paths, Jewish Lights' sister imprint)

Science Fiction/Mystery & Detective Fiction

Criminal Kabbalah: An Intriguing Anthology of Jewish Mystery & Detective Fiction   *Edited by Lawrence W. Raphael; Foreword by Laurie R. King*
All-new stories from twelve of today's masters of mystery and detective fiction—sure to delight mystery buffs of all faith traditions.
6 x 9, 256 pp, Quality PB, 978-1-58023-109-1 **$16.95**

Mystery Midrash: An Anthology of Jewish Mystery & Detective Fiction
Edited by Lawrence W. Raphael; Preface by Joel Siegel
6 x 9, 304 pp, Quality PB, 978-1-58023-055-1 **$16.95**

Wandering Stars: An Anthology of Jewish Fantasy & Science Fiction
Edited by Jack Dann; Introduction by Isaac Asimov
6 x 9, 272 pp, Quality PB, 978-1-58023-005-6 **$18.99**

More Wandering Stars: An Anthology of Outstanding Stories of Jewish Fantasy and Science Fiction *Edited by Jack Dann; Introduction by Isaac Asimov*
6 x 9, 192 pp, Quality PB, 978-1-58023-063-6 **$16.95**

Social Justice

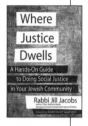

Where Justice Dwells
A Hands-On Guide to Doing Social Justice in Your Jewish Community
By Rabbi Jill Jacobs; Foreword by Rabbi David Saperstein
Provides ways to envision and act on your own ideals of social justice.
7 x 9, 288 pp, Quality PB Original, 978-1-58023-453-5 **$24.99**

There Shall Be No Needy
Pursuing Social Justice through Jewish Law and Tradition
By Rabbi Jill Jacobs; Foreword by Rabbi Elliot N. Dorff, PhD; Preface by Simon Greer
Confronts the most pressing issues of twenty-first-century America from a deeply
Jewish perspective. 6 x 9, 288 pp, Quality PB, 978-1-58023-425-2 **$16.99**

There Shall Be No Needy Teacher's Guide 8½ x 11, 56 pp, PB, 978-1-58023-429-0 **$8.99**

Conscience
The Duty to Obey and the Duty to Disobey
By Rabbi Harold M. Schulweis
Examines the idea of conscience and the role conscience plays in our relationships
to government, law, ethics, religion, human nature, God—and to each other.
6 x 9, 160 pp, Quality PB, 978-1-58023-419-1 **$16.99**; HC, 978-1-58023-375-0 **$19.99**

Judaism and Justice
The Jewish Passion to Repair the World
By Rabbi Sidney Schwarz; Foreword by Ruth Messinger
Explores the relationship between Judaism, social justice and the Jewish identity
of American Jews. 6 x 9, 352 pp, Quality PB, 978-1-58023-353-8 **$19.99**

Spirituality/Women's Interest

New Jewish Feminism
Probing the Past, Forging the Future
Edited by Rabbi Elyse Goldstein; Foreword by Anita Diamant
Looks at the growth and accomplishments of Jewish feminism and what they
mean for Jewish women today and tomorrow.
6 x 9, 480 pp, Quality PB, 978-1-58023-448-1 **$19.99**; HC, 978-1-58023-359-0 **$24.99**

The Divine Feminine in Biblical Wisdom Literature
Selections Annotated & Explained
Translation & Annotation by Rabbi Rami Shapiro
5½ x 8½, 240 pp, Quality PB, 978-1-59473-109-9 **$16.99**
(A book from SkyLight Paths, Jewish Lights' sister imprint)

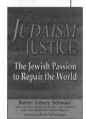

The Quotable Jewish Woman
Wisdom, Inspiration & Humor from the Mind & Heart
Edited by Elaine Bernstein Partnow
6 x 9, 496 pp, Quality PB, 978-1-58023-236-4 **$19.99**

The Women's Haftarah Commentary
New Insights from Women Rabbis on the 54 Weekly Haftarah Portions,
the 5 Megillot & Special Shabbatot
Edited by Rabbi Elyse Goldstein
Illuminates the historical significance of female portrayals in the Haftarah and the
Five Megillot. 6 x 9, 560 pp, Quality PB, 978-1-58023-371-2 **$19.99**

The Women's Torah Commentary
New Insights from Women Rabbis on the 54 Weekly Torah Portions
Edited by Rabbi Elyse Goldstein
Over fifty women rabbis offer inspiring insights on the Torah, in a week-by-week format.
6 x 9, 496 pp, Quality PB, 978-1-58023-370-5 **$19.99**; HC, 978-1-58023-076-6 **$34.95**

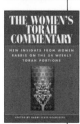

See Passover for *The Women's Passover Companion: Women's Reflections on
the Festival of Freedom* and *The Women's Seder Sourcebook: Rituals &
Readings for Use at the Passover Seder.*

Life Cycle

Marriage/Parenting/Family/Aging

The New Jewish Baby Album: Creating and Celebrating the Beginning of a Spiritual Life—A Jewish Lights Companion
By the Editors at Jewish Lights; Foreword by Anita Diamant; Preface by Rabbi Sandy Eisenberg Sasso
A spiritual keepsake that will be treasured for generations. More than just a memory book, *shows you how—and why it's important*—to create a Jewish home and a Jewish life. 8 x 10, 64 pp, Deluxe Padded HC, Full-color illus., 978-1-58023-138-1 **$19.95**

The Jewish Pregnancy Book: A Resource for the Soul, Body & Mind during Pregnancy, Birth & the First Three Months *By Sandy Falk, MD, and Rabbi Daniel Judson, with Steven A. Rapp* Medical information, prayers and rituals for each stage of pregnancy. 7 x 10, 208 pp, b/w photos, Quality PB, 978-1-58023-178-7 **$16.95**

Celebrating Your New Jewish Daughter: Creating Jewish Ways to Welcome Baby Girls into the Covenant—New and Traditional Ceremonies *By Debra Nussbaum Cohen; Foreword by Rabbi Sandy Eisenberg Sasso* 6 x 9, 272 pp, Quality PB, 978-1-58023-090-2 **$18.95**

The New Jewish Baby Book, 2nd Edition: Names, Ceremonies & Customs—A Guide for Today's Families *By Anita Diamant* 6 x 9, 320 pp, Quality PB, 978-1-58023-251-7 **$19.99**

Parenting as a Spiritual Journey: Deepening Ordinary and Extraordinary Events into Sacred Occasions *By Rabbi Nancy Fuchs-Kreimer, PhD*
6 x 9, 224 pp, Quality PB, 978-1-58023-016-2 **$17.99**

Parenting Jewish Teens: A Guide for the Perplexed
By Joanne Doades Explores the questions and issues that shape the world in which today's Jewish teenagers live and offers constructive advice to parents.
6 x 9, 176 pp, Quality PB, 978-1-58023-305-7 **$16.99**

Judaism for Two: A Spiritual Guide for Strengthening and Celebrating Your Loving Relationship *By Rabbi Nancy Fuchs-Kreimer, PhD, and Rabbi Nancy H. Wiener, DMin; Foreword by Rabbi Elliot N. Dorff, PhD*
Addresses the ways Jewish teachings can enhance and strengthen committed relationships. 6 x 9, 224 pp, Quality PB, 978-1-58023-254-8 **$16.99**

The Creative Jewish Wedding Book, 2nd Edition: A Hands-On Guide to New & Old Traditions, Ceremonies & Celebrations *By Gabrielle Kaplan-Mayer*
9 x 9, 288 pp, b/w photos, Quality PB, 978-1-58023-398-9 **$19.99**

Divorce Is a Mitzvah: A Practical Guide to Finding Wholeness and Holiness When Your Marriage Dies *By Rabbi Perry Netter; Afterword by Rabbi Laura Geller*
6 x 9, 224 pp, Quality PB, 978-1-58023-172-5 **$16.95**

Embracing the Covenant: Converts to Judaism Talk About Why & How
By Rabbi Allan Berkowitz and Patti Moskovitz 6 x 9, 192 pp, Quality PB, 978-1-879045-50-7 **$16.95**

The Guide to Jewish Interfaith Family Life: An InterfaithFamily.com Handbook
Edited by Ronnie Friedland and Edmund Case
6 x 9, 384 pp, Quality PB, 978-1-58023-153-4 **$18.95**

A Heart of Wisdom: Making the Jewish Journey from Midlife through the Elder Years
Edited by Susan Berrin; Foreword by Rabbi Harold Kushner
6 x 9, 384 pp, Quality PB, 978-1-58023-051-3 **$18.95**

Introducing My Faith and My Community: The Jewish Outreach Institute Guide for the Christian in a Jewish Interfaith Relationship
By Rabbi Kerry M. Olitzky 6 x 9, 176 pp, Quality PB, 978-1-58023-192-3 **$16.99**

Making a Successful Jewish Interfaith Marriage: The Jewish Outreach Institute Guide to Opportunities, Challenges and Resources *By Rabbi Kerry M. Olitzky with Joan Peterson Littman*
6 x 9, 176 pp, Quality PB, 978-1-58023-170-1 **$16.95**

A Man's Responsibility: A Jewish Guide to Being a Son, a Partner in Marriage, a Father and a Community Leader *By Rabbi Joseph B. Meszler*
6 x 9, 192 pp, Quality PB, 978-1-58023-435-1 **$16.99**; HC, 978-1-58023-362-0 **$21.99**

So That Your Values Live On: Ethical Wills and How to Prepare Them
Edited by Rabbi Jack Riemer and Rabbi Nathaniel Stampfer
6 x 9, 272 pp, Quality PB, 978-1-879045-34-7 **$18.99**

Holidays/Holy Days

Who by Fire, Who by Water—Un'taneh Tokef
Edited by Rabbi Lawrence A. Hoffman, PhD
Examines the prayer's theology, authorship and poetry through a set of lively essays, all written in accessible language.
6 x 9, 272 pp, HC, 978-1-58023-424-5 **$24.99**

All These Vows—Kol Nidre
Edited by Rabbi Lawrence A. Hoffman, PhD
The most memorable prayer of the Jewish New Year—what it means, why we sing it, and the secret of its magical appeal.
6 x 9, 288 pp, HC, 978-1-58023-430-6 **$24.99**

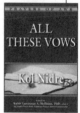

Rosh Hashanah Readings: Inspiration, Information and Contemplation
Yom Kippur Readings: Inspiration, Information and Contemplation
Edited by Rabbi Dov Peretz Elkins; Section Introductions from Arthur Green's These Are the Words
Rosh Hashanah: 6 x 9, 400 pp, Quality PB, 978-1-58023-437-5 **$19.99**; HC, 978-1-58023-239-5 **$24.99**
Yom Kippur: 6 x 9, 368 pp, Quality PB, 978-1-58023-438-2 **$19.99**; HC, 978-1-58023-271-5 **$24.99**

Jewish Holidays: A Brief Introduction for Christians
By Rabbi Kerry M. Olitzky and Rabbi Daniel Judson
5½ x 8½, 176 pp, Quality PB, 978-1-58023-302-6 **$16.99**

Reclaiming Judaism as a Spiritual Practice: Holy Days and Shabbat
By Rabbi Goldie Milgram 7 x 9, 272 pp, Quality PB, 978-1-58023-205-0 **$19.99**

Shabbat, 2nd Edition: The Family Guide to Preparing for and Celebrating the Sabbath
By Dr. Ron Wolfson 7 x 9, 320 pp, Illus., Quality PB, 978-1-58023-164-0 **$19.99**

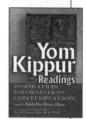

Hanukkah, 2nd Edition: The Family Guide to Spiritual Celebration
By Dr. Ron Wolfson 7 x 9, 240 pp, Illus., Quality PB, 978-1-58023-122-0 **$18.95**

The Jewish Family Fun Book, 2nd Edition
Holiday Projects, Everyday Activities, and Travel Ideas with Jewish Themes
By Danielle Dardashti and Roni Sarig; Illus. by Avi Katz
6 x 9, 304 pp, 70+ b/w illus. & diagrams, Quality PB, 978-1-58023-333-0 **$18.99**

Passover

My People's Passover Haggadah
Traditional Texts, Modern Commentaries
Edited by Rabbi Lawrence A. Hoffman, PhD, and David Arnow, PhD
A diverse and exciting collection of commentaries on the traditional Passover Haggadah—in two volumes!
Vol. 1: 7 x 10, 304 pp, HC, 978-1-58023-354-5 **$24.99**
Vol. 2: 7 x 10, 320 pp, HC, 978-1-58023-346-0 **$24.99**

Freedom Journeys: The Tale of Exodus and Wilderness across Millennia
By Rabbi Arthur O. Waskow and Rabbi Phyllis O. Berman
Explores how the story of Exodus echoes in our own time, calling us to relearn and rethink the Passover story through social-justice, ecological, feminist and interfaith perspectives. 6 x 9, 288 pp, HC, 978-1-58023-445-0 **$24.99**

Leading the Passover Journey: The Seder's Meaning Revealed,
the Haggadah's Story Retold *By Rabbi Nathan Laufer*
Uncovers the hidden meaning of the Seder's rituals and customs.
6 x 9, 224 pp, Quality PB, 978-1-58023-399-6 **$18.99**; HC, 978-1-58023-211-1 **$24.99**

Creating Lively Passover Seders, 2nd Edition: A Sourcebook of Engaging Tales,
Texts & Activities *By David Arnow, PhD* 7 x 9, 464 pp, Quality PB, 978-1-58023-444-3 **$24.99**

Passover, 2nd Edition: The Family Guide to Spiritual Celebration
By Dr. Ron Wolfson with Joel Lurie Grishaver 7 x 9, 416 pp, Quality PB, 978-1-58023-174-9 **$19.95**

The Women's Passover Companion: Women's Reflections on the Festival of Freedom
Edited by Rabbi Sharon Cohen Anisfeld, Tara Mohr and Catherine Spector; Foreword by Paula E. Hyman
6 x 9, 352 pp, Quality PB, 978-1-58023-231-9 **$19.99**; HC, 978-1-58023-128-2 **$24.95**

The Women's Seder Sourcebook: Rituals & Readings for Use at the Passover Seder
Edited by Rabbi Sharon Cohen Anisfeld, Tara Mohr and Catherine Spector
6 x 9, 384 pp, Quality PB, 978-1-58023-232-6 **$19.99**

Spirituality

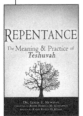

Repentance: The Meaning and Practice of *Teshuvah*
By Dr. Louis E. Newman; Foreword by Rabbi Harold M. Schulweis; Preface by Rabbi Karyn D. Kedar
Examines both the practical and philosophical dimensions of *teshuvah*, Judaism's core religious-moral teaching on repentance, and its value for us—Jews and non-Jews alike—today. 6 x 9, 256 pp, HC, 978-1-58023-426-9 **$24.99**

Tanya, the Masterpiece of Hasidic Wisdom
Selections Annotated & Explained
Translation & Annotation by Rabbi Rami Shapiro; Foreword by Rabbi Zalman M. Schachter-Shalomi
Brings the genius of *Tanya*, one of the most powerful books of Jewish wisdom, to anyone seeking to deepen their understanding of the soul.
5½ x 8½, 240 pp, Quality PB, 978-1-59473-275-1 **$16.99**
(A book from SkyLight Paths, Jewish Lights' sister imprint)

Aleph-Bet Yoga: Embodying the Hebrew Letters for Physical and Spiritual Well-Being
By Steven A. Rapp; Foreword by Tamar Frankiel, PhD, and Judy Greenfeld; Preface by Hart Lazer
7 x 10, 128 pp, b/w photos, Quality PB, Lay-flat binding, 978-1-58023-162-6 **$16.95**

A Book of Life: Embracing Judaism as a Spiritual Practice
By Rabbi Michael Strassfeld 6 x 9, 544 pp, Quality PB, 978-1-58023-247-0 **$19.99**

Bringing the Psalms to Life: How to Understand and Use the Book of Psalms
By Rabbi Daniel F. Polish, PhD 6 x 9, 208 pp, Quality PB, 978-1-58023-157-2 **$16.95**

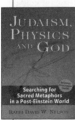

Does the Soul Survive? A Jewish Journey to Belief in Afterlife, Past Lives & Living with Purpose *By Rabbi Elie Kaplan Spitz; Foreword by Brian L. Weiss, MD*
6 x 9, 288 pp, Quality PB, 978-1-58023-165-7 **$16.99**

First Steps to a New Jewish Spirit: Reb Zalman's Guide to Recapturing the Intimacy & Ecstasy in Your Relationship with God *By Rabbi Zalman M. Schachter-Shalomi with Donald Gropman* 6 x 9, 144 pp, Quality PB, 978-1-58023-182-4 **$16.95**

Foundations of Sephardic Spirituality: The Inner Life of Jews of the Ottoman Empire
By Rabbi Marc D. Angel, PhD 6 x 9, 224 pp, Quality PB, 978-1-58023-341-5 **$18.99**

God & the Big Bang: Discovering Harmony between Science & Spirituality
By Dr. Daniel C. Matt 6 x 9, 216 pp, Quality PB, 978-1-879045-89-7 **$16.99**

God in Our Relationships: Spirituality between People from the Teachings of Martin Buber *By Rabbi Dennis S. Ross* 5½ x 8½, 160 pp, Quality PB, 978-1-58023-147-3 **$16.95**

The Jewish Lights Spirituality Handbook: A Guide to Understanding, Exploring & Living a Spiritual Life *Edited by Stuart M. Matlins*
What exactly is "Jewish" about spirituality? How do I make it a part of my life? Fifty of today's foremost spiritual leaders share their ideas and experience with us.
6 x 9, 456 pp, Quality PB, 978-1-58023-093-3 **$19.99**

Judaism, Physics and God: Searching for Sacred Metaphors in a Post-Einstein World
By Rabbi David W. Nelson 6 x 9, 352 pp, Quality PB, inc. reader's discussion guide,
978-1-58023-306-4 **$18.99**; HC, 352 pp, 978-1-58023-252-4 **$24.99**

Meaning & Mitzvah: Daily Practices for Reclaiming Judaism through Prayer, God, Torah, Hebrew, Mitzvot and Peoplehood *By Rabbi Goldie Milgram*
7 x 9, 336 pp, Quality PB, 978-1-58023-256-2 **$19.99**

Minding the Temple of the Soul: Balancing Body, Mind, and Spirit through Traditional Jewish Prayer, Movement, and Meditation *By Tamar Frankiel, PhD, and Judy Greenfeld*
7 x 10, 184 pp, Illus., Quality PB, 978-1-879045-64-4 **$18.99**

One God Clapping: The Spiritual Path of a Zen Rabbi *By Rabbi Alan Lew with Sherril Jaffe*
5½ x 8½, 336 pp, Quality PB, 978-1-58023-115-2 **$16.95**

The Soul of the Story: Meetings with Remarkable People
By Rabbi David Zeller 6 x 9, 288 pp, HC, 978-1-58023-272-2 **$21.99**

There Is No Messiah ... and You're It: The Stunning Transformation of Judaism's Most Provocative Idea *By Rabbi Robert N. Levine, DD*
6 x 9, 192 pp, Quality PB, 978-1-58023-255-5 **$16.99**

These Are the Words, 2nd Edition: A Vocabulary of Jewish Spiritual Life
By Rabbi Arthur Green, PhD 6 x 9, 320 pp, Quality PB, 978-1-58023-494-8 **$19.99**

Spirituality/Prayer

Making Prayer Real: Leading Jewish Spiritual Voices on Why Prayer Is Difficult and What to Do about It *By Rabbi Mike Comins*
A new and different response to the challenges of Jewish prayer, with "best prayer practices" from Jewish spiritual leaders of all denominations.
6 x 9, 320 pp, Quality PB, 978-1-58023-417-7 **$18.99**

Witnesses to the One: The Spiritual History of the *Sh'ma*
By Rabbi Joseph B. Meszler; Foreword by Rabbi Elyse Goldstein
6 x 9, 176 pp, Quality PB, 978-1-58023-400-9 **$16.99**; HC, 978-1-58023-309-5 **$19.99**

My People's Prayer Book Series: Traditional Prayers, Modern Commentaries *Edited by Rabbi Lawrence A. Hoffman, PhD*
Provides diverse and exciting commentary to the traditional liturgy. Will help you find new wisdom in Jewish prayer, and bring liturgy into your life. Each book includes Hebrew text, modern translations and commentaries from all perspectives of the Jewish world.

Vol. 1—The *Sh'ma* and Its Blessings
   7 x 10, 168 pp, HC, 978-1-879045-79-8 **$29.99**
Vol. 2—The *Amidah* 7 x 10, 240 pp, HC, 978-1-879045-80-4 **$24.95**
Vol. 3—*P'sukei D'zimrah* (Morning Psalms)
   7 x 10, 240 pp, HC, 978-1-879045-81-1 **$29.99**
Vol. 4—*Seder K'riat Hatorah* (The Torah Service)
   7 x 10, 264 pp, HC, 978-1-879045-82-8 **$29.99**
Vol. 5—*Birkhot Hashachar* (Morning Blessings)
   7 x 10, 240 pp, HC, 978-1-879045-83-5 **$24.95**
Vol. 6—*Tachanun* and Concluding Prayers
   7 x 10, 240 pp, HC, 978-1-879045-84-2 **$24.95**
Vol. 7—Shabbat at Home 7 x 10, 240 pp, HC, 978-1-879045-85-9 **$24.95**
Vol. 8—*Kabbalat Shabbat* (Welcoming Shabbat in the Synagogue)
   7 x 10, 240 pp, HC, 978-1-58023-121-3 **$24.99**
Vol. 9—Welcoming the Night: *Minchah* and *Ma'ariv* (Afternoon and
   Evening Prayer) 7 x 10, 272 pp, HC, 978-1-58023-262-3 **$24.99**
Vol. 10—Shabbat Morning: *Shacharit* and *Musaf* (Morning and
   Additional Services) 7 x 10, 240 pp, HC, 978-1-58023-240-1 **$29.99**

Spirituality/Lawrence Kushner

I'm God; You're Not: Observations on Organized Religion & Other Disguises of the Ego
6 x 9, 256 pp, HC, 978-1-58023-441-2 **$21.99**

The Book of Letters: A Mystical Hebrew Alphabet
Popular HC Edition, 6 x 9, 80 pp, 2-color text, 978-1-879045-00-2 **$24.95**
Collector's Limited Edition, 9 x 12, 80 pp, gold-foil-embossed pages, w/ limited-edition silkscreened print, 978-1-879045-04-0 **$349.00**

The Book of Miracles: A Young Person's Guide to Jewish Spiritual Awareness
6 x 9, 96 pp, 2-color illus., HC, 978-1-879045-78-1 **$16.95** *For ages 9–13*

The Book of Words: Talking Spiritual Life, Living Spiritual Talk
6 x 9, 160 pp, Quality PB, 978-1-58023-020-9 **$18.99**

Eyes Remade for Wonder: A Lawrence Kushner Reader *Introduction by Thomas Moore*
6 x 9, 240 pp, Quality PB, 978-1-58023-042-1 **$18.95**

God Was in This Place & I, i Did Not Know: Finding Self, Spirituality and
Ultimate Meaning 6 x 9, 192 pp, Quality PB, 978-1-879045-33-0 **$16.95**

Honey from the Rock: An Introduction to Jewish Mysticism
6 x 9, 176 pp, Quality PB, 978-1-58023-073-5 **$16.95**

Invisible Lines of Connection: Sacred Stories of the Ordinary
5½ x 8½, 160 pp, Quality PB, 978-1-879045-98-9 **$15.95**

Jewish Spirituality: A Brief Introduction for Christians
5½ x 8½, 112 pp, Quality PB, 978-1-58023-150-3 **$12.95**

The River of Light: Jewish Mystical Awareness
6 x 9, 192 pp, Quality PB, 978-1-58023-096-4 **$16.95**

The Way Into Jewish Mystical Tradition
6 x 9, 224 pp, Quality PB, 978-1-58023-200-5 **$18.99**; HC, 978-1-58023-029-2 **$21.95**

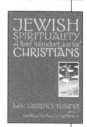

Theology/Philosophy/The Way Into... Series

The Way Into... series offers an accessible and highly usable "guided tour" of the Jewish faith, people, history and beliefs—in total, an introduction to Judaism that will enable you to understand and interact with the sacred texts of the Jewish tradition. Each volume is written by a leading contemporary scholar and teacher, and explores one key aspect of Judaism. The Way Into... series enables all readers to achieve a real sense of Jewish cultural literacy through guided study.

The Way Into Encountering God in Judaism
By Rabbi Neil Gillman, PhD
For everyone who wants to understand how Jews have encountered God throughout history and today.
6 x 9, 240 pp, Quality PB, 978-1-58023-199-2 **$18.99**; HC, 978-1-58023-025-4 **$21.95**
Also Available: **The Jewish Approach to God:** A Brief Introduction for Christians
By Rabbi Neil Gillman, PhD
5¼ x 8½, 192 pp, Quality PB, 978-1-58023-190-9 **$16.95**

The Way Into Jewish Mystical Tradition
By Rabbi Lawrence Kushner
Allows readers to interact directly with the sacred mystical texts of the Jewish tradition. An accessible introduction to the concepts of Jewish mysticism, their religious and spiritual significance, and how they relate to life today.
6 x 9, 224 pp, Quality PB, 978-1-58023-200-5 **$18.99**; HC, 978-1-58023-029-2 **$21.95**

The Way Into Jewish Prayer
By Rabbi Lawrence A. Hoffman, PhD
Opens the door to 3,000 years of Jewish prayer, making anyone feel at home in the Jewish way of communicating with God.
6 x 9, 208 pp, Quality PB, 978-1-58023-201-2 **$18.99**

The Way Into Jewish Prayer Teacher's Guide
By Rabbi Jennifer Ossakow Goldsmith
8½ x 11, 42 pp, PB, 978-1-58023-345-3 **$8.99**
Download a free copy at www.jewishlights.com.

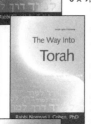

The Way Into Judaism and the Environment
By Jeremy Benstein, PhD
Explores the ways in which Judaism contributes to contemporary social-environmental issues, the extent to which Judaism is part of the problem and how it can be part of the solution.
6 x 9, 288 pp, Quality PB, 978-1-58023-368-2 **$18.99**

The Way Into Tikkun Olam (Repairing the World)
By Rabbi Elliot N. Dorff, PhD
An accessible introduction to the Jewish concept of the individual's responsibility to care for others and repair the world.
6 x 9, 304 pp, Quality PB, 978-1-58023-328-6 **$18.99**

The Way Into Torah
By Rabbi Norman J. Cohen, PhD
Helps guide you in the exploration of the origins and development of Torah, explains why it should be studied and how to do it.
6 x 9, 176 pp, Quality PB, 978-1-58023-198-5 **$16.99**

The Way Into the Varieties of Jewishness
By Sylvia Barack Fishman, PhD
Explores the religious and historical understanding of what it has meant to be Jewish from ancient times to the present controversy over "Who is a Jew?"
6 x 9, 288 pp, Quality PB, 978-1-58023-367-5 **$18.99**; HC, 978-1-58023-030-8 **$24.99**

Theology/Philosophy

The God Who Hates Lies: Confronting & Rethinking Jewish Tradition
By Dr. David Hartman with Charlie Buckholtz
The world's leading Modern Orthodox Jewish theologian probes the deepest questions at the heart of what it means to be a human being and a Jew.
6 x 9, 208 pp, HC, 978-1-58023-455-9 **$24.99**

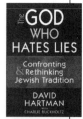

Jewish Theology in Our Time: A New Generation Explores the Foundations and Future of Jewish Belief *Edited by Rabbi Elliot J. Cosgrove, PhD; Foreword by Rabbi David J. Wolpe; Preface by Rabbi Carole B. Balin, PhD*
A powerful and challenging examination of what Jews can believe—by a new generation's most dynamic and innovative thinkers.
6 x 9, 240 pp, HC, 978-1-58023-413-9 **$24.99**

Maimonides—Essential Teachings on Jewish Faith & Ethics: The Book of Knowledge & the Thirteen Principles of Faith—Annotated & Explained
Translation and Annotation by Rabbi Marc D. Angel, PhD
Opens up for us Maimonides's views on the nature of God, providence, prophecy, free will, human nature, repentance and more.
5½ x 8½, 224 pp, Quality PB Original, 978-1-59473-311-6 **$18.99***

The Death of Death: Resurrection and Immortality in Jewish Thought
By Rabbi Neil Gillman, PhD 6 x 9, 336 pp, Quality PB, 978-1-58023-081-0 **$18.95**

Doing Jewish Theology: God, Torah & Israel in Modern Judaism *By Rabbi Neil Gillman, PhD*
6 x 9, 304 pp, Quality PB, 978-1-58023-439-9 **$18.99**

Hasidic Tales: Annotated & Explained *Translation & Annotation by Rabbi Rami Shapiro*
5½ x 8½, 240 pp, Quality PB, 978-1-893361-86-7 **$16.95***

A Heart of Many Rooms: Celebrating the Many Voices within Judaism
By Dr. David Hartman 6 x 9, 352 pp, Quality PB, 978-1-58023-156-5 **$19.95**

The Hebrew Prophets: Selections Annotated & Explained
Translation & Annotation by Rabbi Rami Shapiro; Foreword by Rabbi Zalman M. Schachter-Shalomi
5½ x 8½, 224 pp, Quality PB, 978-1-59473-037-5 **$16.99***

Maimonides, Spinoza and Us: Toward an Intellectually Vibrant Judaism
By Rabbi Marc D. Angel, PhD A challenging look at two great Jewish philosophers and what their thinking means to our understanding of God, truth, revelation and reason. 6 x 9, 224 pp, HC, 978-1-58023-411-5 **$24.99**

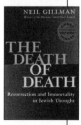

A Living Covenant: The Innovative Spirit in Traditional Judaism
By Dr. David Hartman 6 x 9, 368 pp, Quality PB, 978-1-58023-011-7 **$25.00**

Love and Terror in the God Encounter: The Theological Legacy of Rabbi Joseph B. Soloveitchik *By Dr. David Hartman* 6 x 9, 240 pp, Quality PB, 978-1-58023-176-3 **$19.95**

A Touch of the Sacred: A Theologian's Informal Guide to Jewish Belief
By Dr. Eugene B. Borowitz and Frances W. Schwartz
6 x 9, 256 pp, Quality PB, 978-1-58023-416-0 **$16.99**; HC, 978-1-58023-337-8 **$21.99**

Traces of God: Seeing God in Torah, History and Everyday Life *By Rabbi Neil Gillman, PhD*
6 x 9, 240 pp, Quality PB, 978-1-58023-369-9 **$16.99**

Your Word Is Fire: The Hasidic Masters on Contemplative Prayer
Edited and translated by Rabbi Arthur Green, PhD, and Barry W. Holtz
6 x 9, 160 pp, Quality PB, 978-1-879045-25-5 **$15.95**

I Am Jewish
Personal Reflections Inspired by the Last Words of Daniel Pearl
Almost 150 Jews—both famous and not—from all walks of life, from all around the world, write about many aspects of their Judaism.
Edited by Judea and Ruth Pearl 6 x 9, 304 pp, Deluxe PB w/ flaps, 978-1-58023-259-3 **$18.99**
Download a free copy of the *I Am Jewish Teacher's Guide* at www.jewishlights.com.

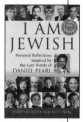

Hannah Senesh: Her Life and Diary, The First Complete Edition
By Hannah Senesh; Foreword by Marge Piercy; Preface by Eitan Senesh; Afterword by Roberta Grossman
6 x 9, 368 pp, b/w photos, Quality PB, 978-1-58023-342-2 **$19.99**

**A book from SkyLight Paths, Jewish Lights' sister imprint*

About Jewish Lights

People of all faiths and backgrounds yearn for books that attract, engage, educate, and spiritually inspire.

Our principal goal is to stimulate thought and help all people learn about who the Jewish People are, where they come from, and what the future can be made to hold. While people of our diverse Jewish heritage are the primary audience, our books speak to people in the Christian world as well and will broaden their understanding of Judaism and the roots of their own faith.

We bring to you authors who are at the forefront of spiritual thought and experience. While each has something different to say, they all say it in a voice that you can hear.

Our books are designed to welcome you and then to engage, stimulate, and inspire. We judge our success not only by whether or not our books are beautiful and commercially successful, but by whether or not they make a difference in your life.

For your information and convenience, at the back of this book we have provided a list of other Jewish Lights books you might find interesting and useful. They cover all the categories of your life:

Bar/Bat Mitzvah	Life Cycle
Bible Study / Midrash	Meditation
Children's Books	Men's Interest
Congregation Resources	Parenting
Current Events / History	Prayer / Ritual / Sacred Practice
Ecology / Environment	Social Justice
Fiction: Mystery, Science Fiction	Spirituality
Grief / Healing	Theology / Philosophy
Holidays / Holy Days	Travel
Inspiration	Twelve Steps
Kabbalah / Mysticism / Enneagram	Women's Interest

Stuart M. Matlins, Publisher

Or phone, fax, mail or e-mail to: **JEWISH LIGHTS Publishing**
Sunset Farm Offices, Route 4 • P.O. Box 237 • Woodstock, Vermont 05091
Tel: (802) 457-4000 • Fax: (802) 457-4004 • www.jewishlights.com
Credit card orders: **(800) 962-4544** (8:30AM–5:30PM EST Monday–Friday)
Generous discounts on quantity orders. SATISFACTION GUARANTEED. Prices subject to change.

For more information about each book, visit our website at www.jewishlights.com